CANADA AND ITS AMERICAS

Canada and Its Americas

Transnational Navigations

Edited by

WINFRIED SIEMERLING AND
SARAH PHILLIPS CASTEEL

McGill-Queen's University Press
Montreal & Kingston · London · Ithaca

© McGill-Queen's University Press 2010
ISBN 978-0-7735-3657-9 (cloth)
ISBN 978-0-7735-3684-5 (pbk)

Legal deposit first quarter 2010
Bibliothèque nationale du Québec

Printed in Canada on acid-free paper that is 100% ancient forest free
(100% post-consumer recycled), processed chlorine free.

This book has been published with the help of grants from the Canadian
Federation for the Humanities and Social Sciences, through the Aid to
Scholarly Publications Programme, using funds provided by the Social
Sciences and Humanities Research Council of Canada, and the Université
de Sherbrooke.

McGill-Queen's University Press acknowledges the support of the Canada
Council for the Arts for our publishing program. We also acknowledge
the financial support of the Government of Canada through the Book
Publishing Industry Development Program (BPIDP) for our publishing
activities.

Library and Archives Canada Cataloguing in Publication

Canada and its Americas: transnational navigations /
edited by Winfried Siemerling and Sarah Phillips Casteel.

Includes bibliographical references and index.
ISBN 978-0-7735-3657-9 (bnd)
ISBN 978-0-7735-3684-5 (pbk)

1. Canadian literature (English) – 20th century – History and
criticism. 2. Canadian literature (French) – 20th century – History
and criticism. 3. America in literature. 4. Postcolonialism in literature.
5. Native peoples in literature. 6. Ethnicity in literature. 7. Culture
in literature. 8. Canada in literature. I. Siemerling, Winfried, 1956–
II. Casteel, Sarah Phillips, 1974–

PS8101.T73C35 2010   C810.9'358   C2009-904895-7

Typeset in Sabon 10.5/13
by Infoscan Collette, Quebec City

Contents

Acknowledgments

Winfried Siemerling would like to acknowledge the support of an individual Standard Research Grant from the Social Sciences and Humanities Research Council of Canada in the preparation of this volume. Helpful also were the research context of the Université de Sherbrooke's SSHRC-supported *Bibliography of Comparative Studies in Canadian, Québec, and Foreign Literatures/Bibliographie d'études comparées des littératures canadienne, québécoise et étrangères* 1930–1995 (see http://www.compcanlit.ca) and of the W.E.B. Du Bois Institute for African and African American Research at Harvard.

Sarah Phillips Casteel would like to thank Rachel Adams, who encouraged her interest in hemispheric American studies at an early stage and with whom she collaborated on a seminar for the American Comparative Literature Association as well as on a special issue of *Comparative American Studies* that layed important groundwork for the present collection. Sarah is immensely grateful to her husband, James, and her sons, Harry and Isaac, for allowing her the time she needed to work on this project. As well, she would like to acknowledge the Social Sciences and Humanities Research Council of Canada for awarding her a Standard Research Grant.

Finally, we are very grateful to our editors at McGill-Queen's University Press as well as to the three anonymous readers for their guidance, insight, and support of this book.

We further thank Maney Publishing and Richard Ellis, editor of the journal *Comparative American Studies* (see http://www.maney. co.uk/journals/cas and http://www.ingentaconnect.com/content/ maney/cas), for granting us permission to print revised versions of the following essays from a special issue on "Canada and the

Americas," co-edited by Rachel Adams and Sarah Phillips Casteel: Albert Braz, "North of America: Racial Hybridity and Canada's (Non)Place in Inter-American Discourse," *Comparative American Studies* 3, no. 1 (March 2005): 79–88; Monika Giacoppe, "'Lucky to be so Bilingual': Québécois and Chicano/a Literatures in a Comparative Context," *Comparative American Studies* 3, no. 1 (March 2005): 47–61; and Maureen Moynagh, "Eyeing the North Star? Figuring Canada in African-Canadian Postslavery Fiction and Drama," *Comparative American Studies* 3, no. 1 (March 2005): 15–27.

Thanks also to the journal *Canadian Literature* for granting us permission to reprint Winfried Siemerling's essay "'May I See Some Identification?' Race, Borders, and Identities in *Any Known Blood*," *Canadian Literature* 182 (2004): 30–50.

CANADA AND ITS AMERICAS

Canada and Its Americas

WINFRIED SIEMERLING AND SARAH PHILLIPS CASTEEL

"All the buses to Aracataca were brightly colored," Michael Ondaatje recalls in a 1978 essay on Gabriel García Márquez, which he addresses to fellow Canadian writer Sheila Watson. Ondaatje writes that the vehicles en route to Márquez's hometown "would take a side road down into the river and soak in it like animals" and notes that he has "terrific slides of the pigs and of the men delivering ice at Aracataca." Yet he finds himself wondering, "What am I doing in this South American town ... photographing pigs photographing ice" (1978, 19). This is a good question, particularly for those of us interested in exploring Canada's relationship to inter-American poetics. Ondaatje's fascination with animals, his poetry-portrayed pigs wallowing in muddy happiness, the easy transfer of qualities between humans, animals, and things, and his penchant finally for the fantastic and the excessive are all familiar, especially to readers of his early work. But the keyword here is perhaps "ice," the frozen fluid whose childhood discovery Aureliano Buendía, in the opening sentence of Márquez's *One Hundred Years of Solitude* (*Cien años de soledad*) (1967), is said to remember when facing the firing squad.

The contrast of heat and ice also opens Ondaatje's *Running in the Family* (1982), a book set in Asia and Canada but illuminated nonetheless by Ondaatje's remarks about dreams, deciphering, writing, mirrors, and death as orchestrated by the author from Aracataca. Ondaatje's essay on Márquez highlights in retrospect certain moments of his own earlier *Coming through Slaughter* (1976) but also forecasts important details and structural features of *Running in the Family* and his subsequent works. Ondaatje observes, for instance, that in *One Hundred Years of Solitude* ghosts begin to replace the members of the Buendía family as they die. This comment introduces us to the temporal and narrative architecture of *In the Skin of a Lion* (1987) and *The English Patient* (1992). Both novels place keys to their reading roughly at their halfway point. At that moment, they send readers searching – ghost-like – and returning (or *revenants*, as the French word for ghosts literally means) to earlier times in the text while also going forward, thus moving in two directions simultaneously. As Ondaatje writes of *One Hundred Years of Solitude*: "About halfway through the book you begin to feel that while you are still moving forward to the end you are simultaneously moving from midpoint to the beginning. Your consciousness is sliding both ways" (1978, 30).

Ondaatje further relates Márquez's ghosts and his handling of narrative time to William Faulkner's remark that "There's no such thing as was, only is" (1978, 30), pointing to the transnational travel of the imagination behind this particular way of conceiving stories. With its rich observations about technique and formal correspondence, the essay thus tenders partial answers to Ondaatje's question about what he was doing "photographing ice" in a South American town that birthed Márquez's Macondo, a place on fictional maps that also show Yoknapatawpha county. Reflections on frozen time and its fluid reversals and permutations (or on the fantastic or the marvellous) are of course neither the prerogative of any single literature or writer nor the sole preoccupation of the essay's author. Yet Ondaatje is clearly deciphering and transforming here formal filaments of a poetics that has traversed the Americas, a set of formal possibilities that individual authors reformulate to shape their individual imaginative worlds and that literary studies seeks to explicate with respect to specific social times and places.

As the example of Ondaatje suggests, the poetics and traditions of other parts of the Americas are powerfully mediated by writers in Canada and Quebec, whether they were born here or, like Ondaatje, immigrated from other parts of the world. Indeed, a number of Canadian writers, including George Bowering, Jack Hodgins, Dany Laferrière, Jacques Poulin, Guillermo Verdecchia, and others discussed in this collection, similarly incorporate a hemispheric awareness into their poetics.[1] Hugh Hazelton, co-editor of the Canadian-Latin American anthology *Compañeros* (1990), has offered a succinct entry point for the Latin American dimension of these mediations elsewhere (2002) and in his contribution to the present collection; his

Latinocanadá: A Critical Anthology of Ten Latin American Writers of Canada (2007) further helps, in Edward Blodgett's memorable phrase, to open Canada "to its several selves" (2003, 20). The Americas comprise not only Latin America, however, but also the United States, whose literary importance for Canada has never been contested. Yet precisely because of the weight and political, economic, and cultural neocolonial tendencies of the United States, this dynamic has proven less than comfortable for the writers and theorists who achieved Canada's declarations of cultural independence in the 1960s[2] and for those who have articulated them since. Despite – and also because of – this discomfort, it seems all but impossible to situate Canada effectively without taking into consideration both its North American and its hemispheric contexts. These often contradictory sets of factors have motivated us, at the current cultural and geopolitical junctures, to seek a fresh collective examination of how Canadian literature locates itself – and can be located – with respect to "its" Americas, those that it perceives and those that it construes.[3]

Inter-American[4] literary and cultural connections have always – and somewhat nervously – been monitored in Latin America (witness José Martí's essay "Nuestra América") and in Canada, mostly with respect to the powerful United States. Meanwhile, since the late 1970s some critics in the United States have been calling for a redefinition of "American literature" that would allow for a more comparative, hemispheric approach (see Spengemann 1978; Scott 1980). Such calls to reconsider the traditional insularity and exceptionalism of United States studies, frequently made with reference to the US's relationship to Latin America, have been echoed with increasing urgency from the mid–1990s through to the present. At the heart of these appeals has been a critique of the term "America" itself – a recognition of the "arrogance," in the words of one scholar (Scott 1980, 635), through which the term has been co-opted by one national literature to the exclusion of other literatures of the hemisphere. Thus the "new American studies" scholarship tends to echo the question posed by John Muthyala in his essay "Reworlding America: The Globalization of American Studies": "By what historical fiat … did the term 'America' come to refer only to a certain region in North America, its history originating in New England, and the term 'American' to refer solely to the English settlers in the seventeenth century and, later, to the people of the United States?" (2001, 96).

Coupled with this critique of the imprecision of the term "American literature" has been a related concern with the parochialism of United States studies (conducted under the name "American studies"). Kirsten Silva Gruesz, for example, in her *Ambassadors of Culture: The Transamerican Origins of Latino Writing*, sets out "to imagine a new form of U.S. cultural history in general: one that would unseat the fiction of American literature's monolingual and Anglocentric roots and question the imperial conflation of the United States with America" (2002, 4). As a result of critics' efforts both to restore the term "American literature" to its broader meaning and to "internationalize" United States studies by resituating it in a global context, the field has seen a rapid expansion in geographical, linguistic, and conceptual terms (see Porter 1994; Wald 1998; Patell 1999; Pease 2001; Pease and Wiegman 2002).

This hemispheric turn is the product of the convergence of a number of trends in literary and cultural criticism. It follows remappings of the field of United States studies by African American, feminist, Asian American, and Chicano critics (Porter 1994, 468), in keeping with which hemispheric American studies in its current configuration has tended to pay particular attention to minority and marginalized discourses (Patell 1999, 169). In addition, the emergence of hemispheric American studies has also been encouraged by the quincentennial "rediscovery" of the Americas and by the recent growth of Caribbean studies, both of which have called attention to alternative visions of the meaning of "America," such as Martí's "Nuestra América" and Edouard Glissant's "L'autre Amérique." Finally, like the popularity of borderlands studies, the hemispheric turn reflects a broader interrogation of the nation as a unit of cultural analysis.5 A particularly telling index of this paradigm shift, then, is the extent to which border zones have displaced the frontier as the key site within United States studies, with the American West itself recast as a multi-ethnic and hybridized contact zone (see Saldívar 1997, xiii; Patell 1999, 172).

Following these transformations of United States studies and cultural criticism, comparative studies has trained its sights on "New World" literary connections. Works like Kirkpatrick Sale's *The Conquest of Paradise* (1990) and Stephen Greenblatt's *Marvelous Possessions* (1991) have re-examined Christopher Columbus and the foundations of "New World" narratives. Literary histories like *The Columbia History of the American Novel* (Elliott 1991) and the *Literary Cultures of Latin America* (Valdés and Kadir 2004) have made it their task to offer perspectives on the literatures and cultures of the Americas that exceed the circumference of one nation alone. Likewise, studies by such scholars as Lois Parkinson Zamora (1997), José David Saldívar (1997), Kirsten Silva Gruesz (2002), Earl Fitz (1991), Patrick Imbert (2004), Roland Walter (2003), Margaret Turner (1995), and Marie Vautier (1998) employ "New World" perspectives or demonstrate on a number of different fronts the value of employing a hemispheric approach to the study of the Americas, an approach that is also currently being explored in conferences, journal issues, and dedicated series from such presses as the University of Virginia Press, the University Press of Florida, and Peter Lang.

Although a variety of models and rationales for hemispheric American studies have been advanced, such work has generally rejected an exceptionalist view of United States cultural production and has moved away from an exclusive focus on "New World" – "Old World" axes in order to uncover inter-American relations of influence, exchange, and correspondence. In the hemispheric paradigm, American literatures and cultures become plural rather than singular, multilingual rather than monolingual. At the same time, the hemispheric turn is very much a pedagogical enterprise that entails a broad rethinking of institutional and disciplinary structures. This perspective has drawn attention to writers, both historical and contemporary, whose literary production lends itself to – and seems to call for – a hemispheric reading. Critics and writers such as José Martí, Herman Melville, William Faulkner, Edmundo O'Gorman, Gloria Anzaldúa, and Edouard Glissant are fast emerging as touchstones of scholarship and course syllabi on the literatures of the Americas. Indeed, it is the tension between the national frameworks that inform more traditional literary critical paradigms and the transamerican orientation of this body of literature that has in part motivated the hemispheric turn. Despite their engagement with such hemispheric dynamics, however, Canadian writers remain notably absent from this corpus.

Whereas hemispheric American studies has by now become established in the United States academy as an approach and a field of study, much less discussed is the question of Canada's place and participation within such projects and perspectives. Canadian culture and criticism are frequently marginalized in hemispheric comparative work, in borderlands criticism, and even in North American studies, partially because of institutionalized pathways and habits that continue to impede scholarly access to this rich material, thus reinforcing traditional disciplinary blindspots (see Adams and Casteel 2005; Siemerling 2005, 8–12). Essay collections dedicated to hemispheric American studies, such as *Do the Americas Have a Common Literature?* (Firmat 1990) and *Poetics of the Americas* (Cowan and Humphries 1997), pay little attention to Canadian writing, implicitly suggesting that if the Americas do have a common literature, it is one that largely excludes Canadian writing.[6] Indeed, the invisibility of Canada in discussions of the literatures of the Americas would appear to confirm Richard Rodriguez's assessment in *Brown: The Last Discovery of America* that from the United States' point of view, "Canada is the largest country in the world that doesn't exist" (2002, 161).

With this volume, we seek to make an intervention into comparative American studies by suggesting several possible access routes into a hemispheric contextualization of Canadian literature. The explorations of these access routes or pathways that are contained in the chapters that follow illustrate not only the benefits that Canadianists stand to gain from a greater openness to hemispheric approaches but also the reciprocal value that a Canadian decentring of US-based models holds for the field of inter-American studies as a whole. In the latter three sections of the collection, "Indigenous Remappings of America," "Postslavery Routes," and "Quebec Connections," we have grouped together case studies that demonstrate how a comparative, border-crossing approach can produce rich results for the study of the literatures and cultures of both Canada and the Americas. Such an approach proves advantageous not only for the study of issues across a wide range of texts but often also with respect to individual border-crossing texts or oeuvres, as the single-author studies in these sections in particular demonstrate. We preface the case studies in these sections, however, with a section that reflects on two related areas of concern that are themselves intrinsic to Canadian literary studies. These concerns seem to us unavoidable and necessary, even though they may complicate the engagement of scholars of Canadian literature and culture with North American and hemispheric perspectives and may indeed have contributed to the still limited visibility of Canadian literature within these fields. Indeed, the very hesitation of Canadianists to participate in hemispheric discussions may serve as an important corrective to some of the more troubling trends in the field of hemispheric American studies as it is currently taking shape, reminding us of the need to attend carefully to national and regional specificities even as we engage with transnational contexts.

The first and more general of these concerns regards future directions of Canadian literary and cultural studies at a time when post- and transnational methodologies have moved to the forefront of critical inquiry (Siemerling 2007). In many respects, the study of Canadian literature is flourishing as never before. The field designates a recognized area of specialization within literary studies, Canadian studies associations around the world promote it, and Canadian authors are internationally successful and garner important prizes. Yet only a few decades after securing its recognized academic position, Canadian literature as an institutionalized field of study is currently facing a number of challenges to which it may be more vulnerable than other comparable fields, including the increasing problematization of "nation" as a category of literary analysis.[7] This problematization of nation appears to be foundational to transnational perspectives such as North American studies and hemispheric studies of the Americas.

A second and more specific challenge for Canadian studies that arises from the hemispheric turn is the necessary hesitation of many scholars of Canadian literature to risk the advances of their hard-won field by engaging in a hemispheric studies that is dominated by a country that, under the designation "American studies," tends to appropriate for nationally limited purposes the name of a continent. With Martí's "Nuestra América" as its central text and with its emphasis on alternative histories and minority discourses, hemispheric American studies is conceived of by many critics as oppositional and contestatory. However, some have questioned whether the hemispheric turn is itself an imperializing move. Patricia Wald, for instance, asks, "To what extent ... is the transnationalizing trend a critique of the limitations of a nation-based analysis, and to what extent does it participate in – and reinforce – the politics of the TNC [transnational corporation]?" (1998, 201). In her study of the Monroe Doctrine, Gretchen Murphy echoes these concerns when she urges us to "interrogate the construction of the hemispheric frame, and examine the powerful tradition that defines America spatially with reference to 'its' hemisphere" (2005, 1).[8]

If such questions trouble United States Americanists, they become of particular concern to scholars located outside the United States, who may note with some alarm that "America" tacitly continues to signify "United States" in a surprising number of avowedly hemispheric academic treatises. Indeed, it often appears to be taken for granted that the United States will remain at the centre of this academic enterprise and that the aim of hemispheric American studies is to rehabilitate United States studies *as* American studies rather than to decentre it. Not surprisingly, then, the suspicion that hemispheric American studies is driven by an imperializing impulse on the part of the United States reinforces a certain reluctance from some Canadian quarters to engage transnational hemispheric or North American approaches. As a result, hemispheric studies has thus far had little presence in the Canadian academy, with very few courses or job postings framed in inter-American terms. The inclusion of hemispheric studies as one of the key terms in a recent call for papers for a prominent Canadian literature conference[9] perhaps signals the beginnings of a shift in this regard, but for the most part, hemispheric projects have been received by Canadianists with skepticism and, on occasion, hostility. This resistance is understandable in the context of the difficult circumstances that attended the full emergence of "Canadian literature" – both discursively and institutionally – in the 1960s, as well as that of a *"littérature québécoise,"* a term circulated roughly from 1963 on (see Siemerling 2005, 120–9). Yet Canadian resistance to hemispheric approaches, although informed by legitimate fears of Canadian literary studies being subordinated to a US-centred theoretical paradigm, paradoxically risks reinforcing the hegemony of the US academy by failing to propose other theoretical paradigms and perspectives. There is a danger, in other words, that a defensive Canadian nationalism and self-protective instinct vis-à-vis the United States may inhibit the development of alternative paradigms of hemispheric American studies that Canadianists, with their historically weak nationalism and acute awareness of the imperial tendencies of the United States, are uniquely positioned to produce.

For indeed, it is crucial to note that the almost off-handed dismissal, on the part of many literary theorists, of the "nation" or the "nation-state" as a category of literary and cultural analysis remains problematic, despite all theoretical arguments against essentialisms, for literatures that had to fight under postcolonial circumstances for national status as late as the 1960s. Are not the projects of "Canadian literature" and *"littérature québécoise,"* for instance, on the verge of being remarginalized after having existed as fully institutionalized fields for only a few decades?[10] Since alternative professional designations in job ads and scholarly self-identification include "postcolonial studies" and, increasingly, "globalization studies" (see Slemon 2007), it may well be tempting to shrug off such presumably postnational developments with an air of theoretical sophistication. Yet the question arises whether certain varieties of cosmopolitanism, postcolonial or otherwise, do not begin to play into the hands of geopolitically dominant nationalisms and power structures.[11] This question becomes particulary pertinent for those who share the hemisphere with the United States, as has been pointed out not only by scholars in Canada (including Cynthia Sugars, Herb Wyile, and David Leahy in the present volume) but also by some in the United States who are interested in "internationalizing" American studies (see, for example, Sadowski-Smith and Fox 2004).

It is not as though the "end" of national literatures has not been discussed with respect to Canadian and Québécois literature. The 2005 "TransCanadas" conference in Vancouver, for instance, dedicated a session to "The Ends of CanLit," and Pierre Nepveu, a leading scholar of *"littérature québécoise,"* asked as early as 1988 whether, after the institutional emergence of the field had been achieved on the grounds of identitarian strategies of reading, it was not time to reflect on the corpus now in different ways, and thus to think about "la *fin* de la littérature québécoise" and a "littérature *post*-québécoise" (1988, 14, original emphasis). United States scholar Gregory Jay, in a comparable move, suggested in 1991 that it was "time to stop teaching 'American' literature" (264) and instead to turn to "Writing in the United States." When challenged by Carolyn Porter (1994) that his project reasserted nationalist boundaries, Jay defended the retention of national parameters by offering the following caveat with respect to other literatures of the Americas: "we should recognize that calling for an end to the study of a national American literature means calling for an end to the study of a national Mexican or Canadian or Colombian literature as well. Do 'we' in the United States want to prescribe such an abandonment of local and regional cultural traditions? Do we have the right? Would

this call for postnationalism return us to the widely discussed observation that the criticisms of identity politics arise just at the moment
when those whose identities have been marginalized demand recognition?" (1997, 182). We think that these questions are indeed pertinent, but we do not believe that they should close off all possibilities
of Canadian engagements with transnational hemispheric studies,
especially if the continued efficiency and reality of "nation" is recognized as a discursive, institutional, and political reality. We concur
with Maureen Moynagh's statement in her contribution to this
volume that "It is not a question of conceiving the transnational as
a kind of deterritorialized abstraction hovering somewhere above
the earth-bound places where people live" but rather of training our
sights on "embedded, place-specific, material, and historical relationships that nonetheless operate across national borders."

Disciplinary concerns notwithstanding, the subsequent case studies
in this volume testify to the fact that the countries of the Americas
share, beyond geographical adjacency, a number of comparable
historical parallels and differences, common legacies as white-settler
societies that derive from their relationships with indigenous societies, slavery, and the imperial powers against which they sought to
define their emergent cultural and political identities.[12] In this respect,
it also seems entirely appropriate to study aspects of United States
culture within the problematic of the postcolonial, as Bill Ashcroft,
Gareth Griffiths, and Helen Tiffin suggested in *The Empire Writes
Back* back in 1989. Indeed, scholars such as Lawrence Buell have
read the emergence of United States national literature in this perspective (e.g., Buell 1992, 2000). That this approach has met with
limited enthusiasm has less to do with the specific claims advanced
by Buell than with the belief that more emphasis should be placed
on the neocolonial pursuits of the United States even as it was establishing its own status against other imperial powers. Postcolonial
work concentrating on United States cultures accordingly has focussed
on black, Native, or ethnic issues within the United States rather
than on its "national" culture.[13] This emphasis does not invalidate
Buell's perspective, but it is clear that a hemispheric approach to the
Americas, like other postcolonial projects, cannot simply proceed
on the basis of parallels and commonalities. It must account for
uneven temporalities and power relations, and thus more than ever
retain the category of the local – of which the historical specificities
of the nation are a crucial mediation. In this regard, Canadianists,

with their sensitivity to US imperialist tendencies, may be particularly well positioned to press for a reorientation of hemispheric American studies toward the analysis of the United States as an empire.

In light of the synecdoche by which the United States habitually comes to be read as the referent of "America," we decided to add a critical twist to our participation in the Second World Congress of the International American Studies Association (IASA), which took place in Ottawa in 2005. The general interest in internationalizing American studies – and in opening the field up to the study of the Americas – was expressed here by the multilingual title of the congress: "Americas' Worlds and the World's Americas/Les mondes des Amériques et les Amériques du monde/Los mundos de las Américas y las Américas del mundo/Os Mundos das Americas, as Americas do Mundo." But the slippery signifier "America" remains problematic even in its pluralized, more clearly hemispheric usage, either urging the emphasis that Martí chose when writing of "Nuestra América" or inviting the question "whose America?" Winfried Siemerling thus playfully transformed the congress title by naming the two sessions that he organized for the 2005 IASA meeting "Canada and Its Americas." These IASA sessions followed on a seminar entitled "Canada and the Americas: Comparative Approaches to Canadian Literatures," led by Rachel Adams and Sarah Phillips Casteel at the 2003 meeting of the American Comparative Literature Association (ACLA) in San Marcos, California. The papers and debates at both the IASA and ACLA sessions demonstrated that there is a strong concern about protecting Canadian culture and literary scholarship in a North American, United States-dominated context. At the same time, they established that there is also considerable interest among both Canadian and non-Canadian scholars in discussing Canadian culture and literature in the wider context of the Americas.

It was striking to us that at other panels at the IASA meeting in Ottawa, few specialists in United States literature interested in internationalizing their field took full advantage of the Canadian conference setting to inquire actively into transnational issues that would include Canadian topics. Little is gained by splendid isolation, however, either for United States Americanists or for Canadianists. Articulations of Canadian vantage points in literary and cultural discussions of the Americas offer important opportunities to increase the visibility of Canada in these debates. Moreover, it is worth emphasizing the perhaps obvious point that a hemispheric American studies need not always or inevitably route itself through the United States (see Sadowski-Smith and Fox 2004, 23),[14] as is illustrated, for example, by the tradition of Canadian-based Latin American scholarship that is represented in the present collection by the chapters by Amaryll Chanady, Albert Braz, and Hugh Hazelton.

With the aim of encouraging a fuller engagement between Canadian and hemispheric American studies, we invited participants in the IASA and ACLA sessions to develop their contributions into chapters for the present volume and commissioned further papers to provide a fuller discussion of the issues and possibilities inherent in an active (rather than reactive) relationship between Canada and "its" Americas.[15] As emphasized above, alongside and in tension with the transnational or hemispheric turn, the national remains a relevant category of cultural analysis. To underscore this point, we open this collection with three chapters that point to some of the risks and challenges attached to a project that would incorporate Canadian literary production into a hemispheric framework. The chapters by Cynthia Sugars, Herb Wyile, and David Leahy – which make up the section "Defending the Nation?" – situate the hemispheric paradigm in relation to postcolonial and other comparative approaches that have been brought to bear on Canadian literature and consider key tensions surrounding the "worlding" of Canadian studies.

As Sugars and Wyile underline so forcefully in their contributions, it is not entirely clear how the theoretical commitment of postcolonial studies to the "local" holds up in its transnational reach when it comes to the question of the nation as a category and site of the local. Accordingly in "Worlding the (Postcolonial) Nation: Canada's Americas," Sugars asks: "How do we transnationalize the postcolonial while still retaining its *post*colonial, and localized, purchase?" Her chapter raises a number of important concerns from the perspective of Canadian studies regarding the hemispheric turn, including the tendency of inter-American studies to take the United States by default as its centre and to exoticize its margins. In "Hemispheric Studies or Scholarly NAFTA? The Case for Canadian Literary Studies," Wyile is similarly conscious of the risks that attend the hemispheric paradigm for a nation whose cultural autonomy has only recently been established and for a national literary criticism that "is in the throes of a process of postnational self-definition." As he notes, "The 'Canadian' part of Canadian literature is being substantially destabilized just at the moment when Canadian literature can be said to have really arrived." Nonetheless, in arguing that the category of nation needs to be retained, and in expressing a certain skepticism and discomfort regarding the hemispheric paradigm, Sugars and Wyile offer the kind of sustained and rigorous engagements with the hemispheric paradigm from a Canadian perspective that so far have been largely lacking from inter-American discourse.

In his chapter, Wyile also introduces the possibility of a "bilateral" approach that would balance comparative perspectives such as the hemispheric paradigm against "a continuing concern for local specificities that might be occluded or effaced by extranational, transcultural perspectives." Thus Wyile ultimately appears somewhat more optimistic than Sugars in pointing to the potential complementarity of national and transnational modes of reading.

Leahy's "Counter-Worlding A/américanité" moves a step further toward envisioning a viable hemispheric literary criticism that would not compromise Canadian specificity. In his chapter, Leahy takes up Gayatri Spivak's concept of "worlding" to consider the problem (posed by Sugars and Wyile) of whether the hemispheric paradigm inevitably replicates imperialist relations of power on the part of the United States. Leahy's response is to propose the concept of "counter-worlding." While recognizing that Canada and Quebec bear their own hegemonic relationships to other regions of the hemisphere, he calls on Canadians "to make USians' versions of *America* strange to themselves," not only in order to counter United States appropriations of "America" but also so that "we may better recognize and understand ourselves and what is worth keeping, modifying, and jettisoning of our own *américanité*." "[I]sn't it time," Leahy asks, "that more Canadians, Québécois, and other peoples within the Americas recognize and address our own *américanité* rather than reproducing the role of reactive colonial subjects in a reductive antiimperial dyad?" The two literary examples of counter-worlding that he cites, Dionne Brand and Paul Chamberland, anticipate the emphasis on black Canadian writing and Quebec writing in two sections of the collection that follow and powerfully illustrate the potential for a counterhegemonic hemispheric vision grounded in a Canadian poetics of resistance.

Bearing in mind some of the provisos cited by Sugars, Wyile, and Leahy, the remaining three sections of this collection then proceed to identify a series of pathways into a hemispheric contextualization of Canadian literary production. The first of these routes is through the "America" of the First Nations. Notably, First Nations and Native American writers like Louise Erdrich and Michael Dorris (*The Crown of Columbus*, 1991), Gerald Vizenor (*The Heirs of Columbus*, 1991), and Thomas King (*Green Grass, Running Water*, 1993) have offered parodies and rewritings of uncritical and outmoded foundational myths of the New World, thus contributing to the possibilities of rethinking a hemispheric approach to the Americas. Both Vizenor and King, it is interesting to observe, use the border between the United States and Canada to make the point that national boundaries are the consequence of white settlement and not primordial facts of thinking and belonging. For as Gregory Jay has written, "borders between the nations of the Americas are less the origins of our history than the products of it" (1997, 182).

King's *Green Grass, Running Water*, for instance, with its many intertextual references, has to be read across the United States-Canada border and thus in a transnational framework, partially because as a First Nations text it criticizes the borders imposed by imperial nations as artificial. Although the text has to be read as a specifically First Nations one, it also requires United States contexts in the treatment of blackness and the character of Babo, with its Melvillian intertext "Benito Cereno" (Siemerling 2005, 89–92). Yet at the same time, *Green Grass, Running Water* also has to be understood as a Canadian text. The character Eli Stands Alone, for instance, who blocks the building of a dam on Native territory in the novel, is readable as a direct reference to Elijah Harper, the member of the Manitoba Legislature who "blocked the Meech Lake Constitutional Accord in 1990" (Flick 1999, 150), thereby creating the current Canadian constitutional status quo. A reading of *Green Grass, Running Water* that pays attention to cultural difference on a national level thus would need to occur simultaneously with a reading that perceives the transnational and transcultural aspects of King's text.[16]

Accordingly, under the heading "Indigenous Remappings of America" we have grouped chapters by Amaryll Chanady, Sarah Phillips Casteel, and Albert Braz that engage simultaneously with national and hemispheric contexts. Rather than remaining within the confines of a single national setting, as studies of representations of the indigene have tended to do, Chanady's "Representations of the Native and the New World Subject" examines such representations in a hemispheric, comparative context by bringing into dialogue

Latin American and North American texts and authors. Her chapter juxtaposes such iconic figures as Catharine Parr Traill and José Martí to illustrate how the indigene was alternately constructed in North and South American settler cultures as Other to the New World nation and as an ancestor that legitimated the settler presence on the land. Chanady's analysis of modes of identification and symbolic filiation with the indigene highlights resonances but also key differences between Latin America and Canada. In particular, her discussion reveals with reference to Canadian texts such as Margaret Laurence's *The Diviners* that although mestizos are "an important paradigm of postindependence identity" and hybrid national belonging in Latin America, "the symbolic integration of the indigene in the Canadian postcolonial subject has been much more difficult, and miscegenation has never become a central trope for an emerging collective identity."

Whereas Chanady focuses on settler colonial and postcolonial literary production, Casteel turns to contemporary diasporic representations of the indigene. Like Chanady's chapter, Casteel's "Indigeneity and Diasporic Belonging: Three New World Readings of Chief Sitting Bull" identifies the search for rootedness as characteristic of New World literatures and takes as its point of departure the extent to which the figure of the indigene has served as a locus of anxieties about New World belonging. "However, if an anxiety about its nonindigenous status troubles Euro-American writing," Casteel asks, "how much more acute must that anxiety be for minority and immigrant writers in the New World?" Observing that contemporary diasporic writers of the Americas are increasingly addressing not only settler societies but also indigenous presences on the land, she proceeds to compare diasporic appropriations of the iconic figure of Chief Sitting Bull by three authors – one Japanese Canadian, one Jewish American, and one Afro-Caribbean. The readings she offers suggest that the figure of the indigene continues to carry considerable currency as a symbol of belonging in contemporary writing of the Americas.

Braz's "Outer America: Racial Hybridity and Canada's Peripheral Place in Inter-American Discourse" brings to a close this section of the collection by arguing for the inclusion of Canada in hemispheric discussions on the grounds that "the Canadian experience can complicate some of the verities about (inter)American life and culture." His chapter makes this case with reference to theories of racial hybridity, citing such well-known Latin American and Caribbean figures as Simón Bolívar, José Martí, José Vasconcelos, and Roberto Fernández Retamar but bringing them into conversation with the Métis nationalist leader and mystic Louis Riel and his concept of *métissage* as well as with several other historical and contemporary attempts to theorize a transracial Canadian identity. Whereas Chanady emphasizes the distance between the Latin American adoption of a mestizo identity and Canadian resistance to integrating the indigenous Other, Braz argues that Riel's embrace of racial hybridity and continental identity has much in common with its Latin American counterparts. Braz emphasizes that racial hybridity is not the privileged purview or distinguishing feature of Nuestra América but rather characterizes aspects of Canadian society and history as well. By highlighting Canada's inter-American connections, he effectively counters the elision of Canada from hemispheric discussions.

Like the colonial fact of white-Native contact, New World slavery was marked by the colonial spheres of imperial nations and later national boundaries yet was not limited by these. As a hemispheric practice, it was part of, or foundational for, the economies, societies, and cultures that became the "New World." Thus slavery and its aftermath provide a second pathway for a hemispheric reading of Canadian literary production. One example is the body of black writing that was produced in Canada West as a result of the Underground Railroad, especially after the 1850 fugitive slave law, which increased even further black immigration to Canada. These texts include, for instance, Mary Ann Shadd's *A Plea for Emigration, or Notes of Canada West* (1852); the newpaper she edited as the first black female editor in Canada, *The Provincial Freeman* (1853–60); its competition, Henry Bibb's *Voice of the Fugitive* (1851–53); a substantial number of written and oral but transcribed slave narratives; and what has been claimed to be the first black novel written in Canada, Martin Robison Delany's *Blake, or the Huts of America* (1859/1861–2) (see Siemerling 2007). Such texts have to be read both across the border and as wider transnational writing practices since the questions of slavery and of emigrationism in many of them clearly exceed North American frameworks. Yet they are also mediated by two particular national contexts that have different consequences. The United States situation has been partially explored by scholarship, but there is also a specifically Canadian context, one that is marked by the complex conditions of reception of these texts that address both the left-behind

United States situation and the new challenges of a nonslavery yet nonetheless often racist and difficult new Canadian environment. Although Upper Canada, for instance, moved to restrict slavery as early as 1793 with Simcoe's Act Against Slavery, scholarly work like Robin Winks's *The Blacks in Canada* (1971) and many other sources demonstrate the difficult experience of blacks even after slavery in Canada officially ceased in 1834.

In addition, this Canadian context must include the consequences for contemporary black writing in Canada of this body of nineteenth-century black writing as well as the problematic elision of race relations from foundational narratives and histories of Canadian literature. This question is at the heart of the texts examined by Maureen Moynagh and Winfried Siemerling in the two chapters that we have paired under the heading "Postslavery Routes." Moynagh's and Siemerling's chapters testify to the fact that the term "postslavery literatures," employed by George Handley in his 2000 study with reference to United States, Caribbean, and Latin American writing, has significant application in a Canadian context as well, albeit with necessarily local and national inflections.

Moynagh's "Eyeing the North Star? Figuring Canada in Postslavery Fiction and Drama" makes the case for reinserting Canada into discussions of postslavery writing of the Americas with reference to contemporary African Canadian writers. As Moynagh points out, in failing to consider this body of fiction, recent scholarship on postslavery writing has unwittingly reinforced the "north star mythology" that Canada is free of the moral burden of slavery that plagues United States historical memory. Writers such as Dionne Brand, Lawrence Hill, and George Elliott Clarke, however, powerfully contest this deeply entrenched Canadian national myth and, in so doing, provide a rationale for hemispheric and comparative approaches to Canadian writing. "A comparative, diasporic poetics is vital for coming to terms with these 'Canadian' texts," Moynagh writes, "since the history of slavery and its legacies, the 'local memories' of which Foucault speaks, are transnational." Her chapter thus represents an important reply to questions such as that of Sugars regarding the status of the local in hemispheric studies by arguing that for Canadian postlavery writing, the local *is* transnational.

Like Moynagh, Siemerling identifies Lawrence Hill as a figure whose literary production requires a reading that crosses national borders and that situates Canadian writing in relation to tropes that have emerged in postslavery literatures of the Americas more broadly. If Moynagh is critical of postslavery criticism for its elision of Canada, Siemerling's "'May I See Some Identification?': Race, Borders, and Identities in *Any Known Blood*" serves as a corrective to the absence of the northern border in borderlands scholarship by revealing an African diasporic Canada-United States borderlands to be a rich site of analysis. With its Harlem Renaissance and slave narrative intertexts as well as its thematization of travel across the Canada-United States border, Hill's *Any Known Blood* incorporates African American locations and histories, but as Siemerling emphasizes, this dimension of the novel does not detract from its "Canadianness." Rather, the border-crossing character of Hill's writing illustrates the relevance of the North American framework to Canadian literary criticism.

The collection concludes with a section on a third pathway, "Quebec Connections," which considers Quebec's links to a variety of sites in both hispanophone and anglophone America. Language emerges as a key focus and ground for inter-American comparison in several of the chapters included in this section. In "Translating in the Multilingual City: Montreal as a City of the Americas," Sherry Simon compares Montreal with two other colonial cities of the Americas: New York City and Mexico City. Her analysis focuses on Montreal's relationship to multilingualism and translation, subjects that have not received sufficient attention in discussions of North American cultural diversity. Yet translation, Simon notes, "is the key to citizenship" in that it is the index of the accommodation and "incorporation of [nonofficial] languages into the public sphere." Making reference both to Néstor García Canclini's understanding of Mexico City as created by the languages that are spoken within it and to Doris Sommer's Brooklyn-inspired "bilingual aesthetics," her analysis highlights tensions between the multilingual city of the Americas and national narratives of identity and belonging.

Monika Giacoppe's "'Lucky to be so bilingual': Québécois and Chicano/a Literatures in a Comparative Context," which also identifies language and multilingualism in particular as a basis for inter-American comparison, brings into focus multilingualism's relationship to gender. Although Chicano/a and Québécois writing have not often been the subject of comparison, Giacoppe identifies powerful thematic resonances between these two literatures. She notes, for example, that hybrid language emerges as a dominant concern of both literatures

because of the extent to which "their vocabulary and syntax bear
the traces of historical – and contemporary – battles for power and
identity." Despite pointing to key differences between the two bodies
of writing, she argues that common historical, political, and religious
factors contribute to the innovative and highly experimental multilingual writing that Québécois and Chicana women have produced.

Notably, Giacoppe's chapter draws Quebec writing into a borderlands framework that has usually been reserved for Chicano literary
production. Patricia Godbout's contribution also maps a Canadian
borderlands by situating the career of the Québécois writer and critic
Louis Dantin, the promoter of the work of Émile Nelligan, in the
context of cross-border migration from Quebec to the north-eastern
United States and return migration back to Quebec in the late nineteenth and early twentieth centuries. Godbout's "Louis Dantin's
American Life" offers new insight into Dantin's career by highlighting the impact of his lengthy period of residence in Boston on his
literary and critical production. Her analysis documents the impact
on Dantin of the United States context as well as of more specific
elements, such as the African American presence. In tracing how
Dantin "progressively and almost despite himself became just as
inhabited by America as he himself inhabited it," Godbout suggests
that his engagement with the United States bespeaks "the awareness
that French Canadians were acquiring of belonging to the American
continent" during this period.

Whereas a number of the essays collected here perform an inter-
American comparison by juxtaposing texts originating from different
regions of the Americas that share generic or thematic features, a
second model of hemispheric studies that emerges in the collection
is one that identifies texts that themselves encompass a transamerican
geography.[17] This second model informs the chapters by Hugh
Hazelton and Catherine Khordoc, which bring the collection to a
close. Hazelton's "Transculturation and National Identity in the
Novel *Rojo, amarillo y verde* by Alejandro Saravia" begins by drawing attention to the presence of Latin American writers in Canada,
to the growth of Canadian studies programs in Latin America, and
to a variety of other forms of literary and cultural exchange between
Canada and Latin America that have contributed to "the development of a comparativist dynamic and framework." Hazelton then
narrows his focus to consider how Alejandro Saravia, a member of
the new generation of Latin American writers in Canada, contrasts

the models of transculturation available in Bolivia and Montreal in his novel *Rojo, amarillo y verde*. Saravia's protagonist finds an antidote to Bolivia's failed search for national identity in "[t]he spontaneous, multi-ethnic – and translinguistic – process of transculturation" that surrounds him in Montreal. Saravia's novel thus manifests the multilingualism that Simon identifies as characteristic of Montreal as a city of the Americas, with Saravia's protagonist remarking that *"Montréal est la première ville nord-américaine avec la plus grande population trilingue* [Montreal is the foremost North American city with the largest trilingual population]."[18]

Finally, in "Looking beyond the Elephant: The Mexican Connection in Francine Noël's *La Conjuration des bâtards*," Khordoc brings to our attention the continental reach of a Quebec writer who "tak[es] Québécois literature out of Quebec" by incorporating Mexican settings and myths, Spanish phrases, and Latin American literary intertexts and techniques. This resituation of Quebec writing, Khordoc observes, "creates a hybrid effect and suggests the possible parallels between different cultures of the so-called New World." Khordoc traces a series of shifts in Noël's poetics from the nationalist, to the postcolonial, to a continental or hemispheric orientation. This trajectory finds its analogue in Québécois literary criticism, which is increasingly opening itself up to comparative approaches. Thus Khordoc joins Pierre Nepveu in arguing for the need to contextualize Quebec writing within a larger framework and to consider its linkages with the rest of the Americas. In Khordoc's view, the implications of this reorientation of both the literary imagination and literary criticism are far-reaching, requiring a re-evaluation of the very category of "Québécois literature" itself.

What becomes visible across the sets of case studies presented in the latter three sections of this collection are the advantages of bringing a wider comparative perspective to bear with respect to the role in Canadian culture, for example, of First Nations cultures, of postslavery writing, or of multilingualism. Inevitably, however, in pursuing these three pathways, this collection neglects other potentially fruitful modes of reading and areas of inquiry that could draw Canadian texts into a hemispheric frame. One such approach is ecocriticism, an interpretive framework whose focus on geography and ecology often serves to problematize geopolitical boundaries. Indeed, as Casteel has argued elsewhere (2007, ch. 3), Canadian writing can be productively read in a comparative hemispheric framework on the basis of its engagement with European modes of representing nature that circulated across New World national literatures. The standard view of representations of nature in Canadian culture (articulated by Northrop Frye in *The Bush Garden* and elsewhere and elaborated by Margaret Atwood in *Survival*) is that, since the contact period, Canadian writers and painters have almost universally depicted nature as unresponsive and lawless and as inducing a sense of repulsion and alienation. A key claim of this line of argument is that this negative response to nature distinguishes Canadian cultural production from an American pastoralism. Yet rereadings of iconic figures of Canadian literature, such as Susanna Moodie by Susan Glickman and other critics, highlight their engagement with pastoral and picturesque modes that circulated across the Americas. Instead of emphasizing the uniqueness of the Canadian response to nature, such critical rereadings suggest that Canada is heir to and shares with other nations of the Americas a common settler colonial discourse about the relationship between New World nature and belonging.[19]

As this example attests, although the approach developed in this collection seems particularly applicable to Native North American and black writing, where national boundaries are both relevant in establishing particular nation-state-defined contexts and insufficient or outright counterproductive as delimiters of the field of study, it is our belief that these examples can be multiplied beyond the cases presented here and that the discourses themselves that structure our fields of study should be as much the subject of our research and attention as the objects they constitute and analyze. Our hope, then, is that this collection may prompt further investigations into other possible routes and pathways that would open up hemispheric readings of Canadian literature and thereby help to render Canadian cultures and literatures more visible within the burgeoning field of hemispheric American studies.

Moreover, although an exploratory project such as the one we have initiated here remains necessarily incomplete, the essays in this collection nonetheless model an alternative paradigm of hemispheric American studies that illustrates how Canadian contributions stand to change existing US-based models beyond mere calls for greater geographical inclusivity. In offering hemispheric readings that decentre the United States, the essays collected here suggest certain key conceptual shifts with regard to the status of the nation in the hemispheric paradigm that the inclusion of Canada in hemispheric discussions will require. The concern expressed at the opening of this collection that the newly won specificity of Canadian literary and cultural studies may be lost or compromised through an engagement with hemispheric or North American studies remains both relevant and legitimate. What the essays map out, however, is neither an undifferentiated, unqualified transnational North American or hemispheric studies that declares issues of nation and state to be obsolete and a quaint residue of twentieth-century inquiry nor a hemispheric studies that would abolish the study of "United States literature" or "Canadian literature" as such. Rather, this collection pursues a contrapuntal approach that carefully reconstructs contextual mediations, including those of nation and state (and of nation-defined literary institutions), as well as mediations of race, ethnicity, class, and gender, while not limiting itself to one national literature in its contextual and comparative reach.

NOTES

1 See Bowering's *Burning Water* (1980), Poulin's *Volkwagen Blues* (1984), and Verdecchia's *Fronteras Americanas* (1993) for their engagements with various dimensions of the myth of the New World. See Hodgins's *The Invention of the World* (1977) and later novels for their links with Latin American magical realism. On Lafferière's transamerican poetics, see Braziel (2005).

2 For the cultural nationalism of the 1960s, literature and literary theory, which we have also chosen as a focus in this collection, constitute a privileged medium, as the influence and relevance of the so-called "thematic critics" – among them Northrop Frye and Margaret Atwood – and of writers like Dennis Lee illustrate. Frye establishes a number of themes he considers central to Canadian literature in his controversial "Conclusion" to the first edition of *Literary History of Canada* in 1965. In the "Conclusion" to the second edition of that text in 1976, he writes: "I am not a continentalist myself" (reprinted in Frye 1982, 74); in his mind, an "independent Canada would be much more useful to the United States itself than a dependent or annexed one would be, and it is of great importance to the United States to have a critical view of it centred in Canada, a view which is not hostile but simply another view" (74–5). Atwood follows Frye's thematic approach in her 1972 *Survival: A*

Thematic Guide to Canadian Literature and portrays Canadian ambivalence and psychological complicities vis-à-vis the United States, for instance, in her novel *Surfacing* (1972). Dennis Lee's essay "Cadence, Country, Silence: Writing in a Colonial Space," a response to the linguistic alienation he felt with respect to United States-dominated language and thought in Canada, has been often cited in postcolonial discussion about Canada. Although all three of these authors have at times pointed to the exemplary role of francophone Quebec authors in articulating cultural identity, Quebec cultural nationalism is expressed mostly in opposition to English Canada, not the United States.

3 We are grateful to Rachel Adams for her earlier work on this topic, both in co-organizing with Sarah Phillips Casteel a 2003 American Comparative Literature Association seminar in which the chapters by Braz, Moynagh, and Giacoppe were originally presented, and in co-editing the special issue of *Comparative American Studies* (CAS) on "Canada and the Americas" that resulted from the ACLA seminar. The present discussion builds on the introduction to the special issue of CAS that Adams and Casteel co-authored in 2005.

4 For the purposes of this introduction, the terms "inter-American studies," "hemispheric studies," and "New World studies" are treated as synonymous.

5 The impact that a transnational perspective has had on United States studies is illustrated by Paula M.L. Moya and Ramón Saldívar's statement in introducing a 2003 special issue of *Modern Fiction Studies*: "The trans-American imaginary is 'transnational' to the degree that 'American' fiction must be seen anew as a heterogeneous grouping of overlapping but distinct discourses that refer to the US in relation to a variety of national entities" (1).

6 One rare exception is John Carlos Rowe's observation in the January 2003 issue of *PMLA* on "America: The Idea, the Literature": "Too often in nineteenth-century United States culture, Canada figures primarily as an imagined place of ultimate freedom and its border a sort of psychic double for the internal border dividing South from North." Rowe insists that "The new comparative American studies must include Canada as a crucial and distinct multiculture ... the study of nineteenth-century transnationality must include not only the Canadian border but also the different and shifting borders imposed on native peoples by the systematic violence of enclosure we know as imperialism" (85). For a more sustained attempt to incorporate a discussion of Canadian material within a broader hemispheric analysis, see Casteel's *Second Arrivals* (2007).

7 Sadowski-Smith and Fox approach this question somewhat differently when they suggest that because of Canada's historically weak nationalism, Canadian studies may be especially well positioned to reconceptualize the category of the nation: "Because of its complex relationship to questions of state-sponsored nationalism and the nation-state as well as its long history of US domination, Canada constitutes an important location from which inter-Americas scholars in Canada, the United States, and other locations could rethink the role of the nation within theories of globalization" (2004, 19–20).

8 Accordingly, Sadowski-Smith and Fox caution that "If Americanists are to internationalize their field without becoming unwitting ambassadors of a US-inspired 'world without boundaries' … they need to travel abroad, engage in scholarly dialogue in languages other than English, and interest themselves in scholarship produced outside the United States and outside their own field. Until they do so, we fear that an Americanist-led hemispherism will only promote a vision of the Americas in which all academic disciplinary configurations are subordinate to those of the United States and in which every region outside of the United States is collapsed into a monolithic other" (2004, 23).

9 The TransCanada 3 conference on "Literature, Institutions, Citizenship" (Mount Allison University, Sackville, NB, July 2009) included "Hemispheric Studies" alongside six other key terms in its call for papers. A conference on "Canada and the Americas: Multidisciplinary Perspectives on Transculturality" (Glendon College, York University, Toronto, spring 2008) also suggested that hemispheric approaches may be gaining ground in the Canadian academy.

10 There are of course important differences between the cultural nationalisms underlying these projects. Both a state-sponsored cultural nationalism like the Canadian one and a more oppositional form like the Quebec one, however, are still preoccupied – as several contributors in the following pages point out – with the further articulation of a communal subject position that until recently has been an emergent one. This postcolonial interest connects them, in fact, with the postcolonial, often diasporic collective subjectivities whose various self-definitions cut across national identities at complex, often oppositional angles.

11 Recent rearticulations of cosmopolitanisms are undertaken mostly in order to theorize globalization and/or to counter exclusions that deny refuge, as for instance, in Jacques Derrida's On Cosmopolitanism and Forgiveness (1997 – trans. 2001). Yet "cosmopolitanism" – like "transnational" – is a double-edged term than can also elide the particular and

the local. If the transnational is not to be conceived by means of falling back upon uncritical versions of cosmopolitanism or universalism, then it has to be derived from some kind of relationship with instances of the particular and the local and their mediated constructions, such as nationally or regionally or culturally specific constructions of race, ethnicity, or gender. Hence the attempts at critical reconstruction of these terms by many theorists – such as in Walter Mignolo's "critical cosmopolitanism" (2000) or Anthony Appiah's "rooted cosmopolitanism" (2005) – or the recent Canadian critiques of cosmopolitanism by Brydon (2004), Moyes (2007), or Sugars in this collection. Instructive in this respect remains the older Canadian native-cosmopolitan debate, launched by John Sutherland's "Literary Colonialism" (1944), in which he attacks A.J.M. Smith's use of that distinction in the introduction to his *Book of Canadian Poetry* (1943); for a detailed discussion, see Kokotailo (1992) and Sugars (2001).

12 In her introduction to *The Usable Past*, Zamora eloquently captures the interplay of difference and commonality that necessarily textures comparative analyses of the literatures of the Americas:

The relative scarcity of comparative studies of literature in the Americas suggests the difficulty of establishing appropriate bases for comparison. Literary production in the hemisphere is vast and various; its traditions and forms did not develop in tandem, nor are its political and social purposes parallel. Comparatists are likely to uncover critical grounds that are comparable but not equivalent, different but not symmetrically so. Thus, I will be exploring differences in order to recognize the outlines of identity, and weighing historical and cultural diversity against shared forms of literary expression. Differences, too, bring texts and writers and readers and cultures together, for in recognizing specific differences we also recognize the shared experience of difference as such – of finitude, limitation, locality. (1997, xii)

13 See the volume edited by Singh and Schmidt, *Postcolonial Theory and the United States: Race, Ethnicity, and Literature* (2000), in which Buell (2000, 214n2) discusses the skeptical reception of some of his previous work.

14 One model for inter-American work that does not route itself through the United States is provided by the comparative Latin American-Canadian essays by Mary Louise Pratt and several other scholars that are collected in *Proceedings of the Xth Congress of the International Comparative Literature Association* (Balakian and Wilhelm 1985), under the heading "Canadian and Latin American Literatures and Their Interdependence."

15 In a subsequent stage in the production of this volume, the contributors had the opportunity to familiarize themselves with and respond to the arguments of the other chapters by consulting preliminary drafts that we posted on a website dedicated to this project.

16 The preceding paragraph and the discussion of African Canadian writing below are directly based on Siemerling's 2005 IASA conference presentation, "Can We Can the Can Can? The Futures of the Study of Canadian Literature."

17 Firmat (1990, 3–4) distinguishes between these two modes of hemispheric analysis by terming them "generic" and "mediative" respectively.

18 French passages are translated here and in the chapters by Giacoppe and Godbout, whereas contributions with more extensive textual analysis of francophone works, like those by Leahy and Khordoc, rely on the original text only.

19 Relatedly, bioregionalism, which concerns smaller geographical units, can contribute to hemispheric approaches by revealing the cross-border biological and cultural contexts that are occluded by political borders in the Americas.

DEFENDING THE NATION?

1

Worlding the (Postcolonial) Nation: Canada's Americas

CYNTHIA SUGARS

The best thing about contemporary writers – and Canadians in
particular – was that no one seemed to know where they were from.

Pico Iyer, *The Global Soul* (2000, 168)

Reading Edward Said's *Humanism and Democratic Criticism* (2004)
is a humbling experience. The essays collected in Said's volume not
only constitute a requiem for the profession of the humanities in
North America but also comprise an ardent defence of the ideal of
radical humanist practice that is very difficult to live up to. Embedded
within his discussion is an analysis of the links between a highhanded
humanist discourse and notions of national identity and homogeneity. This is evident in Said's terminology when he speaks of "nationalistic or Eurocentric humanism" as one and the same (2004, 47)
and defines nationalism in terms of "the affirmative mischief of
exceptionalism and ... patriotic sovereignty" (50). The "whole concept of national identity," Said insists, "has to be revised and, in
most places that I know, is in the process of being revised" (24).
Nevertheless, Said falls back on national constructs to enable his
discussion of the opening up of the social field/imagination and what
he terms the "worldly" realities of citizenship. Particular national
bodies, in his case Palestine and Ireland, are held up as national
entities that are to be applauded for continuing to struggle for cultural sovereignty. The alternative to national-cultural protectionism,
he asserts, "has been national effacement, national obliteration"
(37). But what Said doesn't tell us is why this should matter. Clearly,

for him, it does. But why should we care about national obliteration
if the current nation form needs to be dismantled?

Said's discussion is situated squarely within the context of what
he sees to be an American communal identity. In the name of opening up the national experience to all citizens, he insists that it cannot
be permitted that certain Americans should be allowed the only word
when "expressing or representing that group's experience, which,
after all, is part of the general American experience" (2004, 48).
Notwithstanding this appeal to national expression, his text is an
indictment of the "us-versus-them" impulse of nationalist discourse
(50), even as he calls for a greater attention to the "worldliness" of
all cultural texts, situated, as they necessarily are, within a "real
historical world" (48). Yet if worldliness is to be defined in terms of
the "power, position, and interests" that imbricate every cultural
text, how is it possible to really separate cultural production from
national concerns, and is it even desirable given his insistence on
state protection of the American public intellectual and of the inter-
rogative impulse of "true" humanist inquiry – the "democratic criticism" of his title? Indeed, Said cannot get away from the national,
as his repeated appeals to Palestinian, Irish, or even "American"
experience attest. The national remains the only way of even conceiving of the beyond of nationalism, just as the national is, after
all, at the core of "transnational" studies.

"There is a considerable discrepancy between what we practice as
humanists" through our commitment to a "nationalistically grounded
system of education," Said insists, and "what we know of the wider
world as citizens and scholars" (2004, 55). One might argue that
this discrepancy is visible in another guise: in the ways so many
contemporary critics declare the unfeasibility of the nation even as
they invoke it, and assume it, and require it in the critical moves
they undertake. As Robert Lecker describes it in a Canadian context,
this presents one with the "difficulty of celebrating nation as a function of dismissing it" (2000, 10).

Said's internationally positioned discussion of national constructs
and humanist discourse provides a useful perspective on the role of
Canada within the field of inter-American studies. My focus here is
Canada, but similar arguments might apply to other nations, identities, or regions within the hemisphere. At the outset, it might be
important to engage with the apparent specificity of inter-American/
hemispheric studies as a field unto itself. In opposition to such

configurations as transnationalism and/or globalization, hemispheric studies has the advantage of offering a restricted field of focus. Hence it presumes to defy the overly homogenizing purview of a global context. However, the turn to hemispheric specificity may itself still be too broad, and too diverse, to offer a meaningful conflation. Additionally, as with Commonwealth studies earlier on, inter-American studies contains a default centre – in this case, the United States – that renders every other national context marginal or extrinsic. This problem may arise more from the commonly accepted association of the term "America" than from the field itself, although the very invocation of the "Americas" necessitates some engagement with the presumed given of US dominance. Related to this is the fact that inter-American studies tends to invite an exoticizing of the margins (both within and outside the US). In this sense, Canada, with the exception of Quebec, might be too like the US to stand out in clear cultural or linguistic contradistinction to it and may therefore not be considered exotic or different enough.

In this chapter, I am interested in two fundamental issues that bear upon the question of the desirability of inter-American studies for the study of things Canadian. The first is addressed by Winfried Siemerling and Sarah Phillips Casteel in their introduction to this volume. There, they very ably describe the relative absence of Canada in discussions of inter-American studies, noting that in some instances "'America' tacitly continues to signify 'United States' in a surprising number of avowedly hemispheric academic treatises." The ease with which this slippage takes place makes it important to ask why Canada is marginalized within this discourse and whether the answer might be revealing (both for those who work in the field of Canadian culture and for those involved in the study of the Americas). Is it due to the implicit anti-Americanism of much Canadian cultural theory, or to the incipient nation-based focus in this work (which is there even in interrogations of the nation), or even to a presumed "sameness" between Canadian and US experience? And how do these issues differ from the inter-American contexts of the US in relation to Latin American nations? If the relative absence of Canada in this international context is related to the above points, is this cause for concern? In other words, what is being omitted in the race for hemispheric interrelation?

Second, where does the purchase of the national and the postcolonial reside in transnational theory? I ask this particularly in view

of postcolonialism's commitment to a sense of emplacement (both
in place and in history) and to localized intervention (when I say
local, it is important to remember that the national is one site of
the local). How do we transnationalize the postcolonial while still
retaining its *post*colonial, and localized, purchase? Does the notion
of "hemispheric studies" invite an oversimplification of historical
and discursive phenomena as it overextends scholarly investigation
beyond very useful boundaries? Can the national be retained within
a context of hemispheric studies, in what form, and at what cost?
What happens when the Canadian postcolonial, which is so indebted
to considerations of national space and history, goes global?

This is not to say that there are not important contextually specific
ways of pursuing hemispheric studies. Individual or comparative
studies of specific contexts within the Americas have a great deal to
offer to contemporary studies of global economics, culture, and history, not as a means of imploding national designations but as a way
of highlighting commonalities or differences that transcend and in
some cases precede nation-state boundaries. My concern, perhaps,
is that we advance these inquiries without prescription and, more
important, without the idealizing and often abstract rhetoric that
informed so much early postmodern and postcolonial theory about
the deconstruction of the "nation," particularly as it was applied to
the supposedly liberatory "disunity" of the Canadian state. If presented as a kind of panacea that supercedes and corrects the ills of
nation-based paradigms, an inter-American studies approach risks
becoming hamstrung by an idealizing rhetoric. At the outset, I am
skeptical when these approaches are "theorized" in terms of an
implicit progressivist teleology in and of itself (as an improvement
upon previous theoretical models – for example, nation-based criticism, localized historical approaches, postcolonial studies, and
regional studies). Timothy Brennan has identified how "the intellectual commodity known as cosmopolitanism" (2001, 662) is
automatically associated with such unexamined notions as "open-
mindedness," "decency," and the globally hip (659). In *At Home in
the World*, Brennan elaborates on these "relentlessly positive" connotations of cosmopolitanism to mean "'free from provincial prejudices,' 'not limited to one part of the world,' 'sophisticated, urbane,
worldly'" (1997, 19). In this sense, inter-American studies might
bear similarities to the rhetoric of particular strands of neoliberal
"globalization" that have been guilty of a good deal of idealist

rhetoric about a kind of "new world order." Roy Miki notes how the unravelling of state-constructed notions of national culture in Canada has been succeeded by an equally dubious rhetoric of commodified cultural difference: "In place of a highly state-constructed national identity are the signs of another 'Canada' coming to visibility. This one is configured in the global networks of a corporate commodity culture in which representations of difference take on value as a supplement to economics" (2005, 12). In this mode, not only does Canada become marketable as supremely "multicultural," but the multiple cultures are themselves used to serve the ends of "capital expansion" (16).

I also feel a sense of discomfort when such hemispheric approaches are posited as an extension of the scholarly purview beyond the realm of an assumed *parochialism* (what we might call the return of the colonial cringe). This note of condescension may be particularly disquieting for Canadian scholars since the history of Canadian cultural and national expression has been a long battle against such colonialist designations. Indeed, in the celebrations of moving beyond the nation, one hears echoes of the native-cosmopolitan debate that has so plagued Canadian cultural expression from its beginnings (i.e., the notion that the native, or national, was embarrassingly parochial and aesthetically naive, while the cosmopolitan was somehow free of the taint of national self-absorption and resided in the realm of the transcendentally universal). As I have argued elsewhere, Canadian culture has long been internally ruptured by the false dichotomy of the native and cosmopolitan (Sugars 2001). It is a historical irony that the site of the native most ably came into expression through the importation of supposedly "universal" standards from abroad. If the critical postcolonial move was to enact a revaluation of the "native," in a national context the "native" eventually came to be aligned with a homogenizing embrace, as individual constituents within the nation saw themselves being subsumed within an overarching national narrative. The positing of the terms "native" and "cosmopolitan" as antithetical is part of the problem, but current discourse that seeks to replace the nation with a transnational or global framework sometimes contains a worrying re-enactment of these debates. Certainly, this polarization never held true, as early writers in the Americas were inherently transnational. In Canada the modernist poets of the 1920s, '30s, and '40s – authors such as A.J.M. Smith, F.R. Scott, P.K. Page, and A.M. Klein – were insistent on the necessity of Canadian literature's engagement with international debates and movements, yet they were also committed to a "decolonizing" of Canadian cultural expression in order to counter what they saw as an overweening dependence on imported and outmoded forms. In a 1946 essay entitled "Has Poetry a Future in Canada?" Earle Birney identified the "true cosmopolitan" as "the great world figure [who] had his roots deep in the peculiar soil of his own country" (1980, 76). This argument was no less true of the Confederation writers a generation earlier, many of whom, such as Charles G.D. Roberts, Bliss Carman, Ernest Thompson Seton, and Sara Jeannette Duncan, published and worked in the United States and Britain (and, in Duncan's case, India). Many of these writers were actively invested in transnational literary activities while remaining committed to promoting a Canadian national literature (which they felt went hand in hand with national independence).

This kind of historical memory can get lost when the critical purview is applied to too vast a geographical and historical expanse, what Brennan describes as a form of "intellectual generalism" (1997, 27). To what extent is hemispheric cultural studies merely comparative literature by another name, with all the universalizing, and sometimes dehistoricizing, implications of that project? Said, for instance, refers to the Eurocentric basis of this discourse in terms of "the parochiality of its universalism" (2004, 53). Or worse, in what ways is it impelled by an urge toward novelty or exoticization, which extends into a cultivation of the seemingly exotic as inherently progressive? Might this account for the relative marginality of Canada within this discourse? It is perhaps also comparable to the now outmoded notion of Commonwealth studies, itself a kind of "hemispheric" formulation, which has been widely critiqued for its commitment to a centralizing notion of literary value (the centre being England, with its various Commonwealth satellites) and to a universalizing sense of how the postcolonial "reveals itself" in the margins.

These concerns have a bearing on the constitutive tautology that informs the revised definition of contemporary American studies. John Carlos Rowe's *The New American Studies* is committed to redefining the restrictive field of American cultural studies in order "to transform the traditionally nationalist concerns of the field to address the several ways in which 'America' signifies in the new global ... circumstances" (2002, 3). Rowe looks to what he "hopes" will be a "postnational future" (3). Yet his call for an approach that is "more comparative in scope" and more "sensitive to the global community," one that will address "the multiculture of the United States and the western hemisphere" (4), implies a recognition of and dependence upon national and cultural distinctions that his postnational fantasy would seem to belie. Such group-bounded distinctions are necessary in order for the field to be comparative at all. Rowe's approach also bears a discomfiting resemblance to Ben Wattenberg's description of the US as a "universal nation" (1990). What then stops the postnational field of American studies from becoming "AMERICA" writ large, with US culture as the new (albeit postnational because there would be few alternatives) universal?

It may be apropos to turn to the Canadian author Ray Smith by way of considering the positioning of Canada within the discourse of inter-American, hemispheric studies. One of Smith's most memorable lines defines "North America [as] a large island to the west of the continent of Cape Breton" (1989, 72). If you don't know where Cape Breton is, that is part of the joke. However, while the joke is premised on our knowing where and what North America is, it achieves its effect best if one knows a little about Cape Breton (at the very least, that it is small and fairly rural) and, more than that, a little more about the relation of Cape Breton to the nation of which it forms a part, Canada. The humour of Smith's comment, of course, is that it is topsy-turvy and imagines a diminishment of metropolitan power over the margins: Cape Breton becomes the centre by which North American geography, culture, and politics are measured. He puts the local in a North American context to highlight the absurdity of the marginal as central, while also *revelling* in the notion of the marginal as central, although the joke works only because margins are marginal.

Taken out of context, this quotation would appear to be a call for moving beyond the nation into the realm of the hyper-regional or, alternatively, into the realm of the North American (since the speaker is identifying the location of North America, not Cape Breton). Yet the story from which this quotation derives, entitled "Cape Breton Is the Thought-Control Centre of Canada," is anything but extranational in its impulse. If the title suggests a parodic critique of the arrogance of central Canadian nationalism, the story itself undertakes a further project. In addition to its send-up of Canadian cultural nationalism during the 1967 centennial celebrations, the story also functions as an endorsement of a certain version of national sovereignty in its interrogation of Canadian domination by Americans. First published in 1969, the story is ostensibly about resistance, and yet it is ultimately about paralysis. It concludes on a note of ineffectual, if tongue-in-cheek, apathy: "For Centennial Year, send President Johnson a gift: an American tourist's ear in a matchbox. Even better, don't bother with the postage" (Smith 1989, 75). In what is also a savage satire on US imperialism during the Vietnam War, Smith's story is a parable of the inevitability of failed cross-border communication: the American has lost an ear, while the Canadian's act of rebellion is not heard.

This may seem a somewhat oblique way to launch a conversation about the "worlding" of Canada, but it helps to crystallize a few things. Many of the anticolonial assessments of the 1960s and '70s are, in a sense, inter-American in thrust, even as they are anti-American in their accounts of paralysis in the face of either American imperialism or Canada's marginalization on the international stage. These include such works as George Grant's *Lament for a Nation*, Margaret Atwood's *Survival* and *Surfacing* (and later, *Bodily Harm*), Dennis Lee's "Cadence, Country, Silence" and "Civil Elegies," Leonard Cohen's "The Only Tourist in Havana Turns His Thoughts Homeward," and The Guess Who's "American Woman," from whom the speaker, as in Samuel Beckett's *Endgame*, insists he will escape but never does. The cultural nationalism of these works has come in for a great deal of criticism (even though the plundering "Americans" in Atwood's *Surfacing* are finally revealed to be from Ontario), while their insistently inter-American perspective, if one might call it that, remains evident in much popular Canadian cultural theory today. It is these texts, in turn, that paved the way for many of the more overtly "postcolonial" interventions in Canada in the decades that followed, achieving a movement beyond paralysis into the hefty intranational and international critiques that are imperative and ongoing today. Postcolonialism has enabled the study of the links between culture and geopolitics; perhaps more important, it brought the vector of local history into these considerations. It enabled the national ostensibly to supercede its assumed parochialism within a universalized global context – the sense of the nations within the empire writing back to the centre (or of Cape Breton becoming the cartographic landmark through which North America both achieves and loses its visibility). More recently, the combined interests of the national and the postcolonial have posed a force to be reckoned with – not only when turned inward, to critique the underlying oppressive character of national constructs, but also when turned outward, to interrogate what is an increasingly homogenizing, global order (whether restricted to one hemisphere or applied to "interhemispheric" studies).

In recent decades postcolonialism has launched an important critique of national formations. Indeed, a central paradox of contemporary postcolonial theory, in Canada and elsewhere, is that although its origins lie in the various nationalist decolonization movements of the period following the Second World War, its current incarnation is marked by a disenchantment with nationalism and its attendant colonizing effects. Hence contemporary formulations of the postcolonial and/or hegemonic character of Canadian culture have called for an interrogation of nationalist cultural discourse. These debates are driven by an awareness of the ways that various asymmetries of power, both internally and externally, are perpetuated through narratives that attempt to enforce a group identity. In the contemporary era, writes Pheng Cheah, "nationalism has become the exemplary figure for death" through its common association with "recidivism" (1999, 226). If nationalism has become suspect in the wake of the resurgence of religious fundamentalisms and ethnic nationalisms around the globe, so has the academic community condemned emotional appeals to the homogenizing and exclusionary discourse of national identity.

However, I am reluctant to move from this to a dismissal of the realm of the national in favour of a hemispheric paradigm that appears to offer a means of evading some of these problems and compromises. The turn to intranational constituencies (regions, ethnicities, sexualities, etc.) or to transnational models is potentially as prescriptive and homogenizing as the national formations that such discourses aim to circumvent. According to Neil Lazarus (1999) and Aijaz Ahmad (1994), the problem with many of these antinational arguments is their failure to distinguish between "progressive and retrograde forms of nationalism" (Ahmad 1994, 38). Nor does this imply that one need necessarily reject or wholly embrace any particular national context. As Ahmad points out, nationalism is not necessarily "some unitary thing": "one struggles not against nations and states as such but for different articulations of class, nation and state ... one strives for a rationally argued understanding of social content and historic project for each particular nationalism" (11).

Launching a critique of national constructs is not the same thing as rejecting them out of hand; likewise, to applaud certain instances of national cultural expression is not to endorse them unquestioningly. And by this logic, too, transnational links are not necessarily premised on an erosion of national categories. Rather, as Said suggests, the goal "is to complicate and vary" these categories' "modes of existence" (2004, 41). As Donna Palmateer Pennee notes, "The fact that literary studies can no longer operate as a vehicle for expressing and organizing a would-be homogeneous social structure is not … an argument *not* to use the literary for a heterogeneous but nevertheless shared social structure" (2004, 75). I state this outright because there is an assumption at large that one must either reject the appeals of national constructs altogether or risk becoming complicit with an outmoded, homogenizing system marked by intolerance and intellectual naiveté. This issue requires renewed attention today in what many identify as the contemporary "postnational," yet nevertheless inordinately "national," global era.

It is also important to retain the national and localized purchase of the ongoing anti-imperialist focus of postcolonial studies – in whatever form postcolonial studies is going to take in the future – in order not to participate in a (re)burying of history. This applies not only to the history of Canada's colonial national foundations but also to those easily obscured instances of intellectual prescience and open-mindedness among cultural practitioners in the past. The exhumation of forgotten histories is a relatively recent and unfinished project in Canadian cultural studies, described so well in the work of such writers as Robert Kroetsch, Margaret Laurence, and Rudy Wiebe. This can refer to the shame of an imperial history founded on oppression and violence, as well as to the temptation to paint all of one's predecessors with the same damning brush. One way of reconceiving the latter is to note how Canadian nationalist discourse in the past has sometimes been far more inclusive and progressive than it is credited for being. Early essays and speeches by figures such as Thomas D'Arcy McGee emphasize the inclusive nature of the proposed Dominion in the decades leading up to Confederation. At the time, one of the common arguments against Confederation was that it attempted to unite too disparate a group of people, who were separated by language, religion, ancestry, ethnicity, regional ties, and politics. The supposed homogeneous foundations of the Canadian nation-state were never a given, even though there were heated debates about how the new national imaginary would be configured.

In part, a reassessment of Canadian national expression involves being able to distinguish between enabling and oppressive nationalisms, including a recognition of the ways that the very notion of "Canada" (and, one might add, Canadian "identity") is premised on a slippage from invader to peaceful settler (Brydon 2003a, 57). "We can see this," write Anna Johnston and Alan Lawson, "as a strategic disavowal of the colonizing act. In this process, 'the national' is what replaces 'the indigenous' and in doing so conceals its participation in colonization" (2005, 365). Numerous critics have written about the colonialist foundations of the Canadian nation-state and have launched a call for a return to history in the study of Canadian culture. Himani Bannerji, for example, identifies the two contradictory foundational contexts of the contemporary Canadian nation – a settler colonial state and a liberal democracy – and notes how this contradiction has informed Canadian culture, society, and public policy from their beginnings (2004, 292–3). Imre Szeman echoes her analysis and expresses concern about the current turn toward global capitalist formations; in privileging the global, he argues, we may be in danger of "suppressing our ability to ask deep questions about the political and social function of Canadian [culture] with respect to everyday life in Canada" (2000, 193). Stephen Turner similarly insists on the need to uncover the ways settler societies are premised on an inherent forgetting of history. "An unacknowledged history," he maintains, "will only return in more virulent form" (1999, 37). Since Canada "covered over the violence of its origins by naturalizing itself as a nation" (Miki 2005, 4), it may be important not to forgo the nation as a site of interrogation, particularly as nationalist rhetoric continues to be invoked in popular discourse about national destiny and, indeed, global relevance. Literary attempts at national remembering, such as have been so powerfully undertaken by Joy Kogawa's *Obasan*, Sky Lee's *Disappearing Moon Cafe*, and Joseph Boyden's *Three Day Road*, are important national cultural interventions.

Notwithstanding the narrow insiderism that can result from localized and/or nationalist perspectives, those committed to a postcolonial, antiracist, or otherwise ethically informed study of Canadian culture risk being disempowered by a dissolution of national categories,

particularly in view of the neo-imperialist tenor of present-day
American transnational and global operations. Clearly, a hemispheric
model can be mobilized to assess counterdiscursive approaches to
the United States' global reach, but it must be wary of a too easy
idealization of transnationalism. What is the implied agenda of a
transnational, hemispheric model? How is the *non*-American nation
being positioned? How is the nation-state, as a category, being figured? Gregory Jay puts it succinctly when he comments on the
dubious nature of such radical critiques of nationally circumscribed
fields of study: "Do 'we' in the United States want to prescribe such
an abandonment of local and regional cultural traditions? Do we
have the right? Would this call for postnationalism return us to the
widely discussed observation that the criticisms of identity politics
arise just at the moment when those whose identities have been
marginalized demand recognition?" (quoted in Siemerling 2005, 2).
As Fredric Jameson points out, "in speaking of the weakening of the
nation-state, are we not actually describing the subordination of the
other nation-states to American power?" (2000, 50).

I say all of this, as well, in the context of Canadian-American
relations, where Canadian culture is flatly marginalized in American
cultural studies. I need go no further than the avowedly inter-
American literary association (based in New York) to which I belong
– the Modern Language Association – where my field of study (and
I'm not the first to note this) is designated "literatures other than
British and American." I'm aware, as well, of the relative marginalization of Canada from the international discourse of postcolonialism,
particularly in the various anthologies and primers of postcolonialism that have appeared in the past fifteen years. There has also been
fierce debate about the very applicability of the label "postcolonial"
to a developed settler society such as Canada. If the nation is defunct,
and postcolonialism applies only within a hierarchy of degrees of
"true" postcolonial merit or postcolonial disenfranchisement, and
if Canadian culture is merely an appendage to the all-seeing purview
of institutions like the American Modern Language Association,
then where, finally, *is* Canadian culture if not lost in some ideal of
globalized/hemispheric space?

The position of a Canadian studies scholar is therefore difficult:
how does one include Canada in a transnational, "New World"
context while retaining its already problematic global emplacement?
Can we transnationalize Canadian experience without dissolving it

into the realm of an "American" or "hemispheric" universal, what Frederick Buell describes as America's invention of a "cultural nationalism for post-national circumstances" (1998, 550), or into Wattenberg's euphoric characterization of US hybridity as the "first universal nation" (1990)? Wattenberg's statement easily lends itself to Brennan's critique of how "cosmopolitanism *is* the way in which a kind of American patriotism is today being expressed" (1997, 26, original emphasis). Even Bruce Robbins, who defends politically interventionist and "worldly" notions of internationalism, notes how "the United States has demanded, as a sort of natural right, that its citizens and media be able to pass unhindered across the borders of nations and continents" (1999, 3).

Let me pose two questions that are becoming more pressing as notions of national belonging and national culture become increasingly excoriated. The first question is: To what extent are we monumentalizing the nation by fetishizing the space beyond it? The call to think "beyond the nation," or the notion that we can no longer speak of a "national imaginary," or the sense that we are in a "post-national" era, risks a misrepresentation of the workings and evolving nature of national constructs, not to mention their continued hold on citizens at large. In throwing out the baby with the bath water, what are we losing? What potential for political efficacy, rights negotiations, economic restructuring, environmental initiatives, and advocacy is being sacrificed, particularly when it is crucial to imagine new collectivities in the face of modernity and globalization (Szeman 2003, 202; Saul 2005) and new modes of civic participation and/or interrogation? As Buell argues, "it would be a terrible mistake to ... 'move beyond' forms of critique and advocacy based on ideas of national community and possibilities of change within a national frame" (1998, 580). What lies between the public space of the local and the global? Some critics have argued for the nation's "continuing imperativity as an agent of ethicopolitical transformation in neo-colonial globalization" (Cheah 1999, 250). It provides a way of fostering empowered "identification with an extended community" (McClintock 1995, 353), however heterogeneous that community might be. According to Pennee, "the national remains useful in our attempts to cross the major divide of globalized life – the divide between increasing social fragmentation on the one hand, and an increasing need for alternative methods of social integration, on the other" (2004, 77). This is something worth considering in view of the ongoing and politically interventionist anti-imperialist critiques of national constructs. What is there, really, in the extraterritorial space beyond the nation? *Where* is *there*?

The second question, integral to the first, is: To what extent are we producing essentialist notions of the nation in order to debunk it? And in doing so, are we reifying the homogenizing spectre of the nation, which, after all, it has taken so long to dismantle? Moreover, does such a stance represent an oversimplification of sociocultural history, particularly of what have been sometimes too readily identified as symbiotic links between culture and the state? Homi Bhabha is often identified as one of the prime critics of the nation, and he is frequently used in the service of promoting a move beyond national boundaries. As Lazarus sees it, Bhabha uses "the concept of 'post-coloniality' ... *against* nationalism" (1999, 135, original emphasis). Yet Bhabha himself observes that nation formations cannot be said to have been "superseded by those new realities of internationalism, multinationalism, or even 'late capitalism,' once we acknowledge that the rhetoric of these global terms is most often underwritten in that grim prose of power that each nation can wield within its own sphere of influence" (1990, 1). Indeed, Bhabha's main contribution to these debates is an interrogation of national constructs expressly because they continue to be so meaningful to citizens and because they are inherently unstable, heterogeneous, and evolving.

Anne McClintock offers a convincing addendum to such dismissals of the force of national constructs: "nations are not simply phantasmagoria of the mind but are historical practices through which social difference is both invented and performed. Nationalism becomes ... radically constitutive of people's identities" (1995, 353). To dismiss the viability of the nation form because it is essentially oppressive or homogenizing is to deny its very real effects and to risk disenabling the sites where the nation can be most usefully adapted for oppositional work in the present. To do away with the nation, and the possibility for intranational connections, may therefore be a risky project. It doesn't allow us to oppose the oppressive and restrictive workings of the national body. In other words, it obscures those locations and moments where an effective critique of national power structures can be launched. Moreover, the vector of the nation may be what enables us to resist the imperialist claims of more powerful international constituencies. As Hortense Spillers stated in her 2005 address to the International American Studies Association, "we still have a need for nation-states that protect people."

Within a cosmopolitan context, the nation *is* the local. It leaves open the possibility of a political project that opposes the increasing atomization of global subjects while also responding to the dialectic of sameness and difference within its bounds. Assimilating the nation (in this case, Canada) into the overarching discourse of the postnational risks subjecting it to all the negative repercussions that implies: a caving in to capitalist commodification, a fading into the realm of the homogeneous, a flattening of local styles, a reification of a position of international subordination, a failure to imagine new social relations, and a succumbing to political apathy masked as celebratory cosmopolitan relativism. It also disenables the potential for the Canadian locale to interrogate the American, which, given the present context of global imperialism and the US's "war against terrorism," is something we should be thinking seriously about. All of this appears painfully prescient given Canadian author Rohinton Mistry's post–9/11 experience of being hounded when travelling on a book tour in the United States because he looked "suspicious" and had, well, entered from Canada.

A number of questions emerge from these ruminations: Can Canada afford to be subsumed within the category of hemispheric, inter-American studies? Do scholars and students of Canadian culture have the luxury of being conflated within the larger context of American studies when Canadian studies (and Canadian postcolonialism) still receives such short shrift internationally? Are we proclaiming the subsumption of the Canadian into the alluring liminal realm of the inter-American while we watch the only too tangible American universal become fat on a surfeit of these posthumous postnational satellites?

Yet can Canada afford *not* to be included within these discussions? To opt out of the discussion of inter-American studies altogether may be to segregate Canadian literary study even further, to contribute to its hemispheric invisibility. I therefore ponder these questions with a degree of reserve.

My title, of course, alludes to the term coined by Gayatri Chakravorty Spivak to describe the ways colonized space is made to exist as part of an imperialist, internationalist world order – embodied in her reference to the "worlding" of the Third World (1985, 128). Her definition of the term is largely antithetical to Said's understanding of "worldliness," with which I began this essay. The worlding of the margins becomes a way of inscribing them as colonized and of inscribing imperialist discourse upon those locations. In similar ways the postcolonial might be understood to be "worlded," and hence defused, in the context of international space. Celebrations of cosmopolitanism strive for a similar emplacement of the margins whereby "the local self [is] exported *as* the world" (Brennan 2001, 675, original emphasis). Although this project has a certain appeal, it depends what side of that world, or what section of the hemisphere, one happens to occupy. One person's global is another person's local. If you're standing in Cape Breton, or, for that matter, anywhere north of the 49th parallel, you might start to misrecognize your "home ground" as "foreign territory" (to cite Atwood 1972, 11), or, what may be worse, as deterritorialized liminal (and hence invisible) space.

The journalist and author Pico Iyer, globetrotting inter-American par excellence, has become well known in Canada for his book *The Global Soul* (2000), in which he champions Toronto as his favourite cosmopolitan city. Through Iyer's timely intervention, Canada was securely entrenched on the global map. His discussion is characteristically effusive, decontextualized, and unself-aware. Iyer's heady experience of the city includes "hand[ing] my laundry to the woman from the Caribbean who guarded the front desk of the Hotel Victoria ... Then I'd slip around the corner to where two chirpily efficient Chinese girls would have my croissant and tea ready almost before I'd ordered them. I'd stop off in the Mövenpick Marché down the block – run almost entirely by Filipinas (the sisters, perhaps, of the chambermaids in the Victoria) ... Then, not untypically, an Afghan would fill me in on the politics of Peshawar as I took a cab uptown ... Toronto felt entirely on my wavelength" (2000, 124–5). Any sense of gender and class relations here is entirely absent, while Iyer, the "Global Soul," egocentrically identifies with everyone he meets. "[A] friend," he remarks, "is someone who can bring as many of our selves to the table as possible" (125), which renders all of Toronto, and the globe, a kind of salad bar for his own personal delectation. Not surprisingly, Iyer's idealized depiction of Toronto as the place where "Empire could come to atone for some of its sins" (125) has been criticized for his lack of any real knowledge of the city. And his dehistoricized account of Toronto as a traditional "no-man's-land for various Indian tribes" (120) transformed into a postmodern "meeting place of wanderers" where there is "no ground zero from which everything is measured" (147–48) exemplifies the ways a too easy crossing of borders (between nations, between time periods) slides into vacuous cultural theory.

The leap from this to Iyer's 2002 *Harper's* article on Canadian fiction is therefore not very far. In this piece, he invokes a notion of Canada as an airport transit lounge, "one of the in-between spaces where foreigners congregate" on their way to somewhere else (79). In a similar vein, Yann Martel, upon winning the Man Booker Prize for *Life of Pi* (2001), spoke of Canada as "a good hotel to write from." The worlding of Canada would seem to render the national location irrelevant, or at best amorphous – a convenient stopping ground for writers who want a safe (borderless) place to write from but not to identify with (like the Indian plantation hostel from which the cosmopolitan narrator of *Life of Pi* sits down to write). It would seem, in other words, to deterritorialize and disinherit Canadian cultural and historical space, which I fear could be the fate of Canada (and Canadian scholarship) if subsumed within the albeit restricted space of the New World hemisphere.

NOTE

I would like to acknowledge the assistance of a Standard Research Grant from the Social Sciences and Humanities Research Council of Canada (SSHRC) in the preparation of this chapter and the original conference paper upon which it is based. My thanks also to Brenda Vellino for her astute comments on an early version.

2

Hemispheric Studies or Scholarly NAFTA? The Case for Canadian Literary Studies

HERB WYILE

Because of the influence of globalization, increasing interrogation of the nation as a suitable framework for cultural identification, and growing interest in comparative literature, scholars are giving more and more serious consideration to comparative perspectives on writing in the Western Hemisphere. However, the prospect of hemispheric studies is likely to be viewed by many Canadian literary critics and scholars (among others, undoubtedly) with a good deal of skepticism. To give some sense of why that might be the case, I'd like to draw an example from one of the most influential cultural figures in the Americas – namely, Bugs Bunny. In a *Looney Tunes* episode titled "14 Carrot Rabbit," Bugs is being chased by one of his many nemeses, Chilicoot Sam (a.k.a. Yosemite Sam). The camera zooms back to show Bugs running across a map of North America, Chilicoot Sam in hot pursuit. They start southward from Alaska and cross an apparently blank space into Washington before veering eastward. On closer inspection, faintly printed on that space – which most Canadians would recognize as the location of the province of British Columbia – is the word "Canada." My point here is not to indict Bugs Bunny's creators (to whom I owe a lasting debt for their formative influence on my appreciation of parody, irony, sarcasm, and much more) for their geographical shorthand. As far as the cartoon is concerned, this cartographical asymmetry has a valid narrative foundation: Sam has vowed to chase Bugs "through every state in the union." Still, the image of Canada as a faint and monolithic presence beside a distinct and differentiated United States is a resonant one and provides a visual illustration of one of the primary reasons that scholars of Canadian literature might be wary of hemispheric studies: it threatens to relegate Canadian literature, which has spent roughly the past fifty years shedding its status as terra incognita, to where it once belonged.

It may be telling that my reaction, as a scholar of Canadian literature, to the prospect of hemispheric studies is an automatic, almost knee-jerk, defensive posture vis-à-vis the United States. At the same time, I like to think that I come by this reaction honestly, as it results from the fact that, as Winfried Siemerling and Sarah Casteel state in their introduction to this volume, "Canadian culture and criticism are frequently marginalized in hemispheric comparative work." As the *Looney Tunes* episode suggests, a consideration of a hemispheric approach to literary studies must begin with a recognition of the fundamentally asymmetrical level of knowledge and interest between America and its others, an asymmetry vividly captured by William Watson: "We know about them but they don't know about us. Being Canadian is a little like stalking, albeit involuntary and harmless stalking. And we are very successful stalkers: most Americans have no idea that we are here" (1998, 222).

Whereas it is quite easy for Americans to ignore Canadians, and perhaps understandable that they would, most Canadians do not have the luxury to reciprocate, given the significant influence the United States has on Canada politically, economically, and culturally. No matter how much Canadians may be thoroughly integrated into the popular cultural regime of North America, and however much they may consider themselves (consciously but more often unconsciously) to be honorary Americans, cultural autonomy remains as pressing an issue as political sovereignty and economic control. Indeed, although the current North American Free Trade Agreement (NAFTA) has been beneficial to many sectors of the Canadian economy, the Free Trade Agreement with the United States was vociferously opposed by many Canadian artists and writers in the late 1980s because of anxiety about its effect on Canada's political autonomy but more specifically about the threat it posed to Canadian culture – that it would further erode our perennially fragile cultural autonomy. The intervening two decades since the implementation of the original Free Trade Agreement, which have seen increasing concentration of power and vertical integration in the book industry, and concomitant pressures on small presses (which have played a huge role in cultivating and supporting Canadian literature), have arguably reinforced skepticism about the cultural benefits of deregulation of trade. American violations of provisions of NAFTA (most notably on softwood lumber and beef cattle) in response to domestic economic and political pressures have further entrenched concern on this side of the border about the idea of an open hemisphere, at least in economic terms.

But what does this have to do with the prospect of hemispheric literary studies? Is the implication that a comparative literary hemispheric paradigm would replicate the politics of unequal exchange that currently obtains under NAFTA? Should scholars of Canadian literature steer clear of such a paradigm because it threatens to replicate the current domination of the United States in so many sectors? Although I am not suggesting that a hemispheric approach is neither advisable nor viable, there are grounds for concern that hemispheric studies will take the form of a comparative regime in which the literature of the United States dominates – that in a literary version of "the US and its Americas," Canada, along with all the other "Americas," will be lost in the shuffle.

I am also aware, however, that in exploring this knee-jerk response, I am replicating the very politics that I profess to critique, for that response has firmly positioned the United States as the centre, as that of which one must be wary. Paradoxical as it may seem, Canadians' obsession with being culturally and politically at arm's length from their southern neighbours can have the effect of making Canadians guilty of the kind of cultural insularity of which they regularly accuse their southern counterparts. Alhough perhaps more inclined to comparative approaches than Americans, Canadian scholars are predominantly preoccupied with their own textual backyard, as it were, and are guilty of extending insufficient recognition to literature around the world. However, it's one thing to be insular from a position of strength; it's another thing to be insular from a position of cultural vulnerability – to be defensively insular, as it were. To put it another way, if you are a mouse sleeping next to an elephant, as Pierre Trudeau once described Canadian-American relations, it's hard to see what's on the other side of the elephant.

Nonetheless, critics can and do look across, rather than just within, the borders of those countries that constitute the Western Hemisphere, and there are a number of studies that suggest the value of comparative approaches to the literatures of the Americas. Earl E. Fitz's 1991 study *Rediscovering the New World: Inter-American Literature in a*

Comparative Context, impressive in the breadth of its coverage of the literatures of the Western Hemisphere since pre-Columbian times, suggests the many aesthetic and thematic resonances across those literatures that come from the shared experience of being part of a "New World" discovered and framed by the "Old World." Fitz's study, however, also exhibits the limitations of such approaches in its tendency toward somewhat reductive critical formulations in the process of describing thematic, formal, and historical correspondences across the literatures Fitz studies. For instance, examining the impact of modernism on New World literature, Fitz contends that "[t]he result was a distinctly new literature, avant-garde in its forms, techniques, and imagery but uniquely American" (1991, 145); however, this seeming unity is at odds with the heterogeneous manifestations of modernism in New World literatures that he describes, as indeed is suggested by the title of the chapter in which he makes his claim: "The Five (Six?) Faces of American Modernism." Later, in a chapter on the quest for identity, Fitz argues that an "abiding concern over 'becoming something' turns up again and again in the literatures of the New World" (168); the shortcoming here is not just that such a preoccupation is hardly exclusive to New World literatures (and Fitz here as elsewhere is careful not to cultivate the impression that it is) but also that the chapter itself is so encyclopaedic in its inclusion of writers from across the Western Hemisphere, searching for very different kinds of identity, as to render the unifying theme of identity somewhat banal. Fitz's study makes the compelling case that "the study of Inter-American literature" is "yet another useful approach to our better appreciation of world literature" (234), but the centripetal forces pulling against Fitz's attempts to assert continuities across the literatures of the New World highlight the limitations of such an approach.

Another example of the fertility of comparative approaches is David Jordan's 1994 book *New World Regionalism*, a comparative exploration of the issue of regionalism in the Western Hemisphere, which focuses in particular on Brazilian, Mexican, American, and Canadian literature. Jordan sketches the complicated aesthetic and critical history of regionalism in the context of the "New World" and illustrates, among other things, the metropolitan-rural dynamics that developed around the vexed term in a range of geographic contexts across the hemisphere. The literary texts that Jordan examines under the rubric of "New World regionalism" "indicate how

regional specificity can shape New World fiction to reflect vital conflicts along borders that define personal, regional, and national
identity" (1994, 128). More recently, Winfried Siemerling's *The New
North American Studies* (2005) poses a sustained challenge to nationalist frames of literary construction and locates a transcultural reading of texts in North America against the background of Eurocentric
constructions of the New World in hemispheric terms. And there are
many other fruitful approaches, such as comparative perspectives
on multiculturalism, on the literatures of indigenous peoples, on
fictional representations of history, and on particular genres like
magical realism.

There are reasons, however, why such comparative approaches
are not more numerous in Canada, relative to those studies that
adopt a national framework within which to examine literature
written in and/or about Canada. One of the most important considerations is the relatively nascent status of Canadian literature itself.
One reason an automatic response in some quarters to the prospect
of hemispheric studies is anxiety that it will result merely in the
eclipse of Canadian literature is that Canadian literature, as a relatively autonomous and vigorous literature, or cluster of literatures,
is still a fairly new phenomenon, arguably something that goes back
only to the 1960s. Before that time, it was largely characterized by
colonial subservience, lack of self-confidence, and lack of a supportive domestic readership. That largely stifling colonial influence
extended well into the twentieth century, and Canadian writers'
attainment of an international profile is a relatively recent development. As Canadian literature has established a more robust presence
both domestically and on the international scene, however, critics
and scholars have increasingly come to question national and nationalist formulations of literary and cultural identity, essentially asking:
just what does the "Canadian" part of "Canadian literature" mean?
Literary critical nationalism has been critiqued for its questionable
teleology and organicism, its selective self-definitions, and most
vigorously for its racial, cultural, and regional exclusiveness. As Diana
Brydon observes, "literature, Canada and the notion of a national
literature have all become problematized concepts" (2007, 5). This
questioning of literary and cultural nationalism, indeed, has pro-
gressed to the point at which it might be said that Canadian literary
criticism is in the throes of a process of postnational self-definition.
Scholars and critics are struggling to identify in just what contexts

it is viable to examine literary texts written in and/or about Canada – as exemplified, for instance, by a special millennial issue of the journal *Essays on Canadian Writing* entitled "Where Is Here Now?" (2000) and by the TransCanada conference series organized by Smaro Kamboureli and Roy Miki (including 2007's *Trans.Can.Lit*, a collection of essays developed from the first TransCanada conference in Vancouver in 2005) – with a substantial segment of those critics and scholars inclined to challenge, if not indeed move beyond, a national literary paradigm.

Such interrogations of the nation have come predominantly, if not exclusively, as a result of the increasing influence of postcolonial theory, which has been the primary force behind challenges to the cultural nationalist frameworks that prevailed in Canadian literary criticism through the 1960s and '70s. Indeed, easily the most significant development in Canadian literary studies over the past twenty years has been the eclipse, or at the very least the reframing, of national literary paradigms by postcolonial perspectives. Although postcolonial approaches are increasingly being eclipsed by globalization studies, to the degree that Canadian literature has tended to be located within a transnational comparative literary perspective, it has been one that looks beyond the hemisphere, particularly to other settler-invader cultures such as South Africa, Australia, and New Zealand but more broadly to the constellation of formerly colonized English- and French-speaking cultures. This fundamentally comparative approach to Canadian literature is by now firmly entrenched in Canada, but the attempt to locate Canadian literature within postcolonial studies has not gone unchallenged. As leading Canadian postcolonial critics such as Brydon (1995) and Stephen Slemon (1990) have underscored, there is a good deal of resistance in the international scholarly community to seeing countries like Canada, New Zealand, and Australia – where the aboriginal populations have largely been displaced by European settlers – as postcolonial. On the other hand, as Laura Moss stresses in her introduction to the essay collection *Is Canada Postcolonial? Unsettling Canadian Literature*, the national pastime of musing over Canadian identity has undeniably been displaced by "searching for a postcolonial identity" (2003, vii).

Although there is nothing approaching a consensus on whether Canada is, indeed, postcolonial – or even on whether it might be desirable that it be so – certainly the prevailing assumption has been

that postcolonial theoretical and critical perspectives are highly relevant and useful for examining a range of dynamics in and characteristics of Canadian literary texts. Most critics are ready to concede
that Canada is not postcolonial in the way that India, say, or Nigeria,
or Jamaica is postcolonial, but most critics would also argue that
the point of postcolonial perspectives is not to establish some con-
sensual, monolithic definition of postcoloniality. Rather, the attraction of postcolonial paradigms resides in their utility for examining
and articulating the specific modalities of particular societies that
have been marked by the experience of colonization. As Brydon puts
it, "Postcolonialism is neither a thing nor an essentialized state;
rather it is a complex of processes designed to circumvent imperial
and colonial habits of mind" (1995, 11). Speaking specifically of
Canadian Literature, Donna Bennett argues for the relevance of
postcolonial modes of questioning, just so long as such modes are
neither monolithic nor exclusive:

> The postcolonial model invites us to see – and gives us a new
> way of seeing – the play of tensions within Canadian culture
> as well as the tensions between Canada's culture and that of
> any external centre. Perhaps what it finally helps us to see is
> that there is a collection of cultures within the *idea* of English
> Canada, not so much a mosaic as a kaleidoscope, an arrange-
> ment of fragments whose interrelationships, while ever changing,
> nevertheless serve – by virtue of their container, we might say –
> not only to influence what we see when we look through the
> glass, but also to affect the placement of the other elements in
> the array. (1994, 196–7)

As Slemon notes, however, in the past few years postcolonial critical approaches have experienced a kind of disciplinary crisis, and
"[p]ostcolonial critical study is now in the process of disciplinary
redistribution," a victim in part of reductive critical strategies: "Too
many postcolonialists fitted too many postcolonies to the same conceptual straightjacket. Too many cross-national organizing principles
displaced too many registers of internal national division" (2007,
76). This recognition of the importance of diversity – a recurring
aspect of the debate over the question "is Canada postcolonial?" –
provides another cautionary note to the prospect of situating Canada
within a hemispheric literary paradigm. A routine insistence during

the debate over Canada's status as postcolonial has been on the importance of retaining the contextual specificity of our understanding of Canadian literature – that is, the recognition that Canada had a certain kind of experience, or perhaps kinds of experiences, of colonialism and that in linking Canadian literature to the literature of other societies that had had their own experience of colonialism, it is important not to erode or efface that specificity in the process. This concern, of course, is a variation on a longstanding debate that has emerged repeatedly during the process of Canada's emergence from under the cultural shadow of England, particularly in A.J.M. Smith's notorious distinction between national and cosmopolitan strains in Canadian poetry in his introduction to the first edition of *The Book of Canadian Poetry*: "Some of the poets have concentrated on what is individual and unique in Canadian life and others upon what it has in common with life everywhere. The one group has attempted to describe and interpret whatever is essentially and distinctively Canadian and thus come to terms with an environment that is only now ceasing to be colonial. The other, from the very beginning, has made a heroic effort to transcend colonialism by entering into the universal, civilizing culture of ideas" (1943, 5). Pitting a concern with the local against a more international literary and cultural sensibility has been a perennial critical sport in the context of Canadian literature, with the rhetorical manoeuvres of the one side, as Lianne Moyes argues, frequently mirroring those of the other side: "Arguments for a distinctively Canadian literature tend to universalize regionally or culturally specific characteristics just as arguments for universal literary values tend to mask the values of a particular group" (1992, 29).

It comes as no surprise, then, that a variation of this tension between the local and the universal should resurface in considering the possibility of hemispheric literary studies. Especially because Canada is a relatively marginal country in the international scheme of things and because of its ever-precarious sense of identity, there is good reason to be wary of comparative perspectives, which often establish a common ground by downplaying or effacing those local, contextual specificities that suggest difference rather than commonality, as Smith's embrace of cosmopolitanism suggests. Looking at the history of comparative literature, Susan Bassnett identifies a troubling Eurocentric and liberal humanist universalism in the "Great Books" Western tradition of comparative literature, "with its assumptions

about the humanizing power of great international art" (1993, 36).
She describes the effect of a formalist "avoidance of socio-economic
issues" (36) in which "invasions, colonization, economic deprivation
are all set aside, for what is being considered is literature, and only
literature, as though all writers worked in a vacuum divorced from
external reality" (37). At least certain aspects of the internationalization of culture in our own times, in which the liberalizing effect of
globalization is so often unquestioningly trumpeted by its champions,
threaten to replicate the reductive, exclusive politics of such approaches.
Certainly, it can be argued that, in some ways, cultural globalization
entails a process of cultural dissemination, transference, and inter-
change that retains and respects cultural specificity and cultivates
new and dynamic hybrid forms. As Frederick Buell argues, globalization yields "a decentered set of subnational and supranational interactions ... and these interactions help multiply, invent, and disseminate
cultural differences, rather than overcome them" (1994, 10–11).
However, there are also strains of cultural globalization – represented
most visibly by Hollywood – that amount to a kind of clear-cutting
of the local terrain to prepare the ground for a monocultural harvest,
as it were. Requests routinely faced by Canadian authors of children's
books to purge their books of identifiably Canadian elements for an
American market are another good example. Given the undeniably
homogenizing force of so much cultural production within this kind
of globalized cultural regime, Buell's description of global culture
as a kind of postmodern bricolage – "the detachment of cultural
material from particular territories, and the circulation of it in often
blatantly repackaged, heterogeneous, boundary-violating forms
throughout the world" (27) – is not altogether reassuring.

These tensions between globalization as cultural dissemination,
mutual influence, and exchange, on the one hand, and globalization
as cultural imperialism sporting a Mardi Gras mask, on the other
hand, certainly give pause for thought about embracing a comparative hemispheric perspective. There is a point at which similarity,
or sameness – on which comparative approaches are particularly
reliant – becomes imperializing, and this is an occupational hazard
that needs to be kept firmly in view in the development of hemispheric literary paradigms. This is particularly the case for marginalized (and particularly previously colonized) cultures such as that
of Canada, where recognizing specificity – especially in the shadow of
the elephant – is seen as crucial to cultural survival. Nonetheless, to

be wary of international comparative literary frameworks does not have to entail retreating into essentialist definitions of the "Canada" within which these contextual specificities reside. As Brydon argues, "the nation as a viable cultural form can exist in many different incarnations and certainly does not depend on notions of either authenticity or literary nationalism for its well-being" (1995, 17). Being aware of the extranational links of ostensibly Canadian literary texts is a helpful reminder of the way that most literature is shaped by a diverse range of forces that spill well beyond national boundaries. As Bassnett notes (1993, 13–30), comparative literature has often served historically as a way of superseding nationalist prejudices and insularity (although it has also often worked to reinforce them): "whilst the study of 'national' literatures risked accusations of partisanship, the study of 'comparative' literature carried with it a sense of transcendence of the narrowly nationalistic" (21). The prospect of a comparative approach such as hemispheric studies offers a way out of nationalist frameworks that have proved to be constraining, exclusive, and ultimately porous.

However (as in so many other instances in this poststructuralist universe), there is a reluctance to leave behind certain paradigms that have only just begun to serve as a focus for agency. As has been argued in various quarters, particularly in the contexts of feminism and gender studies and postcolonial theory, there is a profound irony in the fact that the anti-essentialist orientation of so much contemporary critical theory arguably erodes the terrain on which an oppositional agency might be built. Such a concern can also be extended to a previously marginalized (and, in many ways, still marginalized) literature such as Canada's. The "Canadian" part of Canadian literature is being substantially destabilized just at the moment when Canadian literature can be said to have really arrived – that is, to have achieved sustained international attention as "Canadian." To say this is not to subscribe to a teleological narrative of "progress" and "development," notions that have been under steady attack in Canadian literary criticism, as elsewhere, but to recognize the strategic utility of labels, which can have a tactical value without implying a commitment to monolithic and essentialist notions of literary identity. As Donna Palmateer Pennee puts it, "Literary studies organized under the rubric of the national create a space to ask civic questions of state policies and inherited notions of nationalism" (2004, 81). Although disciplinary structures in the academic world are gradually changing, English departments are still largely defined by nation- and period-based criteria, and even though Canadian literature has established a definite place in those structures, that place is still sufficiently newly established that it may not be advisable to give it a firm shaking. As Cynthia Sugars pointedly asks in her introduction to *Home-Work: Postcolonialism, Pedagogy and Canadian Literature*, "In light of the struggle for Canadian literature over much of the twentieth century, to what extent could the various post-colonizings and deconstructions of the discipline, and of pedagogy itself, forfeit the victories that were so hard won earlier on?" (2004, 10).

To steer between the Scylla of a homogenizing, parochial localism and the Charybdis of a potentially imperializing hemispheric scope, then, what is necessary is a bilateral or multilateral development, in which, as Siemerling argues, a "larger comparative perspective" allows us to see "the costs and losses" (2005, 10) of a national literature, even when it is "overtly constructed as discursive multiplicity but nonetheless circumscribed by national space" (9). As the past couple of decades have shown, there is substantial concern about the ossification of nationalist literary paradigms in Canada, but I think reaction to this and enthusiasm for larger comparative perspectives, including hemispheric ones, need to be checked by a continuing concern for local specificities that might be occluded or effaced by extranational, transcultural perspectives.

In principle, hemispheric approaches to literary studies may well offer viable perspectives to complement those approaches that are shaped more firmly by or within the borders of the nation – however much, to evoke the title of a collection on writing by "new Canadians," those borders may be "floating" and thus "free," in the words of M.G. Vassanji, "for an identity, a literature, in the broad sense, to grow, explore, find and define itself" (1999, viii), or no matter how much, as Buell argues, "the territorialization of culture has been undercut and even reversed" and "even 'national' cultures have come to exist more explicitly across, apart from, and even without territories they possess as their own" (1994, 127, 128). Buell contends that a bilateral move has diminished the power of the nation-state and of cultural nationalism and has reconfigured people's relationship to culture across the world: "Focus on the global-local dyad has thus provided ways around nationalism's previous near-monopoly on globally significant cultural differences. It has dramatically expanded the number of communities (or, more generally, 'local sites') people are aware they belong to, and it has made these memberships and identities simultaneously global and local in significance. Thus, along with ending the near monopoly nationalism had on the production of global cultural difference, current emphasis on the global-local has also broken the stranglehold that the nation-state has had on managing worldwide relationships" (298). However, even though Buell rightly stresses the perils of nationalism, the national can potentially serve as a positive and strategic focus for identification, just as the local and the global can be susceptible to the kinds of prejudice, marginalization, and exploitation now routinely attributed to nationalism. As Arif Dirlik argues, the nation-state continues to play a role as a locus for place-based resistance to capitalism. Despite his "anarchistic suspicion of centralized power," Dirlik underscores "the importance of supraplace alliances, including the nation-state, that remain not only as reminders of the need for outside agencies in uncovering the inequalities built into places but also of the need of places, if they are not to become playthings at the hands of capital, for some kind of defense" (2000, xii-xiii).

Indeed, one of the chastening aspects of globalization is that it seems to be binding culture and economics together as (perhaps) never before, and in this respect threatens to be as centralizing and homogenizing as nationalism is accused of being. If a centralizing nationalism is problematic, and we want to pour over the borders as it were, or destabilize them from within, we should be extremely wary of the possibility of simply replicating that hegemonic order on a larger scale. Despite the porousness of culture and its disregard for political boundaries, there are reasons to be wary of embracing a cultural "open border" policy, not least of all the possibility that a continental or hemispheric literary critical orientation will simply reinforce the centralizing of power that has accompanied the reorientation to an economic hemispheric regime. Continental conglomeration of trade relations and other networks of mutual interest, including defence and national security, cushioned by the euphemism "harmonization," is by no means a neat matter of mutually beneficial consolidation but a complex reconfiguration of networks of power, as the history of Canada itself illustrates. In "Just More of the Same? Confederation and Globalization," Michael Clow argues that the reorientation of Canada's economic and political structure in the wake of Confederation, which resulted in the centralization of power and the decline of the economic and political influence the Maritime provinces had previously enjoyed, is being replayed in the current continental integration effected by the free trade agreements and more broadly through Canada's commitment to the ideology of globalization. Canada, in other words, is being systematically "Maritimized" (Clow 2005, 40), reduced to a powerless, northern vestige, as more and more of its ability to steer its fate is bargained away: "The 'harmonization' of Canada's economy and policy with the neo-liberal norms of the American and global economy will undermine any internal democratic processes, and make us helpless to set an alternative course. The Canadian state will be substantially hamstrung to ameliorate the devastation of the population under de-industrialization as long as we remain part of these unions predicated on neo-liberalism" (45). Clow qualifies this seemingly postnational vision by noting that, "[c]ontrary to those who argue that NAFTA and globalization indicate the declining importance of the 'state,'" capital has exploited the mechanisms of the state toward its own "transnational or imperial" ends (47). However, he ultimately argues that in contrast with Confederation, which was a politically overt and relatively democratic process, the emergence of an increasingly borderless economic regime, represented by international trade organizations such as the World Bank and the World Trade Organization, amounts to "the formation of new societies by stealth" (37). "Under the guise of being inter-governmental institutions," these organizations "represent *only* multinational capital – whose members closely collaborate in policy making and adjudication – and governments whose leaders and functionaries now act almost exclusively in the interests of transnational capital" (38, original emphasis). In the process, the political power of more local bodies of governance is considerably diminished: "All these layers of 'extra-parliamentary' governance have the same effect – to limit and subvert, if not eradicate, democracy without the formal imposition of an authoritarian state" (39). Canada, in short, is "goin' down the road."

Parallels between economic globalization and cultural globalization, of course, are far from perfect, but Clow's warnings are nonetheless instructive in that they underscore the potential perils of amalgamation. Adjusting the focus, in this case from a more nationally oriented literary critical focus to a more expansive and fluid inter-American context, necessarily involves an adjustment of emphasis and of relations of power, and developments not just outside the domain of culture but inside it as well (although the borders of culture are likewise porous) suggest that there is good reason to scrutinize that adjustment carefully. To do so is not to promote a defensive, monolithic, garrison nationalism (and Sugars in her contribution to this volume perceptively points to the tendency to conflate those two impulses). Rather, it is to insist that such a shift take place in an equitable, truly global rather than imperializing fashion that sustains the local (whether national or intranational) as it develops the connections between the local and the international.

3

Counter-Worlding *A/américanité*

DAVID LEAHY

According to Gayatri Chakravorty Spivak (1985), "worlding" involves the violent impact of imperialism on colonized spaces and peoples as well as the forms that inscribe imperial discourse on colonized space.[1] Among important examples of "worlding" by inscription, she includes imperial cartography and any "texting, textualizing, a making into art, a making into an object to be understood," as she said to Elizabeth Grosz, that is the result of an "imperialist project['s] ... assum[ption] that the earth that it territorialized was in fact uninscribed" (Spivak 1990, 1).[2] One of her most subtle yet most profound observations is that the simple presence of a British soldier in India "oblig[es] the native to cathect the space of the Other on his home ground" (1985, 248), to concentrate or project his/her material, emotional, and psychic interpellation by the imperial Other onto the very ground he walks and the very air she breathes. It is arguable, of course, that Spivak's notion of "worlding" does not take enough account of the relative autonomy, resistance, and agency of colonized subjects since they are *always already* more than simply subjects who are "othered" by, and thus cathect the imperial Other according to, the many literal and figurative facets of imperialist hegemony.[3] Nonetheless, her characterization of "worlding," as her corpus evidences, is perfectly consistent with the fact that she has been most interested in deconstructing and theorizing the sites and moments of imperialist conquest in which physical and psychic *violence* have been the most intense.

I would like to appropriate Spivak's notion of "worlding" as a tool for interrogating specific aspects of the cultural work of cultural producers within contexts in which the relations of power between an imperial entity and its satellites, neighbours, and allies are generally not so graphically violent as that of India under the British Raj but still tend to function at the more subtle levels that Spivak's emphasis on interpellation addresses. Conventionally, within postcolonial literary studies such an approach is associated with the notion of "counter-discourse." However, as Bill Ashcroft and colleagues note, counter-discourse is most often associated with "challenges posed to particular texts, and thus to imperial ideologies inculcated, stabilized and specifically maintained through texts employed in colonialist education systems" (2000, 56). For the purposes of this chapter, however, I am not interested in "the subversion of canonical [imperial] texts" (57) by counter-discourses but in the ways that an imperial culture may be said to be *counter-worlded*, or *othered*, by cultural producers whose works not only identify cultures' similarities or commonalities with an imperial "centre" or Other but also recognize *and* trouble the ways that the imperial *Other* both interpellates us and is an integral part of our cultures that requires the adoption of paradoxical forms of critique and contestation. Before developing this idea of "counter-worlding" any further, I would also note that as a postcolonial-oriented comparativist of Canadian and Québécois literatures, I am inevitably drawn to considering such an approach vis-à-vis the United States – especially within the immediate context of greater pressures on Canada and Quebec to integrate within the USian imperial nexus in terms of national, continental, and international policies and values, as well as the current academic debates over whether the US should be a subject of postcolonial studies or whether analyses of its cultures, writings, and politics would be well served by the new field of North American studies.[4] Therefore, for the purposes of this chapter, the imperial power under interrogation is the United States of America, and the satellites are Canada and Quebec (and to a tangential degree, the Caribbean). Of course, there are those who refuse to acknowledge the imperial history and adventurism of the United States, just as there are Canadians and Québécois whose sense of themselves and their relationships to our immediate neighbour to the south cannot imagine or fully admit the colonial aspects that underpin and maintain the longest undefended border in the world. I am not about to attempt to convince anyone that USian economic and geopolitical interests – not the defence of democracy or free trade – are truly at the core of USian attitudes and policies toward supposed "rogue

states" like Cézar Chavez's Venezuala or the source of longstanding
USian stratagems to discredit and undermine public healthcare in
Canada. I am also very aware that the objection can be made that
in characterizing the political-economic relationships between the
US and Canada or Quebec as imperial/colonial dyads, I am flattening
out or erasing the multiple ways that Canada and Quebec have been
or are imperialist in their own right and participate in and benefit
materially from the imperialistic aspects of Canadian and Québécois
capital, from the profitability of our international agencies, or from
our national and foreign policies – for example, vis-à-vis First
Nations in Canada and Quebec, the alienation of peasants from the
land in Chad and the Yangtse Valley to the benefit of Canadian and
Québécois corporate interests, or cheap labour from Jamaica or
Trinidad, to allude to only a few of many instances. Furthermore, I
realize that some of my rhetoric can make it appear as though I am
ignoring the ongoing literal and psychic violence toward the multiple
cultural communities and nations that are so pervasive and crucial
to the societies of the US, Canada, and Quebec – as though there
were only one, coherent, USian, Canadian, or Québécois identity or
way of being. The demands by First Nations that their innate and
historical treaty rights be respected, their resistance to the mainte-
nance of the international border between the US and Canada, and
"blacks'" de facto second-class citizenship on both sides of the
49th parallel are among some of the most obvious counter-examples
to the myth of coherent national identities. On the contrary, my
exploration of the nascent concept of counter-worlding, like the new
field of North American studies, can hopefully make a small contribution to the finessing of critical understanding of imperial/colonial
relations on the continent and the subversion of binary, retrograde,
or oversimplified notions of identity.

Having said this, I should also note that for the purposes of this
chapter, I have no interest in revisiting the debate about the definition of "Second World" nations and the consequent implications for
postcolonial resistance theory[5] – although my interest in appropriating Spivak's concept of "worlding" within the context of what has
frequently been identified as "First World" versus "Second World"
relations clearly has implications for how one identifies and critiques
what distinguishes a hegemonic imperial power from its satellites at
more subtle levels than the gross material and political levels of
standing armies, armaments, financial clout, and the like.[6] More

important, I believe that another concept of Spivak's, that of "strategic essentialism," can be used to allay the concern that the concept of worlding does not credit colonized subjects with enough autonomy or agency, that the theoretical and political efficacy of "strategic essentialism" is possibly most pertinent in contexts where the dividing lines between imperial and colonized satellite cultures are most blurred, their material, cultural, and discursive practices most highly integrated or contingent. Spivak sees the strategic identification and politics of "essentialisms ... as [things] one must adopt to produce a critique of anything" (1990, 51).[7] It can be argued that this is always the case whatever the context, whether one is making class, gender, or any other kinds of politics that represent or involve significant classes of people. But in cultures and nations where individual equality and justice before the law, the Constitution, or a Charter of Rights and Freedoms are ostensibly guaranteed but frequently ignored or broken on the basis of cultural and systemic biases against collectivities of people, strategic essentialist politics and critique may be understood as imperative.

Furthermore, as many people of colour and feminists have decried for decades, at the very historical moment when identity politics began to play a socially significant role in raising consciousness about racism and sexism, and in helping to change the public policies that contribute to sustaining and perpetuating them, many practitioners of poststructuralist-influenced theory began to evacuate the radical potential of identity politics in the process of rejecting universalist and essentialist notions of the subject as ultimately retrograde and reactionary. Spivak's response to this phenomenon has consistently been "that the limits of [such] theories are disclosed by an encounter with the materiality of [the] other of the West" (1990, 11) – a materiality that, as this chapter in part explores, our Americanized cultures of spectacle, consumerism, and capitalist "techno-logic" (Chamberland 1990, 73–4) prefer to gloss over when they don't outright blame the victims. In the face of such injustices, to cite Spivak again: "Since the moment of essentializing, universalizing, saying yes to the onto-phenomenological question, is irreducible, let us at least situate it at the moment, let us become vigilant about our own practice and use it as much as we can rather than make the totally counter-productive gesture of repudiating it" (1990, 11).

Taking the aforenoted concepts and concerns into account, I would like to propose that when colonized subjects respond to the ways that imperial cultures "world" us and our societies, our responses can be thought of as forms of "counter-worlding." This term is meant to refer not only to the ways that colonized or subordinate peoples may resist the psychic or ideological violence and hegemony of an imperial presence but especially to contexts where such responses insist on, or are capable of prompting, a new way for imperial Others or subjects to cathect, or imagine themselves and their relationships in terms of, those spaces and peoples they other. I believe this is even more the case, as alluded to above, when the counter-worlding of imperialist powers and cultures is performed by the cultural producers of satellite nations or peoples whose differences are often elided by their proximity to and roles vis-à-vis the imperial heartland, as in cases – such as with blacks or Québécois within Canada vis-à-vis the United States – where there are greater ambivalences concerning the dialectic of the centre-periphery nexus. Nonetheless, a second major distinction between Spivak's characterization of worlding and the literary examples of counter-worlding that I will briefly examine is that when colonized subjects counter-world imperial cultures, their inscriptions rarely have an equivalent cathectic effect socially or psychologically. For their cartographies, texts, or making into art can rarely have the same presence for, let alone an analogous impact on, the hearts and minds of those who benefit from their subordination.[8]

For instance, a writer like Margaret Atwood has had a considerable presence in the United States, effecting a form of highly politicized counter-worlding with a novel like *The Handmaid's Tale*. But its impact within the US is anomalous in comparison with the thousands of Canadian and Québécois published books, or other forms of cultural production, that are not available in the US or have a very limited reception there but that also counter-world it and its empire in a variety of ways. Consider, for instance, Guy Vanderheage's *The Englishman's Boy*, Thomas King's *Green Grass, Running Water*, or Jacques Poulin's *Volkswagon Blues*. In keeping with the important material fact that within the past twenty-five years a writer like Atwood could achieve the presence that she has in the US book market not simply on the basis of the quality of her writing but especially because of the increased hegemony of a US-dominated, "bestseller"-oriented consolidation of Canada's, the hemisphere's, and the West's book trade, we could simply throw up our arms and complain that this is inevitably the nature of the relationship between a large, *hyperpuissante* nation and smaller, satellite ones. Or that

Americans, Canadians, and Québécois are so alike as late-modernist or postmodernist peoples – our consumerist lifestyles so analogous – that cultural production from Canada or Quebec can barely be of interest to USians, that it is not exotic or troubling enough to warrant more attention. However, even though such truisms clearly have bases in fact, I believe that it is exactly because of our proximity to and greater integration within the post-Cold War US empire that now more than ever instances of counter-worlding need to be identified and analyzed. This is not simply a means of asserting national differences and thereby local state sovereignty, nor is it part of a messianic project of saving USians from themselves; rather, a greater awareness of counter-worlding can help us – *other* Americans – to understand how our much vaunted differences can mask or blind us not only to our similarities or alterity vis-à-vis the imperial Other but also to the ways that our counter-worlding of empire can contribute to the rewriting or rethinking of centre-periphery relations, *encouraging the Other "to cathect the space of the [o]ther on [its] home ground."* In short, I believe that a greater appreciation of such counter-worlding, as part of much more "inter-American," "border-crossing approach[es]" to "hemispheric American studies" (to quote Winfried Siemerling and Sarah Phillips Casteel's introduction to this volume), can contribute significantly to the enlargement and enrichment of American studies in much the same way that the shift from "Commonwealth studies" to "postcolonial studies" in the 1980s generated more complex, dialectical understandings of British literary, cultural, and area studies as well as a wider appreciation and distribution of previously marginal "neo/colonial" literatures.

Of course, the disproportionate *rapports de force* that reign can make the efficacy of such an enterprise seem rather daunting, while the idealism of it may even be perceived as laughable, thus reducing one's sense of agency to that of the proverbial fly buzzing a great horned bull (or should that be a Democratic mule *and* a Republican elephant?). Yet isn't it possible that such a defeatist or cynical perspective can pertain only as long as one accepts the myth that *America* is merely the domain of the US and somehow truly distinct and impermeable? Most important, isn't it time that more Canadians, Québécois, and other peoples within the Americas recognize and address our own *américanité* rather than reproducing the role of reactive colonial subjects in a reductive anti-imperial dyad? In other words, I believe not only that we have to make USians' versions of

America strange to themselves – as the title and body of this chapter suggest – but also that in so doing we may better recognize and understand ourselves and what is worth keeping, modifying, and jettisoning of our own *américanité*.

To that end, I will briefly map some of the ways that Paul Chamberland and Dionne Brand have responded artistically to being worlded and, more important, how increasingly their counter-worldings have not relied on a simplistic anticolonial dyad but have explored ways that imperial "inscription" is a dialectical process that can be empowering – even when it makes for disheartening self-reflections. Brand's writing is particularly relevant because of the fact that she is a Caribbean-born-and-raised writer who has since become a Canadian, yet like so many other immigrants her initial attitudes toward Canada were strongly shaped by her perception of Canada as America, as American – a perception that speaks not only to the pervasive power of the mythos of the US for immigrants to *North* America but also to the ways that USian material and cultural power and presence are cathected by immigrants to a place like Toronto. Moreover, as Brand's experiences and knowledge of her adopted country deepened and broadened, along with her Marxist-informed anti-imperial attitudes toward the US, her counter-worlding of *améri-canité* – of the capitalist-driven ways that USian hegemony and values are naturalized, exported to, and adopted by Trinidadians, Grenadians, Canadians, Natives, blacks, and others – has continued to identify and explore how *américanité* is not simply a geopolitical and socio-economic phenomenon but also a general *ontological* problem.

Chamberland's development as a writer and thinker is well worth pairing with Brand's not simply because of the early influence on him, and on many *indépendantistes* of his generation, of Frantz Fanon, black liberation theory, and revolutionary politics but also because of the nuanced ways that he has consistently not only rejected being othered, made into a *nègre blanc* who must "speak white,"[9] but also identified and challenged the ways that the ongoing imperial worlding of Quebec, especially the ever greater integration of the population of Quebec into the socioeconomic or techno-logic of America, undermines the collective vision and politics that prompted the popular rise and successes of the Québécois neona-tionalist movement (as exemplified by the creation of Bill 101),[10] the strengthening of progressive minimum-wage and labour laws, and the implementation and successes of universal healthcare.

Furthermore, Chamberland's writings, like Brand's, consistently interrogate and challenge how *américanité* is not simply a USian phenomenon – and therefore how the US empire's geopolitical and socioeconomic reach and influences can blind us to the ways that our local interests may necessitate adopting strategically essentialist positions.

Dionne Brand has written and spoken very movingly and in original ways as a black female, a Marxist, and a lesbian about the beauty and horrors of life in the Caribbean Islands and *away*, of different forms of revolutionary hope, success, and defeat. She has also increasingly turned her attention to interrogating the gross and more subtle ways that she and others have been worlded, been made strangers to themselves, and resisted colonization while trying to remain vigilant against too facile notions of identity. For the purposes of this chapter, I will concentrate on a few examples of her many autobiographical accounts of the ways that she has experienced British-, USian-, and Canadian-identified forms of "worlding." Her responses to worlding can be understood not only as challenging or subverting such inscriptions but also as developing complex dialogical approaches to language that "subvert the hierarchy that prioritizes Standard English to achieve a new language" and that "embrace contradiction" as well as the "alien other within herself" (Zackodnik 1996, 206). As Teresa Zackodnik has argued, this linguistic embodiment of the doubleness of Brand's identity in terms of colonization and resistance is further enriched by the tripleness of her identity as a lesbian, producing a "synthesis of self and other in her poetry [along] with other lesbian writers, who ... eliminate the hierarchy of subject/object by replacing it with 'a lesbian metaphysic which inscribes the inter/action of a Lesbian Subject and a lesbian Other/ self'" (207).[11] I see no need to reiterate Zackodnik's fine analyses of the ways that Brand's multivoiced, polyphonic foregrounding of and play with heteroglossia, especially since the publication of *No Language Is Neutral*, makes for "a space in which her identity becomes a place of belonging in exile" (206). Rather, I am more interested in considering how her explorations of the doubleness and tripleness of "belonging in exile" may be imagined as troubling imperial space, as wielding forms of counter-worlding that may cause imperial subjects to question the substance, practices, and values of their *Américanité* – "*to cathect the space of the [o]ther on [the*

Other's] *home ground"* – at the same time that such instances of counter-worlding can clarify and critique the ambivalences of satellite nations' own *américanité*.

In *No Language Is Neutral*, Brand confronts what she calls the "lie" of "nostalgia" (1990, 33) – the doubleness or paradox of the longing to return to the landscape, sea, people, and comforts of her upbringing in Trinidad and its impossibility since she has become, through emigration and a variety of personal changes, a tourist in "[t]his place so full of your absence" (33). The sense of alienation upon visiting Trinidad is heightened by her addressing herself in the second person, although it can be simultaneously read as an allusion to the lesbian self she cannot openly be in Trinidad, as becomes more apparent in her uses of the second person later in the poem. The sense of alienation is also heightened by the many ways that the cycle of poems creates strong negative accounts of her experiences as an immigrant in Canada. For instance, a fragmentary allusion to her colonial childhood attraction to the mythos of Canada – "I did read a book once about a / prairie in Alberta since my waving cane-field wasn't / enough" (26) – eventually collides with the actual *American*-identified materiality of Canada's modernity that she is confronted by when she first emigrates to Toronto: "eyes fixed to a skyscraper" – "the concrete / building just overpower me" (25), while "fierce bright windows screaming with goods" provoke the cry of "No wilderness self, is shards, shards, shards, / shards of raw glass, a debris of people" (26). On the surface, the signifying chain of the cold "concrete / building" or the "fierce bright windows" is simply about a general sense of modernist alienation, or the cultural and psychic alienation of a black immigrant from the Caribbean. But its figurative account of the embedded economic and psychic violence of the scene can also be understood as counter-worlding *A/américanité* – after all, America is the birthplace of skyscraper culture[12] – and as perhaps even mocking Canadians' sense of themselves at the beginning of the 1970s as essentially different from USians. Canadians thought of themselves either as citizens of the Peaceable Kingdom of the Great White North or as victims of the "wilderness" – Northrop Frye's (1965) and Atwood's (1972) garrison mentality thesis – but both of these imagined subject-positions were supposedly indicative of Canadians' civilized emphasis on the self in terms of community rather than as individuals. Whether or not a critique of this Canadian mythos is intended by Brand's sentence beginning "No wilderness self," her sense of the violence of the scene, especially when considered from her perspective as an immigrant, troubles the everyday normality of consumerism and capitalism and how, owing to this normality, we generally fail to hear the "scream[s]" of the "debris of people," abroad and at home, on whose backs so many "goods" and "skyscrapers" are built and sustained. Considered in this light, the exclamatory phrase "is shards, shards, shards" is not only a metaphor for the refraction of the light of the "fierce bright windows" or for the fragmented reflections of the passersby but also a metaphor for the violence that is done to colonials, to immigrants, to the self when, as George Grant put it, we "offer" ourselves "on the altar of the reigning Western goddess" (1965, 54).

Although there is nothing terribly new in this kind of critique in terms of its rhetoric, the complexity of Brand's account in *No Language Is Neutral* of the decades by which she "carved from her exile a paradoxical place of belonging" (Zackodnik 1996, 208) and of how she "walk[ed] Bathurst Street" not "until it" *was* "home" but "until it come *like* home" (Brand 1990, 27, my emphasis) speaks profoundly to how one can continue to be worlded, made a stranger to oneself, long after one has emigrated to the imperial centre and its satellites. Although the long duration of Brand's sense of alienation – "Not a single / word drops from my lips for twenty years about living / here" (28) – is slightly difficult to reconcile with her community activism during the same period, it may in part be credited to her leftist politics, and it can also serve as a counterweight to the facile ways that Canadian culture's self-satisfied narrative about multiculturalism tends to elide the more melancholic and tragic aspects of the immigrant experience.

Some other poems in *No Language Is Neutral* allude to her fieldwork in support of the socialist New Jewel Movement in Grenada (under Canadian auspices, I might add), a choice she made in order to try to help create a collective "biotope" of resistance – to foreshadow one of Chamberland's discourses (see Chamberland 1980, 13) – to USian hegemony. It was also clearly, on a more personal level, a means toward "unworlding" herself – that is, until "October 25th, 1983," when, as she put it in a poem after the event, "[A]merica came to restore democracy."[13] The pain of the consequences of that invasion for Brand and the people of Grenada, and its ongoing geopolitical implications, have haunted Brand ever since, but the subsequent years have also led her to produce increasingly complex

accounts of just how thoroughly she had been worlded and the difficulties and necessity of a dialectical sense of resistance. For instance,
in a talk at Toronto's York University in 1997, Brand "attempted
[an] inventory" of "the traces deposited in me both of imperial
domination but also of race, class, and gender resistance," with a
heavy emphasis on the anxieties of "my own accommodations and
acquiescences with domination" (1997, 4).[14] Most of the inventory
revolves around her troubled relationship to the academy – around
the discrepancies between her colonial childhood dreams of escape to
the "green lawns" of a university campus and the oppressive reality
of its bourgeois and racial hierarchies and ignorance. But her account
is especially moving in terms of her sense of her capitulations, of
how her university formation would consistently "satisfy forces
outside of me rather than any propelled by me" (5). Nevertheless,
she also appreciates how her "grandparents" and she were not only
tools of "oppressive ideologies" (6) in her pursuit of education but
"social agents" as well: "facing ... history and deciding, bargaining,
constantly conflicted" (6). "In other words what I'd come to get I
knew I was going to get with all its contradictions" (6).

     Other accounts of personal and collective history, especially in
Brand's A Map to the Door of No Return, create an even thicker
portrait of the conflicted ways that one can experience being worlded.
These accounts move back and forth in time from her British colonial
experiences of material and psychic violence to her experiences of
USian and Canadian manifestations of them, all the while constantly
returning to a complex metaphor of how "the Door of No Return ...
is illuminated in the consciousness of Blacks in the Diaspora [but]
there are no maps. This door is not mere physicality. It is a spiritual
location. It is also a psychic destination. Since leaving was never
voluntary, return was, and still may be, an intention, however ...
There is ... no way in; no return" (2001, 1). As so many Caribbean
writers have done, Brand does a powerful job of summarizing how
"[Trinidadians] were inhabited by British consciousness" (16–17),
how "[t]he news of the BBC is a door to 'over there,' it is the door
to being in the big world" and constantly offers "news of rescue"
(14), "lessons in the proper use of English; ... the proper use of
leather straps; ... the proper use of everything" (15). She remarks
how this process of worlding further meant that "[w]e were also
inhabited by an unknown self. The African. This duality was fought
every day from the time one woke to the time one fell asleep ... One

had the sense that some being had to be erased and some being had to be cultivated" (17).

Concomitantly, Brand's account of her interpellation by the racist trope of the "Dark Continent" gets at its doubleness for the colonial subject: "We floated on an imaginary island imagining a 'Dark Continent.' That 'Dark Continent' was a source of denial and awkward embrace ... No amount of denial, however, dislodged this place, this self, and no amount of forgetting obscured the Door of No Return" (2001, 17). This idea of the long historical violence of being made simultaneously real and mythic to oneself, of what it's like to be worlded such that one becomes "a being living inside and outside of [oneself]" (18), is explored in many powerful ways throughout the book. Two of the most striking examples are Brand's account of Henry Louis Gates's hosting of a PBS film about African civilization and the black diaspora and yet another account of her emigration to Canada and how she was stopped short when she realized that her psychic map of Toronto was actually Afro-American.

In the former example, Brand recounts how in the midst of watching what she expects to be a "dispassionate discussion about the geopolitics" of slavery, Gates suddenly asks an African man in Kumasi (Ghana): "Why did you sell us?" (2001, 31). "Nothing [else] matters," Brand says, "not political history, not colonialism, not all the time in between ... I switch the station, suddenly embarrassed at the question and the answer. There is no answer. The Door of No Return is ajar between them ... Gates, in all his other explorations of the continent, is the quintessential American traveler, oohing and aahing about wonders, skeptical about claims of civilization, lecturing about civilization, fearful about being in Africa ... But here, faced at last with the man from Kumasi, he asks a childlike question to which there is no answer" (32). The visceral power of the scene is reinforced by Brand's subsequent account of "Gates bring[ing] several African-Americans" to a former "slave castle in Ghana ... They stand or sit in various states of emotional collapse as Gates probes them on whether they know that their ancestors were sold by Africans. They reply no. The knowledge seems to add greater sadness to them. The scene is full of silences" (33).

Not only are these anecdotes reminders of the extent to which America, with a capital A, in spite of centuries of resistance, has worlded its Afro-American citizens (and other members of the African diaspora), but they also foreground how even a black-identified liberatory sense of identity, such as Brand was interpellated by before she even set foot in North America, can also make one strange to oneself. Consider Brand's account of her false sense of where she had come to when she emigrated to Canada: "When I arrived at the apartment on Keele Street, Toronto, I was in America" (2001, 115). Although this belief was technically correct in the geographical sense, the rest of the narrative makes clear that in this instance Brand is using *America* in its USian sense and goes on to give a somewhat self-mocking, comic, but nonetheless serious account of how she mistook "Toronto" for the other "America": "I was in America. America was a world already conceived in my mind ... In fact, when I saw it I did not see it; I saw what I had imagined ... It was inhabited by lye-slick-haired dudes, as in Malcom X's autobiography; there were dashikied cadres ... Mothers like Paule Marshall's ... protestors at snack counters ... militants on courthouse steps with rifles. All the inhabitants of this city in America were African-American ... The plane landed in Canada, but I was in America" (117). *Sounds just like Toronto circa 1970, doesn't it?*

Brand's portrayal of her mental map of America at that time speaks to the powerful influence of US-identified forms of black liberation and black nationalism as well as to the historical importance, the necessity even, of such essentialist movements. It can also be understood as a rather sarcastic comment on just how white-identified and quiet race relations in Canada were at that time. So too can it be understood in terms of how her personal experience can be mapped onto a larger historical process in which, as she puts it: "Our ancestors were bewildered because they had a sense of origins," whereas "[w]e, on the other hand, have no such immediate sense of belonging, only of drift" (2001, 118). However, in spite of this sense of drift, of the vicissitudes and difficulties of belonging, much like Chamberland, as we shall see, Brand is highly critical of nationalism. Why? One reason, she says, is that "[e]ach square foot of the Americas has its nationalism. And probably the most powerful of these nationalisms can be experienced in the U.S. But Jamaica, Brazil, Antigua ... are no less virulent" (49). *Virulent.* Like Dr Johnson's famous definition of patriotism as the last resort of the scoundrel, Brand denounces the poisonous, obnoxious, harmful effects of nationalisms' emphasis on "origins." "All origins are arbitrary," she states, adding: "This is not to say that they are not also nurturing, but they are essentially coercive and indifferent. Country, nation, these concepts are of course deeply indebted to origins, family, tradition, home. Nation-states are configurations of origins as exclusionary power structures that have legitimacy based solely on conquest and acquisition" (64). Nor is she very sympathetic to hyphenated identities, to how "[i]n opposition to the calcified Canadian nation narrative we [get] calcified hyphenated narratives," (70) "neo-origins," "cross-nationalisms" (71).[15] Brand does not buy into the "mirror/ image," "invariably conservative" model of Canada as a supposedly multicultural nation (69), and she contests the notion that "Canadian identity has changed over the last thirty or fifty years,"[16] insisting that "[w]e are drawn constantly to the European shape in its definition. A shape, by the way, which obscures its own multiplicity" (72). Not only does Brand put the lie to how Canada is not a "melting pot" – just ask the First Nations peoples who have been and are still often forced to conform to white-identified edicts, lifestyles, and values (need I continue?) – but like Chamberland, she is much more interested in knowing what the Canadian "nation [is] predicated on" (68), whether at some point it will develop the will and the means to become a part of the Americas without perpetuating what Chamberland has characterized as the techno-logic of *Américanité* or what Grant lamented as a supine worship of modernity that fails to distinguish progress from faith in the imperatives of the market as synonymous with the good (1965, 54).[17]

As a result, too many of our myths in *and* of *America* are predicated on imperially driven scripts that do most of us serious disservice or, worse, on myths that world others while erasing, smoothing over, or eliding the *realpolitik* on which they are predicated and that attack and deny the need for alternative identities and scripts. Consider Brand's poignant account of the irony of a black bus driver in Vancouver giving directions to a Salish woman and how they are both eerily of the place and not of it at the same time:

> He is here most recently perhaps from Regina, Saskatchewan, where his mother arrived with her new husband from Toronto, and before that Chicago and still again Bridgetown. And then again the Door of No Return ... He is the driver of lost paths. And here he is telling the Salish woman where to go. The woman from this land walks as one blindfolded, no promontory or dip of water is recognizable. She has not been careless, no. No, she has tried to remember, she has an inkling, but certain disasters

have occurred and the street, the path in her mind, is all rubble,
so she asks the driver through lost paths to conduct her through
her own country. (2001, 220)

Aside from subverting the stereotypical presumption that a black
bus driver in Vancouver is likely an immigrant, or a member of a
static ghetto, and foregrounding the depths of the cultural genocide
against the Natives – especially on the West Coast, where colonization of Natives was the swiftest and most recent – this moment in
A Map to the Door of No Return, like so many others in the book,
speaks profoundly to the necessity of strategic essentialism – to the
defence of local culture and values – as a means of survival and
well-being, without which one can become "lost," subject to "disas-
ters" because one has become a stranger in one's own land. It is also
a small but powerful example of the counter-worlding of *America*
and Canada, of a fundamental racialized aspect of our shared
A/américanité.

Paul Chamberland is probably still most often associated, especially
outside Quebec, with his neonationalist writings of the 1960s – works
like *L'afficheur hurle* (1964a) and *Terre Québec* (1964b). His poetry
and essays of that time are synonymous with the socialist-oriented,
anticolonial-identified journal *Parti pris* and its denunciations of
living "à moitié dans ce demi-pays," of a "Quebec aux mains des
autres livrée prostituée" (1964a, 9, 57). Outraged by the colonial
conditions of francophone Québécois, he dithyrambically juxtaposes
(as in Michèle Lalonde's "Speak White") English Canadian and
USian multinational interests – "200 millions d'anglo-saxons hydre
yankee / Canadian marée polymorphe imberbe à serres nicke- / lées
Standard Oil General Motors" (71) – with an identification of francophone Québécois with other oppressed peoples: "je suis cubain /
yankee no je suis nègre je lave les planchers dans un / bordel du
Texas je suis Québécois" (71). Although such verses passionately
explore what it feels like to be exploited and "worlded," to be made
strange to oneself as a "nègre-blanc" (71), notice how the run-on
syntax suggests the speaker identifies himself to a "yankee" as a
"cubain" ("je suis cubain / yankee"), while the abrupt intervention
of the "no" after "yankee," like the iterative effect of the enjamb-
ment between "cubain" and "yankee," can be read as shifting the
syntax to suggest the speaker's "yankee[ness]." The "no," however,

is also simultaneously a conjunctive hinge for an imperative rejection *and* qualification of what it means to be a "yankee" when one is subordinate ("no je suis nègre") in a powerful suturing of "race" and class: "yankee no je suis nègre je lave les planchers dans un / bordel du Texas" (71).

This *ressentiment*-identified sense of what it meant to be Québécois has often been used to discredit Québécois's desire for independence as ultimately a reactionary, essentialist project.[18] However, such a perspective often fails to take account of just how effective the strategic essentialism of writers and activists like Chamberland was and of the positive collective results that their strategic essentialism has born, such as the political-economic fact that francophone Québécois are no longer predominantly a "class-ethnie." Furthermore, as the verses I have cited suggest, although it may have been too easy in the heady days of the 1960s and '70s to identify with oppressed peoples in significantly different contexts, Chamberland was already quite aware of exceptions to and contradictions within his grouping together of "200 millions d'anglo-saxons." For instance, not only did he consistently map and name Quebec *and* Canada as virtual hinterlands of the United States, but his accounts of the United States rooted the power and reach of the likes of "Standard Oil" and "General Motors" on the backs of the poor within its own borders – its Latinos, blacks, and other "others." That is, not only are international borders and cultures presented as being made permeable and malleable according to the needs of USian capital, but the degradation and violence of the enterprise for colonized peoples and communities *within* the US have always been significant parts of his counter-worlding of it.

In his subsequent writings, Chamberland remains an *indépendantiste*, but he quickly develops new kinds of analyses of *Américanité* that counter-world the US while recognizing other peoples' and nations' reification by and complicity in an increasingly US-dominated world system. One of the first major signs of a new stage in his thinking is *Extrême survivance, extrême poésie* (1978), a recognizably 1970s countercultural work that announces: "j'ai rompu, non sans peine, avec l'activisme révolutionnaire moderne" because of its complicity in the "hypertrophie de la raison" (9) and because he sees its materialist fundaments as being just as destructive of the "biosphere" as "la Machine Antisociale Capitaliste" (13). Although the book's countercultural faith in the imminent disintegration of

industrialism, and thereby of the hierarchy of social classes, in favour
of an "expansion organique de la nouvelle communauté des pro-
ducteurs harmoniques" (21) is now sadly amusing, especially given
how utopic and then darkly foreboding his subsequent writings
became, its critique of "la Machine Antisociale Capitaliste" as reap-
ing an environmental whirlwind – "elle est la Bête de l'Apocalypse"
(23) – today appears to be frighteningly accurate.

The polemic of Chamberland's *Terre souveraine* (1980) was published with an eye toward the 1980 Quebec referendum, but it is
more about a radical, ecological vision that identifies "capitalisme
continental" as a threat to "la différence kébékoise" (10) than it is
supportive of nationalism per se. Chamberland valorizes the sovereignty of Quebec but primarily as a means of saving the local "biotope" (13) in order to develop it as a "laboratoire" (25) in the hope
of creating a cybernetic community that could begin to render hier-
archical concentrations of power useless everywhere (70). Although
Terre souveraine's idealism is also sadly dated, its rather Bauldriardian
analysis denounces "[l]a différence kébèkoise fétichisée – culte mys-
tifié du 'patrimoine'" (51), its celebration of "la 'différence culturelle,'" as a reductive, static, reification of folklore and clichés (52).
This critique of "l'occlusion du vif" (52) not only marks a significant
rejection of traditional nationalism but also foreshadows Chamberland's
ongoing refinement of his counter-worlding of *américanité*.

Although I do not know whether Chamberland had read George
Grant, the increasingly elegiac ways that his poetic series of the 1980s
and '90s, *Géogrammes*, records and deconstructs the global, dehu-
manizing, scale of "[la] Société du spectacle" (1994, 13) concur with
Grant's analysis in *Lament for a Nation* (1965, 54):

Modern civilization makes all local cultures anachronistic ...
It has often been argued that geography and language caused
Canada's defeat. But behind these there is a necessity that is
incomparably more powerful. Our culture floundered on the
aspirations of the age of progress. The argument that Canada,
a local culture, must disappear can, therefore, be stated in three
steps. First, men everywhere move ineluctably toward member-
ship in the universal and homogenous state. Second, Canadians
live next to a society that is the heart of modernity. Third,
nearly all Canadians think that modernity is good, so nothing
essential distinguishes Canadians from Americans. When they

oblate themselves before "the American way of life," they offer themselves on the altar of the reigning Western goddess.

In the light of this citation from Grant, consider the following lines by Chamberland from *L'assaut contre les vivants* (1994, 13): "un forcené (terme du code actualitaire) se suicide / *live* devant la camera. Les spectateurs applaudissent au punch final. / Non, je n'ai pas inventé ça." Or these ones from *Le multiple événement terrestre* (1991, 175):

pendant que les pluies acides désagrègent la statue de la Liberté, Dart Vader fait des syllogismes, il dit qu'il y a des États terroristes, qu'ils s'attaquent aux États-Unis, donc que « nous avons le droit de nous défendre. »

[E]n juillet le Nicaragua distribuait deux cent cinquante mille fusils à la milice populaire de crainte d'une invasion américaine.

Tout se passé comme si le « monde extérieur » ne répondait plus ... *Comme si je n'existais pas* ... la complexe résultante d'hallucinations innombrables. Je parle du monde *humain* bien sûr, car les arbres, les ciels sont prodigieusement « réels. »
  Dieu n'existe pas.
  L'homme non plus.
  Rien qu'un sautillement par l'encombrement des hallucinations concrétées, qui soutirent une continuelle attention. (Original emphasis)

[U]n jour ils verront le soleil se lever sur mars, quand toute la colonie y sera installée, aux alentours de 2005   qui ? – les membres de la *Civilisation synergétique*, des Américains enthousiastes et fortunés   ils ont leur quartier general à Fort Worth au Texas, *Caravan Dreams*: arts martiaux/cinéma/ boîte de nuit.

I cite these passages at length without developing a close reading not only because I've decided – as much as is possible within the context of an academic discourse – to let these words in another language speak for themselves but also because their signs and traces of *Américanité* are graphic reminders of how Chamberland, and myself,

or you are worlded by "the American way of life." Moreover, these
concrete examples of Chamberland's parodic counter-worlding of
US-identified ways of being interpellate the reader via some of the
sites ("la statue de la Liberté"; "Fort Worth") and the social classes
("[les] Américains enthousiastes et fortunés") of America's symbolic
and political-economic hegemony, while simultaneously juxtaposing
these with other americans' worlded erasure ("*Comme si je n'existais
pas*") and complicity (i.e., via the well-nigh universal violence as
recreation and consumerism of shopping malls with their "arts
martiaux/cinéma/boîte de nuit") as well as with still other americans'
resistance ("la malice populaire de [Nicaragua]"). I could enumerate
more of the artistically and linguistically innovative ways in the
Géogrammes that Chamberland counter-worlds the United States
and the violent impacts of its *americanization* of satellite cultures
and values, but I am even more strongly drawn to backtracking to
an essay by Chamberland that was published in 1990, in translation,
for a special issue of *The Massachusetts Review*. I will forgo a summary of Chamberland's analysis of the immediate political scene in
Canada and Quebec in 1989–90 that led him to conjecture in the
essay's title that "Independence Is for 1993." What is most pertinent
about the essay are the ways that Chamberland so artfully links a
rejection of traditional Québécois nationalism with a claim for
the need to save Quebec's local culture from "*disappearance*" (69):
"The sentimental exaltation of identity, of the Québécois being, has
burnt out ... It seems that from now on such bombast is no longer
needed ... To sustain the hypostasis of a Québécois 'nature' would
amount to enclosing ourselves in a narcissistic self-representation ...
The nationalist exaltation conceals the fear of the Other, an impotent
fascination which summons defeat and which defeat reveals" (66–7).
Chamberland chooses instead to define Quebec's "distinct society" on
the basis of the "undeniably locatable difference – [of] language" (67),
and as he had done in *Terre souveraine*, he proposes the independence
of Quebec as a potential means of resisting what he now characterizes as "Techno-capitalis[m's]" "cloning of the anthrope" (70).

Yet Chamberland no sooner champions this strategic essentialist
will to "difference," how "linguistic difference which supports cultural difference ... constitutes a resource for resistance to techno-
capitalist leveling" (1990, 72–3), than he warns that "Quebecois
nationalists who persist in seeing English (or American) only as the
language of culture ... commit a grave error ... [Since] [o]*ne could*

very well be a Quebecois nationalist and at the same time conform blindly to techno-capitalist logic. [And w]hether we speak French or not, if all of our life speaks techno-language, obeys techno-*logic*, it would be perfectly useless, ridiculous, to struggle for our difference [since] in the guise of living-in-French in Quebec, a non-culture would spread blithely" (73–4, my emphasis). To my knowledge, this essay has never drawn any public or academic responses, be it from USians or other americans – say in Toronto or Trois-Rivières – but its critique of how techno-capitalism simulates difference (71) only to impose "the pitiless logic of the Same" for the sake of "money" and "Power" (74) and its qualification of techno-capitalism's *Américanité* while recognizing its geopolitical amorphousness are important reminders to USians and other americans that although cultural differences are often worth defending and promoting, they can also blind us to our complicity in our own subjugation, to the doubleness of the ways that our desires for progress can make us all "outsiders," even when we truly believe we're not.

As I trust the selected examples of cultural production by Dionne Brand and Paul Chamberland demonstrate, their counter-worlding of the US involves artistic and critical strategies that identify and critique the negative, imperialistic aspects of *Américanité* while simultaneously foregrounding how the *othering* of other *americans*, both within and outside the borders of the United States, is not only politically-economically, culturally, and psychically destructive but also inevitably perpetuates a symbolic dyad of oppression and reaction. In counter-worlding USian power and values, and especially in attempting to *"cathect the space of the [o]ther on the [O]ther's home ground,"* Canadian and Québécois cultural producers such as Brand and Chamberland not only perform important acts of cultural resistance but concomitantly make us more aware of our own *americanité*, of important aspects of our alterity vis-à-vis the US and its *American* culture and values, and of the questionable consequences of ignoring and failing to resolve the consequent social ambivalences and contradictions. As a result, we can be better placed to recognize and imagine the value of strategically essentialist ways of being and, ideally, of making politics without resorting to merely reactionary or static ideologies or biases, such as state or racial nationalism for its own sake, or to perpetuating the culturally, and hence politically, homogenizing techno-logic of capitalism. Likewise, the benefits for

"American studies" – and by extension its USian subjects — as I and my colleagues in this collection argue in our various ways, should be much greater than any imagined or real losses to its disciplinary or cultural focus.

Ché Guevara once wrote that he envied North American revolutionaries because "you live in the heart of the beast." However, the accolade can be faulted for underestimating the extent to which it is difficult as a result not to become one with the beast. Brand's and Chamberland's counter-worldings of A/américanité are, in my estimation, small but important cultural explorations of the diverse ways that such self-betrayal as a result of being worlded can be resisted and overcome to the benefit of all peoples of the Americas.

NOTES

1 See also Ashcroft et al. (2000, 241–2) and Cherry (2002).

2 This interview by Elizabeth Grosz was first published as Spivak (1984–85).

3 For a theoretical summary of the ways that I am using upper- and lower-case versions of the Other/other to distinguish between the superordination of the imperialist or colonialist vis-à-vis the subordination of the Native or the colonized, see Ashcroft et al. (2000): "Other/other" (169–71) and "othering" (171–3). Analogously, throughout this chapter, variations on American/american and Américanité/américanité (Americanness/americanness) are meant to signal distinctions between a USian imperial-identified sense of America or what it is to be an American and those of other peoples of the Americas who are nevertheless americanized. For critiques of the neglect or erasure of the agency or resistance of the colonized, of the diminishment of their power in their own right that is often implicit in postcolonial theorizations, see Mukherjee (1994) and Parry (2004).

4 As this very collection attests, this field is rich with critical and theoretical potential. See also Siemerling (2005).

5 For one of the most pithy yet comprehensive accounts of this issue, see Slemon (1990).

6 Analogous general terms that often muddy one's ability to identify and differentiate the relations of power between "Western" or "Northern" states are "developed nations" and "postindustrial economies." To my way of thinking, the latter term is perhaps the most odious. Not only does it circulate quite freely and widely without its meaning being

questioned, but it masks the ongoing importance of the competition for industrial production and its profitability within and between "developed" nations. Consider, for instance, how Canada and Quebec remain – in the midst of their supposed status as postindustrial economies – extremely dependent on the wealth and export of natural resources in the form of raw materials and hydro- or nuclear-generated electricity. Nor should Canadians and Québécois forget that the "hinterlands" of the United States – such as West Virgina, Maine, and the Dakotas – have their own troubled histories with American centre-periphery issues that are profoundly imperialist in nature.

7 This interview by Walter Adamson was first published as Spivak (1986).

8 Signs of how the contrary is true in contexts like Britain, Canada, Quebec, and France deserve a whole other essay on how the continued presence of othered immigrant subjects, especially those who have become second- or third-generation "nationals," can have profound impacts that challenge the hearts and minds of traditional "white" inhabitants of the shire, or *citoyens*, and can cause the latter "to cathect the space of the [o]ther on [their] home ground." However, I believe that it is too early to say whether in the majority of such cases the relatively recent *making strange* of the imperial homeland will lead to the creation of truly democratic, ethno-pluralistic, hybrid cultures in the medium to long term or whether, as much of what's going on in France and Australia these days suggests, it will lead to greater social conflict, especially along racialized and religious lines for some time to come.

9 This was originally an insulting, coercive, idiomatic term used in various parts of North America to enforce the speaking of English among immigrants and other non-English speakers, such as the French Canadians in Quebec and New England. For a powerful, poetic, counter-discursive appropriation and counter-worlding of this chauvinistic term's enforcement of English as the superordinate language of international capital, see Lalonde (1979).

10 Bill 101 is the provincial law, passed in 1977, that implemented the Charter of the French Language, which made French the official language of Quebec. Its most positive accomplishment has been Quebec's consequent success at integrating immigrants into the French majority culture.

11 In this instance, Zackodnick is citing Englebrecht (1990, 86).

12 For a vivid, detailed account of the importance of skyscraper culture to the practices and symbolism of modernity and *Américanité*, see Douglas (1995).

13 If my memory serves, the poem "Grenada, October 25th, 1983" was printed as a broadsheet/poster in an issue of *This Magazine* in 1984.

14 As the source of this attempt, Brand (1997, 4) credits Edward Said's
   citation in *Orientalism* of Antonio Gramsci's insistence on the necessity of compiling such an inventory.
15 One might be tempted to draw an analogy with Neil Bissoondath's
   (1994) critique of Canadian "Multi-Cult," but unlike Bissoondath,
   Brand clearly has no faith in the ability of the Charter of Rights and
   Freedoms to establish a level, nonracial playing field based on
   common citizenship.
16 A case in point is how systemic racism in Canada generates twice as
   much unemployment among young adult blacks in comparison with
   the general population, even though their average level of education
   is now higher than that of whites.
17 For analogous comments by Brand, see her film *Listening for
   Something ... Adrienne Rich and Dionne Brand in Conversation*
   (1996).
18 For a significant example of this position, see Angenot (1997).

INDIGENOUS REMAPPINGS OF AMERICA

4

Representations of the Native and the New World Subject

AMARYLL CHANADY

Throughout the Americas, the Native peoples were often described as the Other of a newly emerging society of settlers and immigrants – an Other that had to be "civilized," displaced, eliminated, or persuaded to fade away quietly before the advances of colonization. At the same time, the "Indian" was often represented as the basis of New World specificity in a symbolic identification with imaginary non-European ancestors. The mestizos, or "half-breeds," by comparison, were frequently regarded as degenerate "human hybrids" or unfortunate victims of colonization, destined to disappear or to perpetuate their misery in poverty and alcoholism on the margins of society. In many Latin American nations, however, the mestizo also became an icon for the inclusive New World subject in a gesture of differentiation not with Europe but with the United States, the emerging colossus to the north. A comparative discussion of the variety of discursive constructions of the Native and the mestizo in the Americas sheds light not only on the parallels but also on the differences between the ways that the nations represented their internal others, often in conjunction with discourses of identity stressing the uniqueness of the New World. From the "vanishing Indian" in Canada to the countercultural Native in the United States in the 1920s and the mestizo pillar of the new inclusive society in Latin America, the divergent figures of the indigene reflect the cultural, demographic, and political specificities of the nations of the Americas.

In Canada, as in the rest of the Americas, the settlers were often symbolically set in opposition to the Natives, who were equated with the wilderness. In a recent study, Laura Smyth Groening (2004) argues that Canadian writing has always been characterized by a Manichean allegory, in which barbarian, violent Natives close to nature and instinct, are contrasted with the Europeans, seen as civilized, rational, and hardworking. Even when the allegory is revalued, and nature is seen as positive, the allegory based on a binary opposition between self and Other remains intact. An interesting exception is the autobiographical writing of Susanna Moodie and Anna Jameson, in which the female narrators describe various types of social interaction with Native women. Groening stresses the importance of gender in the representation of the indigene since the women writers' identification with Native women deconstructs the Manichean allegory of male writers of the time (2004, 49–60). However, the allegory is very much present in the work of other colonial women writers, such as Catharine Parr Traill, who emigrated to Upper Canada from England in 1832. Traill's differentiation between the indigene and the European settler resembles that of many male writers who saw the Native as an idle nomad: "These old settlers and their children have seen the whole face of the country changed. They have seen the forest disappear before the axe of the industrious emigrant; they have seen towns and villages spring up where the bear and the wolf had their lair. They have seen the white-sailed vessel and the steamer plough those lakes and rivers where the solitary Indian silently glided over their lonely waters in his frail canoe" (Traill 1969, 17). This quotation, taken from Traill's *The Canadian Settler's Guide* (1855), encapsulates some of the main oppositions of the paradigm of what I will call the motif of the "founding nation," in which the Native is symbolically excluded from nation-building, and the act of founding a new society is considered the exclusive domain of the European settlers. Reflecting on the present comfort of the old settlers compared with the "toil and privation" of their beginnings in Upper Canada, Traill contrasts the "industrious emigrant," artisan of the founding nation, with the "solitary Indian," who symbolizes the exact opposite.

Although Traill avoids the most extreme formulations of the negative pole of the European-Indian opposition, the binary structure of the description and the laudatory reference to the "industrious emigrant" must be read in the context of the centuries-old civilization-barbarism dichotomy. The industrious emigrant brings to mind his stereotypical opposite, the Indian who founds nothing, builds nothing, and expends energy only when absolutely necessary for survival or to wage war. Whereas the emigrant founds towns and villages, and travels in sailboats and steamers, the Indian "silently glides over ... lonely waters in his frail canoe" (Traill 1969, 17). The opposition is not only one of technological progress (steamer versus canoe) but also one of social interaction since the town connotes sociability, as do the sailboat and steamer, built for the transport of groups of people, in contrast to the canoe of the "solitary" Indian travelling over "lonely waters." Traill's description also contrasts the strong and stable steamers and sailing ships with the "frail" canoe, the relatively sedentary lives of the colonizers living in permanent settlements with the nomadic wanderings of the Indians, and the settlers' transformation of nature with the Indians' blending, or living in harmony, with it. The opposition between nature and culture is aptly symbolized by the contrast between the steamers that "plough," a metaphor suggesting a relatively permanent change in the land, and the canoes that merely "glide," thus leaving the land undisturbed, or only momentarily disturbed. The two elements of the binary opposition suggest not only a contrast between permanence and transitoriness but also one between industry and leisure, as well as invoking the more general paradigm of agricultural activity versus hunting-and-gathering, a dichotomy more explicitly developed elsewhere in Traill's accounts of early settler life, to which I will return below. In this description of the changes brought about by the emigrants, the present is characterized by the settlers' permanent towns and solid steamships, whereas the past, depicted only in the process of transformation, is identified with forests, the lairs of bears and wolves, and the Indians' canoes. Thus not only are untamed nature, animals, and Native inhabitants symbolically associated in the nature paradigm, in opposition to that of the founding nation conceptualized as culture, but they are also explicitly conceptualized as the absence of culture, a lack that is gradually eliminated by the industry of the settlers.

Traill derives great satisfaction from contemplating the achievements of the colonizers in their transformation of nature, as is evident in the continuation of the passage cited above:

They have seen highways opened out through impenetrable swamps where human foot however adventurous had never trod. The busy mill-wheels have dashed where only the foaming rocks broke the onward flow of the forest stream. They have

seen God's holy temples rise, pointing upwards with their glit-
tering spires above the lowlier habitations of men, and have
heard the sabbath-bell calling the Christian worshippers to
prayer. They have seen the savage Indian bending there in mute
reverence, or lifting his voice in hymns of praise to that blessed
Redeemer who had called him out of darkness into his marvellous light. And stranger things he may now behold in that
mysterious wire, that now conveys a whispered message from
one end of the Province to the other with lightning swiftness;
and see the iron railway already traversing the Province, and
bringing the far-off produce of the woods to the store of the
merchant and to the city mart. (1969, 17)

Here, the "savage Indian" is shown as the beneficiary of evangeliza-
tion, linked with the civilizing mission in a passage where "darkness"
is associated not only with heathenism but also with the absence of
technological enlightenment and where "marvellous light" refers not
only to the revelation of God but also to civilization in general.

Although amenable to certain aspects of civilization, however, the
indigenous inhabitants are contrasted with the settlers not only by
the fact that they are the beneficiaries of enlightenment, while the
settlers do the enlightening, but also by their explicit exclusion from
the category of the agents of civilization. In *The Backwoods of
Canada*, a selection of letters written to her mother between 1832
and 1835, Traill informs her readers that many Indians "can both
read and write fluently, and are greatly improved in their moral and
religious conduct," and that they are "well and comfortably clothed,
and have houses to live in," but she adds that they are "still too much
attached to their wandering habits to become good and industrious
settlers" since they periodically "leave the village and encamp themselves in the woods along the borders of those lakes and rivers that
present the most advantageous hunting and fishing-grounds" (1986,
36). She describes them as particularly skilful in their traditional
pursuits, such as spear-fishing, in which they are "very expert ... the
squaws paddling the canoes with admirable skill and dexterity";
ice-fishing, "in which these people also excel" (67); and duck-
shooting, in which they are "very successful" and thus imitated by
white settlers (68). But even though the Native inhabitants are admired
for their skill in certain areas, in which they may even teach the settlers, they are explicitly constructed as the Other of the founders of

the new nation: "Their summer is not our summer. Like the people it is peculiar to this continent. – *They* reap while *we* sow. While *they* collect, *we* scatter abroad the seed for the future harvest" (1969, 232, original emphasis). It is a question of differences not merely between cultures, and between the geographical and climatic characteristics of North America and Europe, but also between culture (in the etymological sense of farming, as well as in the sense of culture as general social and intellectual improvement) and nature since the Europeans cultivate the land (they *sow* and *scatter*), whereas the Indians harvest available food sources (they only *reap* and *collect*). Agriculture is of course considered a prerequisite for establishing a civilized community.

Although many Latin American writers also constructed Natives as barbarians, idlers, obstacles to culture, or simply the Other of the civilizing process, the following quotation from the Cuban poet, intellectual, and revolutionary José Martí illustrates a very different motif: "We ... feel the inflamed blood of Tamanaco and Paramaconi coursing through our veins" (quoted in Fernández Retamar 1989, 19–20). Although many indigenist intellectuals advocated the integration of the marginalized indigenous sectors of society and expressed a sincere concern for their continuing exclusion, the symbolic constitution of a specifically Latin American identity based on the indigene corresponded to a need to create a symbolic filiation and historical depth among Creoles (the descendants of white Europeans) who no longer identified with the former colonizer. The symbolic filiation with the indigene was often a conscious strategy with specific political ends, which would explain the continuing contradiction between official ideologies of ethnic inclusion and the actual treatment of minorities. But identification with the indigene also involved a deep desire for rootedness. The quotation from Martí is a particularly illustrative example of the emotional nature of this kind of identification.

Even though symbolic filiation is more prevalent in Latin America, it also existed in former British colonies since the perception of a lack of rootedness and historical depth is shared in varying degrees by all settler societies. In a wide-ranging study of literary images of the Indian in Canada, Leslie Monkman explains the importance of the representation of the indigenous people by the need to create a sense of history, culture, and identity in a continent perceived as new: "For these writers, the Indian is no longer a foil for white culture but rather an indigenous ancestor in a land where the white man is still an immigrant. Red heroes fill the vacuum created by the absence of white aboriginal traditions on this continent, and the dream of a distinctive national literature focuses on the history and heritage of the red man" (1981, 5). He subsequently discusses the nineteenth-century poet Charles Sangster, who represented indigenous heroes as substitutes for the lack of feudal castles (96). Monkman argues that Canadian authors perceived the Indian as an ancestor and identified with indigenous myths and historical figures since the latter were "vehicles for the definition of the white man's national, social, or personal identity" (163).

This indigenous Other is just as much a product of the social imaginary as is the contrastive Other of the motif of the founding nation. Jane Tompkins's comments on the imaginary Indians of her childhood would apply to many authors and intellectuals who identified with the indigene: "My Indians, like my princesses, were creatures totally of the imagination, and I did not care to have any real exemplars interfering with what I already knew" (1986, 101). Contrary to the idealized metropolitan depiction of the indigene as Europe's irreducible cultural Other, New World identification with the internal Other frequently involves not only the seduction of lifestyles associated with freedom from the constraints of civilization but also a process of collective self-representation and the symbolic creation of a New World specificity. The indigene is thus not only a fictional Other described with a certain nostalgia for simpler lifestyles that supposedly avoid the vices of civilization but also an Other that can be taken as both a positive model for the nation as a whole and a marker of difference with respect to Europe. In other words, the author, intellectual, or politician may strongly identify with the indigene and experience a sense of psychological or cultural affinity on an individual basis and at the same time identify indigenous culture with that of the nation in a collective self-representation based on the internal Other.

Identification with the indigene can of course involve adopting an outsider position with respect to mainstream society, especially in the United States and Canada. In his study of fictional representations of the Amerindian in the United States, Michael Castro explains that young countercultural poets of the late 1960s and early '70s "identified with" Native peoples and thought of themselves as "tribal," "communal," and critical of the "destructive qualities of America and Western civilization – the lack of respect for human and natural

life that we saw as responsible for the tragedy of Vietnam" (1983, xii).
They experimented with new forms of poetry and public performance
that they considered "akin to ancient American tribal forms in the
way they sought to serve the spiritual needs of community" (xiii).
As Castro points out, many of the poets he discusses based their
portrayal of the Native on the noble-savage stereotype, "both in its
sense of the inadequacies of Western man, and its accompanying
sense that the Indian possessed qualities we lack and need" (xvi).

But the Native is not merely an object of individual identification
for young poets and intellectuals dissatisfied with modern society.
Several earlier poets presented the Amerindian as a model for the
entire collectivity. Walt Whitman, for example, considered the North
American Native to be a "vital resource, in touch with the spirit of
the American continent and offering, for an emerging American
consciousness and identity, 'new forms' of language and lifestyle"
that will create a necessary connection to place and foster certain
personal values (Castro 1983, xvii-xviii).

Castro discusses three poets of the 1920s – Vachel Lindsay, Hart
Crane, and William Carlos Williams – for whom the Amerindian
served as a "symbol of both the American continent and a new
American identity based on a harmonious relationship – a mystical
participation – with the land" (1983, 49). Lindsay, for example,
establishes an explicit symbolic filiation with the Native inhabitants
of the land through "Our Mother Pocahontas" (the title of his poem)
while denying white ancestry (49) in a "miraculous acquisition of
the Indian's bloodline and spirit" (53). This act is accompanied by
a rejection of "gray Europe's rags" (Lindsay's expression, 50) and
by a eulogy for the new land of promise, plenty, and renewal. With
respect to Williams, Castro explains that the poet urged his compa-
triots to become "Indian-like" in order to establish a sense of rootedness in the new continent (65). In "First People: Indians and Eskimos
as Symbols," the Canadian author and critic Margaret Atwood
argues that many Canadian authors also "adopted" the Amerindians
as their "true ancestors" and turned to indigenous myths and legends
as source material for their own writing in the same way that
European writers used Greek myths and the Bible (1972, 103).

The examples of "identification" alluded to above – the term is
used by Atwood (1972) and Castro (1983) on several occasions, as
well as by numerous other critics in their discussion of fictional
representations of the indigene – do not illustrate the same process.

Countercultural poets consider indigenous culture a better societal model than their own urbanized environment and feel a strong affinity with idealized Native lifestyles, other authors adopt the indigene as a symbol of the American continent in their construction of a new imagined community, and yet others use indigenous legends as thematic material. Using the indigene (or another internal Other, such as the country-dweller) as a nationalist symbol around which political discourse, and especially a rhetoric of solidarity, can be developed is of course not exclusive to the Americas but may even characterize European nationalist discourses. However, the Euro-American authors' explicit invocation of a symbolic filiation with the indigene (Lindsay's Pocahontas poem and Martí's lines) involves more than the search for nationalist symbols for political purposes. When Atwood asks "what do you do for a past if you are a white, relatively new to the continent and rootless?" (1972, 104), she is alluding to a perceived lack among members of the settler community who reject the colonial heritage and attempt to create an alternative past that will function as a marker of specificity for the new imagined community. The fictitious nature of this symbolic filiation is even more evident in Euro-American self-representations than in European inventions of the past. When Atwood points out that "it might well be argued that a knowledge of our origins is 'in truth' much more likely to require the exhumation of a pile of dead Scots Presbyterians and French Catholics" (105), she is undoubtedly right. But the need to create a new usable past is very obvious among many authors, intellectuals, and politicians.

Some of these strategies of "identification" have nothing to do with an actual sense of affinity and community with the indigene. In his study of Mexican attitudes toward the Native population and the mestizo, the twentieth-century critic Agustín Basave Benítez refers to the symbolic cultural filiation with the indigene as a "virtual expropriation of the indigenous past by the Creoles" (1992, 19). He attributes to this "expropriation" both a strictly political motive and a desire for a more positive self-image when he explains that Creole intellectuals used the indigene to legitimate their struggle against Europe, claiming a non-European cultural tradition according to which they would no longer be seen as degenerated Spaniards who create defective copies of metropolitan institutions. He also points out that the Creoles "appropriated the splendor of the dead Indian" and deliberately ignored the "misery of the living Indian" because they could not "consider such a specimen as their compatriot"; in spite of their enthusiasm for the "mythical warrior of Anáhuac," they did not feel the "slightest affinity with the Indian in the street, and even less with his culture" (19).

In Quebec, francophone writers sometimes occupied a more contradictory position. Although they represented the Native as threatened, excluded, displaced, and belonging to a culture well on its way to dying, they also established a certain affinity between the Native and their own culture, even when the indigenous culture was not idealized. Gilles Thérien argues that the imaginary Indian has become a mirror of the Quebecker, whose francophone culture is no less threatened (1987, 17).[1]

A particularly interesting example of identification in Latin America is the representation of the emerging postindependence nations as hybridized, the mestizo being held up as the icon of a specifically New World collective subject. Martí is one of the thinkers most frequently associated with the paradigm of the mestizo nation, at least by many contemporary Latin Americanists, having coined the felicitous expression "nuestra América mestiza" (our mestizo America) (1972, 312), which was eventually to become a singularly effective ideologeme in the constitution of a positive Latin American identity. But although this expression has frequently been brandished as a valorizing marker of difference with respect to supposedly "purer" societies in North America and Europe, less attention has been paid to what exactly Martí meant by "mestizo America." A perusal of his main writings on hybridity and miscegenation reveals that the expression does not refer to a continent inhabited largely by members of a "new race" resulting from the miscegenation of Europeans, Amerindians, and Africans, akin to José Vasconcelos's (1961) problematic "cosmic race," which the Mexican educator developed in an essay of 1925, four decades after Martí wrote his most influential speeches and essays. Although Martí often uses the term in the sense of racial miscegenation between individuals, he generally uses it to refer to the multiracial composition of Latin American society. In his most widely read essay, "Nuestra América" (Our America), he introduces the expression "nuestra América mestiza" in the same passage in which he provides a metaphorical definition in apposition: "nations with bare legs and Parisian dress-coat" ("pueblos de pierna desnuda y casaca de París") (1972, 312). This is a metaphor neither for the mingling of European and non-European races nor for the

acculturation of Amerindians or Africans since it is the collectivity
that is personified as hybrid. Martí stresses this when he refers on
the same page to the "discordant elements" of America and the
"disjointed continent." The Amerindian and the African, constituting
the internal Other from the perspective of the dominant Creole sector
of society, are not presented as having merged with the hegemonic
groups. On the contrary, intranational (Cuban) and intracontinental
diversity is constantly emphasized by Martí.

The term he prefers in most passages concerning racial diversity
is therefore "hybrid" (híbrido). Although the latter term also refers
to persons of mixed racial origins and is thus partially synonymous
with mestizo, it is a more general term, which includes, without being
restricted to, the racial mingling of Europeans and Amerindians.
Hybridity was understood in various ways by nineteenth-century
proponents of racialist theories, including the homogenizing amalgamation of races in a completely new race, the imperfect mixing of
races in which original racial characteristics remained visible and
unevenly distributed, and the simple coexistence in the same nation
of different ethnic groups (for a very useful account of the European
conceptualization of hybridity, see Young 1995). It was hardly a
neutral term since it was associated with the pejorative connotations
of racialist theories that considered the "human hybrid" to be a
degenerate type and mingling between Caucasian and non-Caucasian
races to be a source of degeneration of the (Aryan) race. It certainly
did not have the central status it has today in postcolonial theory.
Martí's awareness of the negative implications of racial hybridity
are obvious when he claims elsewhere, in an obviously dialogic
rejoinder to the racialist beliefs at the time, that Cuba is "more
favoured than harmed by the mixture of its races" ("más servido
que herido por la mezcla de sus razas") (1972, 184). It is also evident
in the passage in which he expresses admiration for the "Indian
Juárez," who fought successfully to preserve Mexican independence
from foreign intervention and contributed to the country's subsequent international prestige, in spite of its being a "hybrid nation,
the nation of a million whites and seven million Indians" ("nación
híbrida, la nación de un millón de blancos y siete millones de indios")
(112). Martí is of course using the term "hybrid" in the sense of
racially diverse, not in the sense of miscegenated, but the range of
meanings of the term as well as the absence of a clear distinction

between these meanings in Martí's writings make any favourable stand on hybridity in any of its meanings a strong rejection of the negative associations of the term.

His admiring reference to Herbert Spencer as one of the two guiding lights, together with Simón Bolívar, of Latin America (Martí 1972, 303) is highly problematic in this context, since Spencer distinguished between the mingling of proximate races (e.g., Caucasian), which he regarded as positive, and that of distant races (Caucasian and non-Caucasian), which he saw in a very pejorative light (Vasconcelos expresses similar reservations at the beginning of *La raza cósmica*). Martí in fact oscillates between revalorizing a national/continental characteristic that was generally considered negative and trying to prove that it is possible to achieve greatness in spite of the internal dissentions caused by colonization and racial heterogeneity. When he explains that Latin America replaced "poison" with "sap," that it started off as a "drain" ("sentina") but is now becoming a "crucible," and that this "hybrid and original land, fashioned out of divisive Spaniards and grim and terrified aborigines, with its spattering of Africans" ("tierra híbrida y original, amasada con españoles retaceros y aborígenes torvos y aterrados, más sus salpicaduras de africanos") managed to compensate for its "disorder and treacherous mixture of our origins" ("desorden y mezcla alevosa de nuestros orígenes") by the "soul of the harmonious and artistic land" ("alma de la tierra armoniosa y artística") (1972, 302–3), he is not praising hybridity as such but presenting it as an obstacle to be overcome. What is interesting in this passage is not only the idea that different races can eventually create a new society instead of engaging in a battle at the end of which the "stronger" races reduce the weaker ones to perpetual servitude, or even exterminate the less successful ones, but also the idea that the natural environment could exert a positive influence on the new society. In the early 1780s, the Jesuit scholar Francisco Clavijero (1958) had already criticized racialist theories stressing the deleterious influence of tropical climate, which was believed to lead to the physical and moral degeneration of the European settlers, and had praised the natural attractions of the continent. In his essay "Nuestra América," Martí thus echoes Clavijero in his valorization of the Latin American environment, which deliberately contradicts certain received ideas. He foresees a positive future for his continent because of its spirit of moderation (again contradicting a widespread belief in the excesses of colonial and postindependence Latin America) and the "serene harmony of Nature" in the "continent of light" (1972, 313).

Hybridity, however, also becomes a marker of difference with respect to the newly emerged political and economic power to the North, namely the "other America." The expression "nuestra América mestiza" occurs in an essay that expresses strong reservations about the strength of the United States and its intentions regarding Latin America, especially Cuba. Martí establishes an opposition between the America of Lincoln and the America of Juárez (1972, 297) and between the country in which slavery was officially abolished and the continent on which a person of indigenous heritage actually rose to power. Although "hybridity" is generally used by Martí in the sense of racial heterogeneity, not in that of miscegenation, the distinction between North and South based on *mestizaje* involves more than the degree of heterogeneity. Both North and South are composed of many races and ethnic groups, as Martí points out in his essay, in which he describes the hybrid origins of the United States, composed of Puritans, Quakers, Catholics, Swedes, Frenchmen, Scotsmen, and Germans (298), besides the indigenous and Afro-American populations. But he considers North American liberty "egotistical and unjust" since it is erected on the bent backs of an entire slave race (299), while Indians are hunted like wolves (298). Whereas Latin America accepts a leader of Native origin (Juárez), North America "drowns its Indians in their blood" ("ahoga en sangre a sus indios") (309). The difference between North and South is thus not racial and ethnic hybridity (in the sense of heterogeneity) as such but the way that the internal Other (non-European) is integrated into society. In this essay Martí sees mestizo America as an example of integrated and harmonious heterogeneity (he will contest this view in other essays), whereas he considers North America to be one of hierarchy and marginalization. Greater social and political integration of racial groups also entails a greater degree of miscegenation, such that the mestizo (heterogeneous) continent ("nuestra mestiza América") inevitably also contains mestizos in the literal sense of the term (persons of mixed race). Martí in fact uses the two meanings of mestizo alternately. When he claims that in Latin America the "autochthonous mestizo has vanquished the exotic Creole" ("mestizo autóctono ha vencido al criollo exótico") (310), the differentiation between the terms "mestizo" and "Creole" makes

clear that "mestizo" is here to be taken in the literal sense, and this
is corroborated, at least partly, by his opposition between the "blond
nation" to the North and the "swarthy men" ("trigueños") to the
South (317). The expression "nuestra América mestiza," by contrast,
has a broader and more indefinite meaning that includes not only
the idea of racial miscegenation but also that of racial and cultural
heterogeneity, as well as that of tolerance for and integration of different racial groups within society.

The negative representation of the external, threatening Other
becomes constitutive of the contrasting utopian portrait of the Self,
as it would later also become for Vasconcelos (1961). This utopian
portrait is at times situated retroactively during the wars of independence, described by Martí as a collective rising of all the races and
classes of Latin America in which Creole members of the church
conversed with Indians and poor whites marched alongside mestizos,
accompanied by singing African ex-slaves, squadrons of gauchos,
and resuscitated indigenous tribes (1972, 301–2). But generally, the
utopian society is brandished as the goal of successful Latin American
nation-building and explicitly situated in the future, in which love
and friendship between all will reign. Martí opposes the desired Latin
American liberty, which should be "humanitarian and expansive,
not local, not of race, not of sect" ("humanitaria y expansiva, no
local, ni de raza, ni de secta") (303), to the "sectarian" liberty in
North America, which concerns the locality or the individual rather
than humanity in general. He describes the United States as a country
of pilgrims without masters or slaves (in spite of his comments elsewhere on the enslavement of African Americans) and of adventurers
without any law but their own, solitary and feared companions of
the leopard and the eagle (299).

In a singularly contradictory rhetorical strategy, the imaginary
constitution of the mestizo nation (or, generally, continent) as toler-
ant and humanitarian is based on the positing of a northern nation
as racist and sectarian in order to counteract the racism and internal
divisions that actually characterize Latin America, according to Martí
himself. A negative Other is thus constituted in opposition to a positive Self that does not yet exist. It is significant that in those passages
in which Martí unfavourably compares the North to the South, he
remains silent about those Latin American defects that he criticizes
in other speeches and essays or even in other passages of the same
text. *Mestizaje* becomes an ambiguous marker of difference that is

constantly deconstructed by Martí. In fact, the function of the ideologeme of *mestizaje* is progressively transformed from one of differentiation between Self and Other into one of differentiation
between the present and the future collective Self. His rejection of
· the possible annexation of Cuba by the United States and his criticism of the "excessive individualism" (1972, 83) of the "authoritarian, greedy and aggressive Yankee" ("yanqui autoritario, codicioso
y agresivo") (157) who would arrive in Cuba with his monopolies
and destroy all other commercial activities and maybe even send his
freed African slaves there in order to get rid of them (188) makes it
necessary to reconceptualize the ideologeme of the mestizo nation
or continent not so much as a marker of difference in order to constitute a specific differential national or continental identity but as a
rallying cry in a deliberate political strategy of national and continental reconciliation and solidarity in the face of an external threat.

In a recent book on "mestizophily" in Mexico, and more particularly in the writings of the politician and scholar Andrés Molina
Enríquez, Basave Benítez defines the term *mestizofilia* as the belief
that racial and cultural miscegenation is desirable and describes the
main premise of Molina Enríquez's thought as follows: "that the
mestizos of Mexico … are Mexicans by antonomasia, the authentic
depositaries of Mexicanness," and "that Mexico cannot become a
developed and prosperous nation until it completes the process of
miscegenation and succeeds in the ethnic homogenization of the
population through the racial fusion of the Indian and Creole minorities in the mestizo masses" (1992, 13).[2] Basave Benítez correctly
emphasizes the connection between the identification of Mexicanness
with *mestizaje* and the search for a national identity and criticizes
the application to Latin America of European theories of nation,
developed in an entirely different context. However, the opposition
he establishes between his own continent, in which states existed
before nations were created, and Europe, in which nations supposedly preceded states (14), is somewhat simplistic, especially in view
of the fact that he refers to Hugh Seton-Watson's (1982) distinction
between various types of national movements in Europe, namely
gradualist (England and France), integrationist (Italy and Germany),
and separatist (Hungary and Romania). Although it was generally
easier to identify certain ethnic characteristics, such as language, as
markers of identity in Europe, there was no such thing as an essentialist nation preceding statehood there either. The nation as imagined

community was created in various ways, such as identifying with a particular government, sharing the same official and usually state-fostered "memories" of the past, reading the same books and newspapers, and believing in the same national heroes. Neither did particular "nations," in the ethnic sense, always give rise to independent states since different states may share the same language (Germany and Austria). On the other hand, as Walker Connor (1994) and numerous other political scientists have pointed out, there are few European states in which only one language is spoken (not only patently multi-ethnic Russia but even France with its Breton and Basque minorities and Italy with its numerous dialects that can only be considered dialects, not "proper" languages, for political reasons). There is thus no equation between a supposedly stable ethnic group ("nation" in the sense in which Basave Benítez uses it, and which he claims preceded the European states) and the nation[-state] that must be created. The semantic slippage between nation and nation-state (the term *nación*, used by the Mexican scholar, has the same double meaning as that of "nation") allows for a neat dichotomy between Europe, which has pre-existing nations, and Latin America, which must create them, but obscures the fact that nations are always created, even though this may come about in different ways. Certain strategies of symbolic nation-building are in fact common to European and Latin American nations, namely the marginalization of nonhegemonic ethnic groups and languages in the constitution of a homogeneous imagined collectivity by the government and cultural elites. Latin American nations thus differ from European ones not in that their identity, contrary to that of European nations, had to be defined, as Basave Benítez suggests (1992, 15), but in the particular way that they were symbolically constructed.

Miscegenation has a very different function in Canadian literature. Rather than a symbol for a new hybrid nation different from the European nations that colonized the Americas, miscegenation is generally represented in a negative manner. Although negative portraits of mestizos are ubiquitous in Latin American writings, where they are described as particularly cruel mediators between the colonial or Creole overseers and the exploited Indians, or as the degraded and impoverished remnants of a glorious indigenous past (see Arguedas 1975), they have entered the national imaginary as an important paradigm of postindependence identity. In Canadian literature, "half-breeds" are generally portrayed as torn between two cultures and afflicted by a strong self-hatred, as well as hatred of the white culture, to which the father often belongs. In a discussion of the Métis writers Maria Campbell, Lee Maracle, and Beatrice Culleton Mosionier, Laura Smyth Groening (2004, 131) examines how Métis women "explore the practical consequences of living with a mixed-race heritage" that includes not only racism but also the in-between status of those who can identify neither with treaty Indians nor with white Canadians. She also describes Duncan Campbell Scott's characters as "tormented by their dual heritage: haunted by their past, displaced by their present" (103). She argues that for white writers, "hybridity" is often a politically correct term for assimilation (143) and that Native people "were not really imagined as mingling racially and culturally with Europeans to produce a new nationality" (98). In her discussion of Charles Mair's poem "Tecumseh," she quotes the injunction of a figure called the Prophet that "Red shall not marry White," concluding that "the poets and playwrights of colonial Canada ensure that no Indian or mixed-race children thrive" (85).

In her discussion of Margaret Laurence's *Diviners*, in which the Métis patriarch Lazarus Tonnerre contemplates the bodies of his dead daughter and grandchildren, Groening points out that the image of death and destruction "replicates the most dangerous trope in Canadian literature: the Indian as the member of a dead and dying people" (2004, 21). The Métis are assimilated to the ubiquitous motif of the dead and dying Indian, which has replaced that of the howling savage of the numerous historical accounts of Indian warfare in early Canadian writing. The disappearing Métis, however, are not just Indians, although Groening rightly points out that they are assimilated to them in their inevitable destiny as a disappearing culture. They are also a people of mixed race, and the importance of this is illustrated by Laurence's 1966 short story "The Loons." At the beginning of the story, the Tonnerre settlement is described as situated on the outskirts of Manawaka and portrayed as "a chaos of lean-tos, wooden packing cases, warped lumber, discarded car tires, ramshackle chicken coops, tangled strands of barbed wire and rusty tin cans" (1986, 143). Their status as outcasts is highlighted by the spatial configuration of their settlement, which is built "below" Manawaka, in the centre of a cluster of trees "at the foot of the Town hill" (143). What is particularly interesting is the description of the Tonnerres as "French halfbreeds" who "spoke a *patois* that was neither Cree nor French" and who are considered by the white narrator's Grandmother MacLeod to be "neither flesh, fowl, nor good salt herring" (143). They are neither Native nor European: "They did not belong among the Cree of the Galloping Mountain reservation, further north, and they did not belong among the Scots-Irish and Ukrainians of Manawaka, either" (143). The lack of racial and cultural purity is emphasized throughout the story, as Vanessa, the white protagonist, is intensely disappointed in Piquette, the Métis girl who is invited to spend the summer at the white family's cabin. Before she meets her Métis playmate, she dreams of her as an exotic "daughter of the forest, a kind of junior prophetess of the wilds" (146), only to discover that Piquette is a "dead loss" as an Indian (147) since she knows nothing about nature and is not even interested in the natural beauty surrounding the summer cabin. Piquette eventually marries a white man and dies in a fire with her two mixed-race children. Although the final sentence of the story identifies Piquette with the loons who disappear with the encroachment of civilization, and thus confirms the motif of the dead and dying Indian, the emphasis on the mixed race and cultural degeneration of Piquette as well as on her death and that of her mixed-blood children also points to another motif: the scandal of hybridity.

Piquette's fate thus signals a major difference in the constitution of the New World subject in Canadian and Latin American writing. Whereas the new collective subject in Spanish-language texts has frequently been conceptualized in terms of the symbolic appropriation of the indigene or the amalgamation of the indigene and the white Creole in a new hybrid nation, the symbolic integration of the indigene in the Canadian postcolonial subject has been much more difficult, and miscegenation has never become a central trope for an emerging collective identity.

NOTES

1 For a more in-depth discussion of the representation of the Native in Quebec literature, see Chanady (1999, 123–93).
2 "son los mexicanos por antonomasia, los auténticos depositarios de la mexicanidad"; "M. no puede convertirse en una nación desarrollada y próspera mientras no culmine su proceso de mestizaje y logre homogeneizar en lo étnico la población mediante la fusión racial de las minorías de indios y criollos en la masa mestiza."

5

Indigeneity and Diasporic Belonging: Three New World Readings of Chief Sitting Bull

SARAH PHILLIPS CASTEEL

The literatures of the Americas, particularly in their colonial phase, are fundamentally preoccupied with the problem of belonging, or what Lois Parkinson Zamora has called "the anxiety of origins" (1997, 5). They are characterized (to a greater or lesser degree) by a keen awareness of their lack of both compelling myths of origin and strong national literary traditions. In New World writing, anxieties about belonging and origins often manifest themselves in depictions of the figure of the Indian, whether negative or positive. For although indigenous peoples of the Americas are seen as obstacles to European settlement of the land, they also represent an authentic connection to that land for which the new arrival longs. The problem of belonging haunts the literatures of the Americas, which often seek to establish their difference from Europe via an identification with the Indian but must also acknowledge their own lack of indigeneity. To "go native" – and the related phenomenon that Philip Deloria terms "playing Indian" (1998) – become one means of laying claim to New World belonging, of establishing the legitimacy of the Euro-American presence in the New World.

The figure of the Indian as a locus for anxieties about New World belonging has been valuably explored in the context of the settler literatures of both North and South America.[1] However, if an anxiety about its nonindigenous status troubles Euro-American writing, how much more acute must that anxiety be for minority and immigrant writers in the New World? Increasingly, minority and immigrant writers of the Americas feel the need to address not only the settler society but also prior indigenous presences on the land. Thus, for example, Caribbean Canadian writer Dionne Brand's novel *What We All Long For*, which portrays the urban Toronto landscape of second-generation postimmigrant alienation, opens with the observation that the myriad ethnic neighbourhoods of Toronto all "sit on Ojibway land but hardly any of them know it or care because that genealogy is wilfully untraceable except in the name of the city itself" (2005, 4). In acknowledging indigenous claims to the land, contemporary diasporic writers such as Brand must negotiate traditional Euro-American narrative solutions to the problem of belonging, including the trope of "going native."

The currency of the figure of the Indian in contemporary diasporic discourse becomes particularly evident when we adopt a hemispheric mode of reading. Indeed, although the literary obsession with indigeneity has tended to be discussed within a national framework, its transamerican character invites a hemispheric approach. If, as Amaryll Chanady demonstrates in the present volume, the figure of the Indian is a focus for anxieties about belonging across a series of New World national literatures, my aim here is to show how the legacy of such patterns of representation can be traced across contemporary diasporic writing of the Americas as well.

To this end, I will offer as a case study the evocation of the nineteenth-century Sioux leader Chief Sitting Bull in the work of three diasporic authors of the Americas: Joy Kogawa, Bernard Malamud, and Derek Walcott. Tracing the circulation of Sitting Bull among these three authors from Canada, the United States, and the Caribbean both suggests the continuing reliance of contemporary writers on the figure of the indigene to construct a sense of New World belonging and indicates that we are addressing a hemispheric, rather than narrowly national, problematic. By the same token, resituating a celebrated Canadian text, Joy Kogawa's *Obasan*, in a comparative American framework generates a more sharply critical reading of the novel than those produced within the national and ethnic contexts in which *Obasan* is more standardly considered. Indeed, the comparison with Malamud's and Walcott's appropriations of Sitting Bull reveals not only the currency of the figure of the indigene in contemporary diasporic writing but also the risks entailed in reinscribing settler colonial narratives of indigenization.[2]

The presence of Sitting Bull, an iconic figure of US national history, in not only the US but also the Canadian and Caribbean texts under consideration here is suggestive of the cultural dominance of the United States in the hemisphere. Accordingly, the choice of Sitting Bull as an anchor for my discussion may seem questionable given some scholars' charge that the recent paradigm shift from nation to hemisphere in US American studies is driven by an imperializing impulse that seeks to subordinate other American literatures to US-centred readings, concerns, and vocabularies. As is discussed in the introduction to this collection, Canadianists in particular are wary of the "transnationalizing impulse" (Wald 1998, 202) that has fuelled the expansion of US American studies, and they have objected that those postcolonial countries in the hemisphere with historically weak nationalisms may not be quite so eager to abandon the nation.[3]

As a result, Canadianists have largely absented themselves from hemispheric conversations. Hemispheric approaches have not taken hold in the Canadian academy as they have in the US; on the whole, they are not reflected in course syllabi or in job postings, and they remain marginal in Canadian scholarship.[4] Compounding this trend, a notable feature of hemispheric American studies as it is currently configured is its lack of attention to Canadian material. US Americanists, while endeavouring to establish relationships between the US and Latin America and to a lesser extent the Caribbean, have with a few rare exceptions almost entirely neglected Canada.[5] By focusing here on a well-known Canadian novel, Joy Kogawa's *Obasan*, I seek to bring greater visibility to Canadian literature within hemispheric discussions that have marginalized Canadian material. At the same time, I hope to suggest an alternative configuration of hemispheric studies that would move beyond the project of rehabilitating US American studies in order to illustrate the benefits that Canadianists stand to gain from a fuller engagement with inter-American approaches.

The example of *Obasan* will demonstrate how broadening the field of analysis beyond the national framework can bring to light neglected aspects of a much-discussed text. In particular, a comparative and inter-American approach reveals how the analogy that Kogawa establishes between indigenous and diasporic displacements is challenged and problematized by other diasporic authors. The hemispheric framework that I will elaborate illustrates both the urgency of rereading *Obasan* with a more critical appreciation of its relationship to longstanding New World narrative structures and the necessity of broadening discussions of the representation of the indigene to include contemporary minority and immigrant discourses.

Obasan's powerfully corrective historical vision and aesthetic strengths have been extensively discussed in the secondary literature. Yet the extent to which Kogawa's call for a more inclusive model of Canadian belonging is predicated on an image of the Indian as connected to nature has been largely overlooked. Indeed, the novel's reliance on an image of the Indian as one with nature and on a related analogy between Japanese Canadian and First Nations experiences of dispossession has received little comment. Both *Obasan* (1981) and its sequel *Itsuka* (1992) propose that First Nations peoples have been subject to forms of dispossession since European contact that align them with Japanese Canadians. The affiliation with First Nations peoples in turn effects a rapprochement between Kogawa's Japanese Canadians and the Canadian landscape from which they have been alienated. This analogy is fundamental to *Obasan*'s articulation of Japanese Canadian belonging, as a key passage about Chief Sitting Bull, an emblem of Native American dispossession, reveals.

It is worth recalling that Sitting Bull is himself a border-crossing figure who spent several years in exile in Canada between 1877 and 1881 after the Battle of the Little Bighorn and who claimed that he was at least as much a British Indian as he was an American Indian (MacEwan 1973, 10–11, 103). Kogawa alludes to Sitting Bull's experience of Canadian exile in the opening scene of *Obasan*, in which the protagonist, Naomi, describes her uncle, a Japanese Canadian fisherman who is forcibly dislocated from the coast to the Prairies during the Second World War:

Everything in front of us is virgin land. From the beginning
of time, the grass along this stretch of prairie has not been cut.
About a mile east is a spot which was once an Indian buffalo
jump, a high steep cliff where the buffalo were stampeded and
fell to their deaths. All the bones are still there, some sticking
right out of the side of a fresh landslide.
Uncle could be Chief Sitting Bull squatting here. He has
the same prairie-baked skin, the deep brown furrows like dry

riverbeds creasing his cheeks. All he needs is a feather head-
dress, and he would be perfect for a picture postcard – "Indian
Chief from Canadian Prairie" – souvenir of Alberta, made in
Japan. (1994, 2–3)

In this passage, Kogawa at once evokes the colonialist tropes of
virgin territory and the vanishing Indian and undercuts these tropes
by introducing the more contemporary image of the Japanese-made
souvenir. Yet underlying the satirical reference to the commodification of the Indian chief is an assertion of a basic parallelism between
Japanese Canadian and First Nations historical experiences that is
reaffirmed and extended at various points throughout *Obasan*.[6] In
addition, the landscape imagery that Kogawa employs to characterize
Uncle Isamu's facial features asserts a connection with nature that
both he and Sitting Bull embody.

The initial parallelism between First Nations and Japanese
Canadians that Kogawa introduces in the Sitting Bull passage is
periodically reasserted throughout the novel as a means of binding
Japanese Canadians to the physical environment. Kogawa deepens
the analogy with First Nations peoples in a dream sequence in which
Naomi imagines herself in a forest together with another woman
and a man:

They have been here before us, forever in the forest ... They move
on a heavily treed slope that rises sharply to our right. The
woman's back is bent. Slow and heavy as sleep, her arms sway
and swing, front to back, back to front. For a flickering moment
she appears as she once was, naked, youthful, voluptuous.
    But the mirage fades. Her face is now harsh again and angular
as quartz – square, a coarse golden brown. Her body, a matching
squareness, is dense as earth. With a sickle she is harvesting the
forest's debris, gathering the branches into piles. (1994, 34)

Naomi soon joins the woman in the laborious task of clearing the
forest, while a British martinet oversees their efforts. In this scene
of patriarchal and colonial oppression, both the Canadian land and
its inhabitants are subjugated to the British officer's will; the martinet
wields absolute control over the indigenous woman, Naomi, and
nature itself.[7] Like the Sitting Bull passage, the dream undercuts the
colonialist trope of virgin territory by highlighting the historical

suppression of First Nations peoples and the natural environment that this trope masked. However, at the same time as Kogawa challenges this colonialist discourse, she reproduces certain of its features. The timeless indigenous woman represents an ancient way of life; she has been in the forest "forever." The woman was once "naked" and "voluptuous," a description that evokes primitivist fantasies of the eroticized indigenous female body. The woman's physical movements are ape-like, as though she were half-animal. Finally, the woman is strongly identified with nature: in contrast to the martinet, who maintains a marked distance from nature, the woman has a body as "dense as earth."

Kogawa's persistent emphasis on the natural piety of the Indian attests to the influence of New World and primitivist discourse on her writing. In keeping with a practice that dates back to Christopher Columbus's letters, Kogawa presents indigenous peoples as continuous with the landscape, such that the degradation of the woman and of nature are coterminous. This purported intimacy between indigenous peoples and the land has been both exploited and parodied by Canadian First Nations writers. Jeannette Armstrong's novel *Whispering in Shadows* (2000) advances a narrative of reconnection with the earth in its affiliation of First Nations and ecological concerns. Tomson Highway's *Kiss of the Fur Queen* (1999) and Thomas King's *Truth and Bright Water* (1999), by contrast, heavily ironize the trope of the Indian's privileged relationship with nature in scenes in which First Nations characters display varying degrees of ineptitude and lack of enthusiasm on camping trips.

Lacking any such ironic overtones, Kogawa's alliance of Japanese Canadians and First Nations peoples in *Obasan* enables her to associate Japanese Canadians with the physical environment, bolstering her characters' claims to Canadian belonging. This strategy becomes more pronounced in Kogawa's sequel to *Obasan*, *Itsuka*, in which Naomi finds a lover and companion in the unlikely person of a French Canadian priest, Father Cedric. Cedric has Métis ancestry[8] and woos Naomi by taking her into the wilderness of the Laurentian Shield, affirming his indigeneity by demonstrating a powerful intimacy with the Canadian landscape. Walking through the woods with Cedric, Naomi senses "the touch ... not so much of history as of prehistory" as well as "the breath of his ancestors" (1992, 134). Naomi's quest for belonging is fulfilled both by the political victory of Japanese Canadian redress and by her joint union with the Métis and the Canadian land, with which Cedric has brought her into closer contact.

In *Itsuka* the emblem of the Japanese connection to First Nations Canadians is the "Japanese Haida rattle" that Cedric inherits from his father and later gives to Naomi, symbolically conferring on her an (indigenous) Canadian identity.[9] Cedric relates the rattle's history to Naomi:

> Back in the early 1900s, Japanese miners and fishermen had settled on the Queen Charlotte Islands. At the time of the Japanese Canadian round-up in 1942, a few of the men fled to the more remote islands and were sheltered by the Haida ...
> The isseis and their protectors ate the same food – sea-weed, herring roe, young ferns, berries. The sun and sea joined them. Children were born. Moon-faced children. Babies with Japanese eyes. And there were dark-skinned children on the islands as well – offspring of slaves in flight from the south. One of the issei fathers carved this rattle for his child. (1992, 108)

This Japanese Canadian myth of origins highlights cooperation between First Nations and Japanese Canadians and concretizes the symbolic alliance that *Obasan* had introduced by alluding to miscegenation and the birth of Japanese Haida children. The narrative of the rattle supplies a sense of belonging that had previously eluded Kogawa's protagonists. It also anticipates Naomi's sexual union with Cedric. In a scene of lovemaking in the wilderness (207–8) that echoes other such Edenic episodes found throughout New World writing, Naomi recovers the connection with nature and with Canada that her family's forced removal from Vancouver had severed. *Itsuka* thus conforms to the primitivist plot in New World literature of the protagonist who is revitalized through interracial sexual contact with the Indian.

Primitivist longings also characterize an episode in *Itsuka* in which Naomi accompanies her Aunt Emily to Hawaii, a "nisei paradise" of communal togetherness: "The extravagant moist air on this island is thick with the sweet scent of fruit and flowers and there are ferns and fringe trees ... On the streets, we blend into a collage of races. We're both tanning quickly and beginning to look like the 'locals.' If belongingness was all that mattered in life, Aunt Emily says, she'd move to Hawaii in a flash" (1992, 85). Kogawa's idealized depiction of Hawaii as a place of harmony with nature and of uncomplicated belonging – of "hominess" to use Marianna Torgovnick's term (1990, 185) – recalls the European primitivist fantasy of the ideal other place (often located to the south). In contrast to the alienated condition of Kogawa's Japanese Canadians, the Japanese Hawaiians are fully at home in their landscape: "Hawaii's niseis, Aunt Emily says, are as unbent as free-standing trees. Unlike us crippled bonsai in Canada, they've retained community here" (Kogawa 1992, 85). The difficulty with this primitivist solution to the problem of belonging is that it relies on an escapist fantasy of a retreat into nature and therefore is difficult to sustain. Naomi's Hawaiian idyll is soon ended and she must once again confront the more complex realities of her Canadian life. After her sojourn in Hawaii, Naomi returns to Toronto to continue her work on behalf of the cause of Japanese Canadian redress. The culminating event of *Itsuka* is the Canadian government's capitulation in 1988 to the Japanese Canadians' demands for compensation. Naomi's quest for belonging is fulfilled both by this political victory and by her joint union with the Métis (Cedric) and the Canadian land, with which Cedric has brought her into closer contact.

Both *Obasan* and *Itsuka* propose that since European contact First Nations peoples have been subject to forms of dispossession that align them with Japanese Canadians. This affiliation with First Nations peoples in turn effects a rapprochement between Kogawa's Japanese Canadians and the landscape from which they have been alienated, forming the basis for the protagonists' claims to Japanese Canadian belonging. What is so striking about this dimension of Kogawa's novels is how closely it parallels earlier Canadian and New World literary plots in which the hero is indigenized through contact with the Indian and his landscape. Kogawa's writing thus provides a key example of the reinscription of the settler colonial fantasy of indigenization in contemporary diasporic writing, one that can be further illuminated through comparison with readings of Sitting Bull in the work of two other diasporic writers of the Americas.

Bernard Malamud and Derek Walcott also prove to be powerfully attracted to the figure of the Indian and to Chief Sitting Bull in particular, and like Kogawa, they suggest that Sitting Bull's story has an important resonance for other dispossessed peoples. Yet the readings of Sitting Bull that they develop in the contexts, respectively, of

Jewish and African diaspora experience in the Americas suggest a conception of the relationship between indigenous and diasporic identities that diverges from that of Kogawa. Although Sitting Bull is not referred to by name in Jewish American author Bernard Malamud's posthumously published novel *The People* (1989), this Jewish Western contains strong echoes of Sitting Bull's biography. Malamud is more hesitant than Kogawa, however, to associate too closely his displaced protagonist with the narrative of Native American dispossession.

Malamud's hero, Yozip Bloom, is a Russian Jewish greenhorn who in the 1870s American West inadvertently becomes the representative of an Indian tribe that is in the process of negotiating its land rights. When we first meet Yozip, he is "drifting westward, a decent direction" (1989, 3), peddling dry goods and doing other odd jobs along the way. As Yozip wanders the country attempting to find a sense of purpose, he appears profoundly disoriented: "He moved into Idaho, stopping off for a while at Moscow. Nothing in Moscow reminded him of Moscow" (4). At issue throughout the manuscript is Yozip's uncertain status in the New World, his confusion as to whether he is a native or a non-native: "An officious Jew he met in Wyoming told him he spoke with a Yiddish accent. Yozip was astonished because he now considered himself to be, in effect, a native. He had put in for citizenship the day after he had arrived in the New World, five years ago, and figured he was an American by now. He would know for sure after he had looked through the two or three official documents his cousin was keeping for him for when he got back from wherever he was going" (3). As Yozip soon discovers, the members of the tribe are also profoundly disoriented. Like Yozip, "the People" are non-citizens who are continually threatened with dispossession, and both Yozip and the tribe struggle with the English language that they are attempting to acquire. The People are in danger of losing the land that has been granted to them, and after witnessing Yozip inadvertently commit an act of heroism, they induct him into their tribe and ask him to act as their representative in their treaty negotiations.

In *The People*, Yozip's condition of dispossession and that of the tribe serve to mutually amplify one another. It is on the basis of their shared experience of dispossession that Yozip identifies with the tribe and their resistance to the white settlers. (Pocatello, the Idaho town in which Yozip meets the tribe, is named for the leader of the Shoshone people who led the struggle against the settlers in the late nineteenth century.) At the same time, however, Malamud's manuscript maintains a constant tension with regard to Yozip's status as a "new Indian." At first, Yozip's induction into the tribe appears to remedy his problem of belonging, as he comes to learn the People's language and adopt their style of dress and many of their customs. Yet his Indianness is constantly being called into question by the white society, by the tribe members, and by Yozip himself. This ambiguity is heightened when the tribe is forced to flee its land and attempts to escape to Canada (recalling Chief Sitting Bull's 1877 flight to Canada). Yozip, who has been elected chief and renamed "Jozip," is called upon to lead the tribe into safety and to determine its tactical strategy. However, his ability to do so is limited by his distinct cultural background and his politics, for he is an avowed socialist, pacifist, and vegetarian: "What kind of warrior chief was a Jew who lived among a tribe of Indians with peace raging in his heart?" (Malamud 1989, 75), he asks himself. As a result, Yozip makes poor decisions on the tribe's behalf that lead to the People's repudiation of him: "'You were a fool to think you are the equal of an Indian,' Indian Head said. 'This trek to Canada has destroyed many of the People'" (82).

Malamud also contrasts the tribe's intimate rapport with their land – "this land that lives in our heart," as Chief Joseph puts it (1989, 13) – with the immigrant Yozip's perpetual state of disconnection from his environment: "If only a man knew where to go. It shamed him still to think that one place was as good as another. What does one attach himself to?" (16). Because Yozip's relationship with the land is so dissimilar to that of the People, he is extremely uncomfortable in his role as a spokesperson for the tribe in its land negotiations. When the chief of the tribe decides to send Yozip to Washington, DC, as his envoy, Yozip protests: "'What do I know from strange cities?' ... 'How can I tulk with my short tongue? Where will I find the words? When I open my mouth to tulk they will laugh at me'" (27). The chief is insistent, however:

"We are sending you to Washington to speak with your eloquence on our behalf. We send you to speak for our tribe that has chosen you to be our brother ..."
    But Yozip was still worried. "What can a greenhorn do for you in such a city as Washington? Suppose they say I am not yet a citizen and so they keep from me my citizen papers?"
    "None of us have citizen papers," said Indian Head. (28)

Thus even though there is sympathy and overlap between the Indian and Jewish perspectives in *The People*, Malamud is careful not to conflate these perspectives. Instead, Malamud continually calls attention to the distance separating Yozip from the rest of the tribe and, by extension, to divergences between diasporic and indigenous narratives of (un)belonging.

Like Malamud, the St Lucian writer Derek Walcott, despite devoting both a play and substantial portions of his epic poem *Omeros* (1990) to the story of Sitting Bull, is reluctant to draw too neat a parallel between Native American narratives of dispossession and other New World experiences of displacement. This reluctance is suggested by the absence of Sitting Bull from Walcott's play *The Ghost Dance* (1989). The play is set in North Dakota after the Battle of the Little Bighorn in the days leading up to the massacre of Native Americans at Wounded Knee in 1890, and it mimics the generic conventions of a John Ford Western, with all the requisite stock figures and props. It offers a counternarrative to Manifest Destiny not by presenting a Native American perspective on the Ghost Dance as perhaps one might have expected but instead by portraying the ambivalent, conscience-stricken responses of the white men and women who witnessed the growth of the Ghost Dance movement.

The Ghost Dance centres on the widow Catherine Weldon, a friend and former secretary to Chief Sitting Bull, who attempts to warn him of the danger he faces in encouraging his people to participate in the Ghost Dance and who seduces Major McLaughlin, an Indian Agent, in order to extract information about the army's plans. Catherine rejects as "madness" the Ghost Dance, a messianic movement that taught that the old life before the arrival of the white man could be recovered through acceptance of the new religion and the ritual of the dance. Catherine is white but also marginalized, a border-crossing figure who refuses to respect racial and cultural boundaries.

If Catherine claims that she "find[s] no difficulty / at all in crossing the mute line, the boundary / that separates us from the Sioux" (Walcott 2002, 223), she is not the only character in the play to question white authority and to cross boundaries. Even Sitting Bull's arch antagonist Major McLaughlin declares himself "exhausted by all the brutality" and asks, "why do we pale faces presume our superiority?" (143). McLaughlin himself has an Indian wife, while Lieutenant Brandon is engaged to Lucy, an Indian woman who is attempting to assimilate into white Christian society. Yet the waning of Catherine's friendship with Sitting Bull, the weakening of the two soldier's romantic relationships with Indian women, and Lucy's failed conversion to Christianity point to the pressures under which such cross-cultural alliances come as the hostility between the Sioux and the white settlers escalates. These pressures culminate in the murder of Sitting Bull and his sons by McLaughlin's Indian police at the end of the play.

Thus while the play highlights contact between cultures – the intermarriages and other forms of interaction and hybridization that shape the society of the late-nineteenth-century American West – it also traces the hardening of identities as the conflict intensifies. Catherine in particular resists this polarization through her sympathy for the Sioux and her friendship with Sitting Bull. "Why, for that matter, couldn't we become Indians?" Catherine asks; "Why do the Indians have to turn into us?" (Walcott 2002, 150). Walcott's American West is a space of contact and mutual influence, of the indigenization of whites as much as the whitening of Indians. Yet the events leading up to the 1890 massacre at Wounded Knee mark an irreparable rupture. According to Catherine, there is no erasing what has transpired; the United States will be foreever haunted by the legacy of Native American dispossession.

Walcott pursues his interest in Sitting Bull and the Sioux in *Omeros*, in which his reading of the Native American West becomes part of a larger commentary on New World societies and the historical legacies of displacement that plague them. In *Omeros* the incorporation of Native American material works to expand the scope of the poem and to advance a hemispheric perspective on what might otherwise appear to be more narrowly Caribbean concerns. Walcott suggests through his inclusion of Native American themes – and concomitantly of indigenous Caribbean presences – that a Caribbean identity and sense of place must be defined in plural, cross-cultural terms. The incorporation of Native American material into what is ostensibly a poem about Caribbean homecoming serves to advance a conception of Caribbean society as one of contact, interaction, and layered histories. The epic framework is a capacious one that makes space for a plurality of voices and geographies, enabling the poet/narrator to move back and forth from the Caribbean to the United States of the poet's exile, establishing relationships between the two regions. The US passages of the poem reference a New World slavery past that links the Caribbean and the United States; less obviously perhaps, they also allude to indigenous histories of dispossession that span the two regions. There is "[o]ne elegy from Aruac to Sioux," a poignant line of the poem asserts (Walcott 1990, 164).

Toward the end of book 3 of *Omeros*, the St Lucian fisherman Achille fantasizes that he is a soldier in an American Western. As Bob Marley's "Buffalo Soldier" plays in the background, a highly cinematic Western scene unfolds in Achille's imagination, accompanied by a reggae beat, "Red Indians bouncing to a West Indian rhythm" (Walcott 1990, 161). The Caribbean locale is transformed into the American West: Achille's oar becomes a rifle, the stern of his boat becomes a saddle. He envisions himself shooting at "savages" who fall "like Aruacs ... / to the muskets of the Conquistador" (162). This brief allusion to the indigenous peoples of the Caribbean is subsequently developed in the following scene when Achille, while raking leaves in the yard of the blind old man Seven Seas, uncovers archaeological evidence of the island's Arawak inhabitants. When Achille unearths a stone totem, he is disturbed by the discovery and "wrenches" the totem out of the ground, "hurling" it away.[10]

Achille's gesture of jettisoning evidence of an indigenous past is one that the poem as a whole does not support. Instead, Walcott calls attention to a suppressed indigenous Caribbean past through a thematic focus on Native American history. In addition to repeated but brief allusions to the indigenous Caribbean presence, such as the reference in the poem's opening lines to the island's Arawak name, "Iounalao," *Omeros* gives sustained attention to the late-nineteenth-century phenomenon of the Ghost Dance and to the events that led up to the death of Chief Sitting Bull. Walcott's attention to indigenous peoples of the Americas – both Caribbean and North American – reflects his cross-cultural poetics and his inclusive vision of Caribbean identity. In particular, Walcott's somewhat controversial emphasis on Native American material serves to locate the Caribbean in a hemispheric American context.[11]

Revisiting episodes of Native American history that he had earlier explored in *The Ghost Dance*, Walcott situates this material within a new framework in *Omeros* that makes its resonance with regard to the Caribbean more explicit. Book 4 is set in the United States and deals with the narrator's period of exile in Brookline, Massachusetts, where he finds himself depressed, isolated, and adrift after the break-up of his marriage. In the midst of these autobiographical musings, the scenery suddenly shifts to that of the American West, to the Dakotas, where the narrator allows a Crow horseman to "pass / into the page" of the poem (1990, 175). At this point the narrator begins to draw what initially seems a rather self-indulgent analogy between his marital difficulties and the broken treaties and hardships suffered by the Sioux. The themes of loss and betrayal link the two episodes in a complex mapping of the poet's personal and romantic life onto Native American history. The analogy at first appears reductive, collapsing the historical into the personal and identifying the suffering narrator with the oppressed Indian whose treaty agreements have not been respected. Yet as the poem continues, it soon broadens out from the personal to engage broader historical themes. References to American slavery are woven into stanzas about the Trail of Tears, drawing connections between the forms of dispossession that beset Native and African Americans and, by extension, the African diaspora in the New World.

As she does in the play, Catherine Weldon takes up considerable space in the poem.[12] The history of Native American dispossession is told largely through her eyes and voice, contributing to the multiperspectival character of the poem. By ventriloquizing Catherine, Walcott broadens the perspective of the poem and privileges the possibilities for cross-cultural sympathy that Catherine represents. By the same token, it is significant that as in *The Ghost Dance*, Walcott does not make a Native American character the focal point. Instead, by filtering the story of the Sioux through Catherine, he maintains a deliberate distance from the Native American material. Although Walcott incorporates the story of Native American dispossession into his broader narrative, linking it to the Middle Passage and to New World slavery, he does not assert a one-to-one identification between indigenous and African diasporic experiences in the New World.

The world of Walcott's *Omeros* is not one of contained ethnicities in which boundaries are firmly maintained but rather one of dynamic interaction – if not always identification – among the variety of peoples who inhabit the Americas. For Walcott, a Caribbean sense of place must register the plurality of Caribbean (and New World) societies, as well as competing claims to the landscape. The epic mode in Walcott's rendering remains preoccupied with themes of exile and homecoming, but home is no longer achieved through the coercive force of empire and Manifest Destiny: Walcott's characters are engaged in "founding not Rome but home" (1990, 301). Accordingly, prior presences on the land are not effaced so that new presences might be substituted. Instead, the landscape is suffused with layered histories. Equally, the historical experiences of oppression of various peoples cannot be collapsed together, even if there are parallels and continuities among them. Toward the end of the poem we learn that a St Lucian villager's romance with a Cherokee woman in Florida has failed; the gap between West Indians and "true-true Indian[s]" (317) remains a meaningful one.

Unlike Kogawa, then, Malamud and Walcott maintain a constant tension between the diasporic and the indigenous, an approach that coincides with James Clifford's (1994) observation that diasporic and indigenous peoples tend to employ diverging and even conflicting narrative strategies in constructing their identities and claims to belonging.[13] Malamud's immigrant Jewish protagonist is at best a reluctant leader of the Indian tribe and is eventually disavowed by the People. Walcott highlights points of identification but also disconnection between West Indians and "true-true Indians," between the Middle Passage and the Trail of Tears. Relatedly, visual artists Jin-me Yoon and Isaac Julien present jarring juxtapositions of indigenous and diasporic peoples of the Americas in their installations, troubling the assumption that there is a natural solidarity between these groups. In Yoon's *A Group of Sixty-Seven* (1996), sixty-seven Korean Canadian subjects pose in front of an Emily Carr painting, partially obscuring a Native Northwest Coast village and asserting a diasporic presence at the cost of an indigenous one. Julien's installation *True North* (2004) raises similar questions through its uncanny rendering of what has conventionally been portrayed as a benevolent interaction between the early-twentieth-century African American polar explorer Matthew Henson and the Inuit he encountered.[14] It is these tensions between the diasporic and the indigenous that seem to me to be absent from Kogawa's novels.

Reading a diasporic Canadian text such as *Obasan* in hemispheric terms enables us to identify the extent to which it participates in a broader New World struggle to find a sense of belonging and suggests that an anxiety about achieving an indigenous status is one that continues to perplex New World writing. At the same time, situating *Obasan* in its hemispheric context reveals the relationships of competition as well as solidarity that may develop between diasporic and indigenous peoples in the Americas. The broader field of analysis made available by a hemispheric framework thus foregrounds not only the continuing currency of the settler colonial trope of "going native" in contemporary diasporic writing but also its attendant challenges for the diasporic author.

NOTES

1 On North America, see Goldie (1989), Berkhofer (1978), Deloria (1998), and Hundorf (2001); on South America, see Wasserman (1994), Chanady (1994), and the essays collected in Camayd-Freixas and González (2000). For a comparison of Latin American and Canadian discursive traditions of representing the indigene, see Chanady's essay in the present volume.

2 The comparative analysis that I develop in the present chapter builds on my earlier work on Kogawa and Malamud in the context of landscape representation. See Casteel (2007) for a more extended discussion of both Kogawa's and Malamud's texts.

3 See, for example, Traister, who summarizes from a Canadian perspective the power imbalances involved in the enterprise of hemispheric American studies: "the deconstruction of the idea and borders of the U.S. nation-state and, by definition, of the nations arrayed on its territorial borders, exhibits the very *privilege* of Americanist theoreticians in relation to other North Americans" (2002, 46, original emphasis).

4 If the hemispheric trend has been greeted with suspicion by many Canadianists, one notable exception may be scholars of First Nations studies, whose use of a hemispheric framework long predates the recent reconfiguration of American studies. Indigenous peoples' relationship to national borders in the Americas is frequently contestatory, as Thomas King's story "Borders" (1993) and annual Iroquois border-crossing rituals attest (see Grinde 2002; Luna-Firebaugh 2002).

5 For a fuller discussion, see Adams and Casteel (2005). Among US scholars, two notable exceptions are Claudia Sadowski-Smith and Claire Fox, who in a 2004 article take inspiration from Canadian studies in their critique of current assumptions that inform the field, including its monolingualism and its tendency to apply US vocabularies of race and ethnicity to other regions of the Americas.

6 For example, immediately following the Sitting Bull passage, Naomi describes how the Native children whom she has taught could pass for Japanese and "vice versa" (Kogawa 1994, 3). Subsequently in the novel,

the analogy is underlined when we learn that Slocan, the town where the Japanese Canadians find shelter from the disruptions of the Second World War, had originally been a place of refuge for First Nations peoples fleeing smallpox and other ills.

7 Although not all critics have read the woman as indigenous, in my view her indigeneity is strongly suggested by such features as the "golden brown" colour of her face as well as by the other elements that I have identified here.

8 "His mother, he says, was swarthy and small ... Her thick black hair was in one long braid to her waist. She was, he believes, the great-granddaughter of a Métis woman" (Kogawa 1992, 107).

9 See Fee's (1987, 21) discussion of "totem transfer," in which the transfer of an object from Native to newcomer symbolically validates the land claim of the newcomer.

10 Hamner (1997) interprets this gesture as reflecting Achille's superstitious fear of the Arawak, but in my reading it has a broader significance in the context of the poem's preoccupation with not only indigenous Caribbean but Native American pasts as well.

11 Walcott has been widely faulted for his inclusion of Native American motifs in *Omeros*, which critics view as distracting from the poem's Caribbean themes.

12 Catherine Weldon's letters to Chief Sitting Bull served as a key source for both the play and the poem (see Bensen 1994, 119).

13 In his essay "Diasporas," Clifford observes:

> Diaspora exists in practical, and at time principled, tension with nativist identity formations ... what are the historical and/or indigenous rights of *relative* newcomers – fourth-generation Indians in Fiji or even Mexicans in the southwestern United States ...? How long does it take to become "indigenous"? Lines too strictly drawn between "original" inhabitants (who often themselves replaced prior populations) and subsequent immigrants risk ahistoricism. With all these qualifications, however, it is clear that the claims to political legitimacy made by peoples who have inhabited a territory since before recorded history and those who arrived by steamboat or airplane will be founded on very different principles. (1994, 308–9, original emphasis)

14 For a detailed discussion of the treatment of indigeneity in the work of Yoon and of Julien, see Casteel (2007, ch. 6).

6

Outer America: Racial Hybridity and Canada's Peripheral Place in Inter-American Discourse

ALBERT BRAZ

Canada! ... Canada is so far away, it almost doesn't exist.
                                                    Jorge Luis Borges

I don't even know what street Canada is on.
                                                    Al Capone

Canada is one of the largest countries in the Americas, indeed the world. Or, as Richard Rodriguez jokes, at least for the people of the United States, it is "the largest country in the world that doesn't exist" (2002, 161). In any case, for such a territorial colossus, Canada is barely acknowledged in inter-American discourse. There are two main explanations for this peculiar state of affairs. First, Canada remains extremely ambivalent about its spatial location. Second, hemispheric studies have become increasingly oriented along a United States-Hispanic America axis. Consequently, Canada is seldom considered in continental dialogues, whether they originate in the United States or in Spanish America. This general elision of Canada, I argue in this chapter, is regrettable for several reasons, not the least the fact that you can hardly attain a real understanding of the continent if you exclude such a large portion of its land mass. No less significant, the Canadian experience can complicate some of the verities about (inter)American life and culture. This is particularly true of racial hybridity. For such prominent thinkers as Simón

Bolívar, José Martí, José Vasconcelos, and Roberto Fernández Retamar, racial crossing is one key element that differentiates "Nuestra América" from Anglo-America, the United States. However, what they do not seem to realize is that two racially mixed communities, or nations, the Métis and the Halfbreeds, blossomed in the so-called Great White North. Moreover, the leader of one of those groups, Louis Riel, became one of the great exponents of racial hybridity and continental identity in the Americas. Indeed, as I will try to demonstrate, Riel's writings underscore the urgency of placing inter-American studies in a truly continental context.

Besides Canada, the only other large country in the Americas that is routinely ignored in hemispheric discussions is Brazil. So marginalized discursively are the two countries that one perhaps should label them "Outer America," a geographic entity that both is and is not part of the continent.[1] For that reason, too, it might be worth contrasting them. There are obviously major similarities and also major differences between Canada and Brazil, beginning with the fact that Canada's official languages are the imperial English and French and Brazil's the less dominant Portuguese. As Neil Besner has noted, the two giants are "exemplary instances of colonial cultures that at once differ sharply in the shape of their colonial pasts, and share provocatively similar dispositions to their quite different colonial legacies, which have developed asymmetrically in different, and differently conceived, landscapes and geographies, invaded, settled, and narrated by different colonial powers" (2005, 24). Building on Roberto Schwarz's concept of "misplaced ideas" (1992, 19–32), Besner asserts that, like all present and former colonies, Canada and Brazil "constantly reproduce and carry forward with them the colonial perception of inauthenticity and imitation" (2005, 26). One characteristic that the two countries definitely share is the tendency to view the world through European eyes, which has led them to downplay their geographical locations, including their spatial connection to each other. For example, in her travelogue *Brazilian Journal*, the poet P.K. Page documents how less than fifty years ago Canada could send ambassadors to Brazil without their knowing "the rudiments" of its national language (1987, 2). Perhaps even more telling about the magnitude of Canada's lack of interest in the land of the samba is the reception of Page's own book. Page openly admits that she never mastered Portuguese during her two-year sojourn in Brazil as the wife of Ambassador Arthur Irwin (26, 108). Yet Canadian critics have not deemed it necessary to verify her sweeping generalizations about the way the Portuguese language explains the behaviour of Brazilians, seemingly accepting her claim in a more recent memoir that, after her stay in the South American country, "I was Brazilian" (2006, 46).

Needless to say, Canada's historical indifference toward Brazil is fully reciprocated. In fact, I will now use a Brazilian text to illustrate how casually Canada is often erased in the continent's culture. More specifically, I will briefly examine Carlos Diegues's *Bye Bye Brasil*. Diegues's film is a lament for a vanishing popular art form, the travelling circus. The small troupe of performers at the centre of the movie is conducting what appears to be one of its last tours of Brazil's north-eastern interior, as the circus is about to be displaced by modern technology, notably radio and television. The troupe, which bears the already heavily Anglicized name Caravana Rolidei (Holiday Caravan),[2] is led by a magician with the equally hybridized name of Lord Cigano, or Gypsy Lord. When he reaches one backlands town, the self-described Master of the Fantastic informs spectators that he has the power to make the dreams of all Brazilians come true and inquires what they desire him to do. Someone asks for prosperity and progress, and someone else for eternal life. But Lord Cigano responds that he will do something much more wondrous: he will make it snow in Brazil. Or, as he phrases it, he will make it snow in Brazil the way it snows in all civilized countries, which he then proceeds to enumerate: Switzerland, Germany, France, England, and the United States. Significantly, the one land he never mentions is Canada. What also becomes apparent is that, for Lord Cigano, snow countries are essentially countries with cultural capital – in short, those states of which it can be said that, to paraphrase Al Capone, you know what "street" they are on (quoted in Colombo 2000, 426). Canada does not appear to have much cultural capital and thus is not a snow country, even though it gets large amounts of snow. Actually, judging by Lord Cigano's list, one of the defining characteristics of snow countries, with the exception of Switzerland and parts of the United States, is that they do not receive an inordinately high snowfall.

Another intriguing aspect of *Bye Bye Brasil* is the name it gives to the United States, a name that, as is usually the case with almost anything involving the Great Republic, also has serious ramifications for Canada. Lord Cigano refers to the United States as "os Estados

Unidos da América do Norte," not exactly the same as the translation provided in the English subtitles: "USA." The political motiva-
tion for restricting the United States to the northern half of the
continent is both transparent and justifiable. Many Latin Americans,
as is evident in the region's common parlance, simply refuse to sur-
render the continent's name to a single polity, no matter how mighty.
Nevertheless, this taxonomical realignment – underlined by the wide
acceptance of the term "the United States of North America," as
well as by references to "the North American President" and "the
North American Secretary of State" – has major consequences, particularly for the region's two other countries, Mexico and Canada
(Braz 2008, 122). However, the fates of those two nations are quite
dissimilar. Mexico is absorbed into the Latin American world.
Canada, in contrast, is driven off the map.

   The effacement of Canada implicit in the North Americanization
of the United States is probably not as insidious as it may first seem.
After all, Canada's engagement with the Americas as a whole is so
peripheral that almost no one in Canada appears to have noticed
the development. That said, this invisibility has repercussions since
other entities can define a country in ways that have very little to
do with its own reality, or at least its history. Racial hybridity is a
case in point. Discussions of the ethnocultural differences between
Latin America and the United States invariably contrast the "mestizo" character of Our America with the whiteness of the Other
America, presumably including Canada (Martí 2000, 290; Fernández
Retamar 1989, 4).[3] Yet, if what characterizes Latin Americans is
their being "a motley of Indian and criollo" (Martí 2000, 291), then
they have much more in common than they realize with a segment
of the Canadian populace, the Halfbreeds and the Métis, the latter
being the group that produced Riel (historically, the main difference
between the Halfbreeds and the Métis is that the Halfbreeds were
predominantly English-speaking and Protestant, whereas the Métis
were primarily French-speaking and Catholic; today both groups
tend to speak English and to define themselves as Métis).

   Louis Riel, who was born in 1844 and died in 1885, is an extremely
problematic figure in Canadian culture, so perhaps I should explain
why I have chosen to incorporate him into the Canadian family.
Even though he has emerged as the most popular personage in the
country's history (Braz 2003), he passionately resisted having the
Métis enter the Canadian Confederation. His second military clash

with Ottawa, of course, culminated in his being hanged for treason
on 16 November 1885. Moreover, the verdict may not have been as
untenable as is now commonly believed. As late as August of that
year, he was writing to Grover Cleveland to remind the US president
of "the advantage of annexing the Northwest to the great american
republic" and to ask that Cleveland "blot out" the "international
line ... from lake Superior to the Pacific ocean" (1985, vol. 3, 187).[4]
In that same letter, Riel, "as american citizen," suggested that the US
consul to Winnipeg "be appointed governor General of those vast
territories" and Riel his "First Minister and secretary of the Northwest"
(187–8). Furthermore, this was not the first time the Métis leader had
expressed his desire to follow a political "plan of action deferential
to the united States" (1985, vol. 2, 7). During the Red River crisis,
some fifteen years earlier, he had appealed to another US president,
Ulysses S. Grant, to protect him and his people from what he termed
"a foreign power and ... a foreign jurisdiction," namely Canada (1985,
vol. 1, 111). It is true that, despite his lack of enthusiasm for the
Canadian experiment, Riel was very proud of his *Canadien* ancestry,[5]
as is evident in a poem like "Le peuple Métis-Canadien français":

Métis et Canadiens ensemble
Français, si nos trois éléments
S'amalgament bien, il me semble
Que nous serons un jour plus grands.
(1985, vol. 4, 324)

Also, Riel and his people lived (and, in the latter's case, continue to
live) in an area that has long been part of Canada, the Red River
Valley of Manitoba, which perhaps might justify his posthumous
Canadianization. Still, one should not ignore that Riel often expressed
considerably warmer feelings toward the United States than toward
its northern neighbour, the "fraude immense" and "tyrannie colos-
sale" (1985, vol. 3, 299) whose citizens ironically would embrace
him as one of their own and transform him into their quintessential
national icon. Indeed, Riel's numerous appeals for support to leading
US political figures underscore not only the fragility of the Métis
position in much of the second half of the nineteenth century but
also his own affinities with the United States.

Along with his Métis nationalism, which played such a crucial
role in the two North-West conflicts with Canada in the 1860s and

1880s, Riel is best known as a mystic. Following a religious epiphany
at Saint Patrick's Catholic Church in Washington, DC, on 8 December
1875,[6] he became convinced that "God [had] anointed him" the
"prophet of the new world" (1985, vol. 3, 261). Believing that "idées
révolutionnaires" were corrupting the Vatican, Riel concluded that
the only way the Catholic Church could save itself would be by
relocating to the Americas. Thus he decided to "séparé de Rome,"
transfer the Holy See to his hometown of Winnipeg, and elect a new
pope from the New World (144, 146). Less well known about Riel,
however, is that his political and religious ideas are inextricably
linked to his concept of *métissage*, the racial hybridity he believed
would characterize the inhabitants of what became western Canada.
Moreover, his notion of racial mixing appears to have developed in
response to the political realities confronting his ethnonational group.
Throughout his life, Riel identified with the French-speaking Catholic
Métis, whom he usually described as a "branche" of the French
Canadian tree, who desired "grandir comme cet arbre, avec cet arbre,
ne point se détacher de lui, souffrir et se réjouir avec lui" (1985, vol. 1,
368). However, his schism with the Catholic Church caused a major
rift between him and his Quebec cousins. This was particularly true
after he started proclaiming not only that the Catholic hierarchy was
corrupt but also that, once French Canada had accomplished its
glorious task of spreading Catholicism in the New World, because
of the "infirmités de la vieillese," it was imperative that "sa mission
passé en d'autres mains," those of the Métis (1985, vol. 2, 119–20).
One of the consequences of the quarrel with Quebec was that Riel
was forced to engender alliances between the Métis and other groups,
notably with the English-speaking Protestant Halfbreeds.

Such a political and cultural reorientation necessarily also required
that he accommodate the new community's cultural, religious, and
racial duality. This is precisely what he did, by envisaging the Métis
as a transracial nationality. Both Natives and newcomers, maintained
Riel, were destined to fuse into a new nationality, the Métis nation.
The reason that all other ethnocultural groups would welcome
becoming part of this global *métissage*, he reasoned, was that the
term Métis was not restrictive. As he wrote to a French Canadian
friend from Red River in 1877, outlining why the new people that
had emerged in the North-West could not bear the old name "canadien-
français" but must adopt a new moniker that better captured its
own history and genealogy:

Je crois que le nom métis est de nature à favoriser la fondation d'une puissante nationalité dans le Manitoba et le Nord Ouest. C'est un nom qui signifie mélange. Jusqu'ici il a servi à designer la race issue du sang mêlé des européens et des Sauvages, mais il est également propre à dénommer une race d'hommes, qui se recruterait du mélange de tous les sangs, entr'eux; et qui, tout en passant dans le moule canadien-français, conserverait le souvenir de son origine, en s'appelant métisse. Le nom métis serait agréable à tout le monde, parce qu'il n'est pas exclusif et qu'il a l'avantage de mentionner d'une manière convenable, le contingent pour lequel chaque nation contribuerait à fonder le peuple nouveau. Et à ce point de vue je crois qu'il serait difficile de donner comme base à notre nationalité dans le Manitoba et le Nord-Ouest, une idée plus large et plus forte que l'idée métisse. (1985, vol. 2, 120)

According to Riel, the reason the Métis were so at home in the New World had a great deal to do with their dual biocultural heritage. Interestingly, he traced his people's sense of belonging at least as much to their European ancestry as to their aboriginal one. In fact, while exhorting the Métis to be "fiers d'être français," Riel stated that their collective identity was bound to the French language, which he described as "l'une des plus belles langues du monde, et certainement la plus polie de toutes" (301). As he elaborated:

Le mot français, Métis, est dérivé, du participe latin, Mixtus, qui signifie Mêlé: il rend bien l'idée dont il est chargé.

Toute appropriée que l'expression anglaise correspondante, Halfbreed, fût à la première génération du mélange des sangs, maintenant que le sang européen et le sang sauvage sont mêlés à tous les degrés elle n'est plus assez générale.

Le mot français, Métis, exprime l'idée de ce mélange d'une manière aussi satisfaisante que possible; et devient par là même un nom convenable de race. (1985, vol. 3, 278)

For Riel, the Métis were "un peuple neuf, mais civilisé" (283), and it was unquestionably their European ancestry that set them apart from the First Nations. In short, the Métis were not merely an in-between people but also a civilizing one, the hybrids that would bring European civilization to their aboriginal relatives.

Needless to say, Riel's concept of *métissage* is not without its contradictions, especially from an aboriginal perspective. Actually, as one reads his writings on the subject, one cannot help but notice his ambivalence toward the First Nations. Riel often praised his aboriginal ancestors, the ancestors through whom the Métis had acquired their "titre" to the land (1985, vol. 3, 279). At the same time, he systematically distinguished between the Métis and the First Nations, usually presenting the New Nation as "superior" to its aboriginal forebears. For instance, Riel boasted that the Métis were "les hommes qui domptèrent ces nations sauvages par leurs armes" (284), the people that "a toujours eu l'honneur de vaincre ses ennemis indiens" (274). He also asserted that, with the Métis, "Les bonnes qualités canadiennes-françaises / Corrigent les défauts de Notre Sang Indien" (1985, vol. 4, 326). Riel clearly believed that not the least significant of his people's roles was to be mediators between their two ancestral groups. More precisely, the Métis appeared to have been created to "elevate" the First Nations to the level of the Europeans. As he wrote, the reason the "crees are the most civilized indians of the Canadian Northwest" was that "they have been for a good many years in constant communications with the halfbreeds" (1985, vol. 2, 240). Indeed, as one ponders his ideas on racial hybridity, one is not exactly surprised that the "prophet" of the New World had such an exalted view of his European heritage that he declared not only that "presque tout mon sang vient de la France" but also that, through his mother, he was "un des princes descendants de Louis xi" (1985, vol. 2, 72; vol. 3, 209).

Even though Riel is the most prominent champion of racial hybridity and continental identity in what is now Canada, he is not the only one. Another proponent of racial hybridity is the poet Pauline Johnson, who was no less contentious than the Métis politician-mystic when it came to the relations between Natives and newcomers in the Americas. Although she was the daughter of an English mother and a Mohawk father (himself of mixed ancestry), Johnson was a Mohawk by "Canadian law" (Strong-Boag and Gerson 2000, 3) and tended to identify with her father's people. In much of her writing, Johnson celebrated aboriginal life before the arrival of the Europeans. However, she also devoted numerous poems and stories to the romantic relations between the two groups and to their mixed offspring, works that are usually quite critical of the general Euro-Canadian attitude toward racial hybridity. Like Riel, Johnson seems extremely conflicted on the subject. In fact, some critics claim that her "idealization of the unhyphenated Native" reflects her profound fear "that Native North America was dying" and that "[m]ixed-race peoples might be its only heirs" (Strong-Boag and Gerson 2000, 198). The complexity of Johnson's views on race and racial mixing are conspicuously evident in a poem like "A Cry from an Indian Wife," the text that first brought her to the attention of the Canadian public. Written in 1885, the poem has the Indian woman of the title sending her husband off to fight the "white-faced warriors, marching West to quell / Our fallen tribe that rises to rebel" (Johnson 2002, 14). Yet, even though "A Cry" was obviously inspired by the North-West Rebellion, the Loyalist Johnson never once mentioned the dominant aboriginal party in the conflict, the Franco-Catholic Métis. In contrast, in her story "The Shagganappi," she explored the experiences faced by a Red River boy of mixed French and Cree ancestry, "Fire-Flint" Larocque, as he attends an exclusive school in central Canada. Larocque has become disheartened, having realized that many of his white schoolmates look down on him since he does not even belong to a "tribe; he is a halfbreed" (262). But his spirits are uplifted by no less a figure than the governor general of Canada, who tells Larocque (and his classmates) that "you have one of the proudest places and heritages in the world; you are Canadian in the greatest sense of that great word" (263). That is, contrary to the prevailing view held at the school and, by extension, in much of the country, Johnson implied that, rather than being of sign of degeneracy, racial mixing was the ultimate marker of inter-Americanness, of citizenship.

An even more unequivocal champion of what used to be called racial amalgamation is the influential literary journalist and writer William Arthur Deacon. Both in his prophetic 1933 book *My Vision of Canada* and in a long, unpublished 1935 letter to Grey Owl, the English-born naturalist who pretended to be of mixed Scottish-Apache ancestry, Deacon contended that the most effective way of "Canadianizing the Canadians" (1935, 3) was by "hastening" the intermarriage between Natives and newcomers "to form a united race to hold and enjoy the land for the best advantage of all" (2–3). As he elaborated, "Many people of both races dislike blending; but it always goes on. Nature takes care of that. Human beings who live together get to like each other and breed." Deacon, who was of English, Irish, and Welsh descent, claimed that this phenomenon was

evident "everywhere," from Mexico, which "today has all but oblit-
erated the Spaniard," to Ireland, which has "more actual English
blood ... than Irish." Canada would be no exception, and he asserted
that the "French and English must blend eventually, and Indians
must come into the common stock" (3).

Deacon's ideas on the racial fusion of Natives and non-Natives
were not disinterested, as he candidly admitted. He maintained that
newcomers such as himself had "stolen the Indians' land" and had
"to square ourselves." But since it was "too late in the day to do it
by getting out and handing the land back," he felt that the only way
they could pay this "debt" was by amalgamating themselves with
aboriginal people (1935, 3). Such a racial fusion would thus constitute one of the foundational stones of his future Canada, a country
he prophesied was destined for "world dominance" (1933, 1) and,
by the year 2000, would "exercise undisputed intellectual leadership
in the world" (279). Still, Deacon's views were informed by more
than his utopian nationalism or a collective sense of guilt, the feeling
that "the inevitable result of usurping the Indians' country is that the
dark-skinned survivors must be drawn into permanent blood union
with other Canadians to form the new type" (1935, 3–4). They also
reflect the fact that much racial mixing had already occurred in
Canada. As Deacon noted, "It is impossible at this date to know
how much Indian blood our French-speaking Canadians represent"
(1). Likewise, the Scottish fur traders who worked for the Hudson's
Bay Company in the Prairies "took Indian wives as a common practice," and their influential progeny were now "liberally infused with
Cree blood" (3). In other words, Deacon argued, he was not invent-
ing a hybrid past for Canada but simply acknowledging it.

More recently, Uma Parameswaran has also articulated a vision
of Canada as a hybrid nation. In an essay entitled "Driving into the
New Millennium on a Trans-Canada Highway That Has Only Entry
Ramps," the Indian-born Winnipeg writer asserts that there is "an
increasing awareness that Canada's cultural diversity demands a
reconfiguration of our pedagogical maps" so that young people will
be able "to see themselves in terms of country and identity." As she
adds, she foresees "the 'brownification' of Canada," in which "separate races give rise to mixed-race generations" (2000, 91–2). Although
there are similarities between Parameswaran's idea of Canada and
Deacon's, there are also substantial differences. For example, by
stressing the affinities between aboriginal Canadians and nonwhite
newcomers as people of colour, she blurs their rather disparate

territorial claims. Perhaps because of her focus on the welfare of so-called visible minorities, and their sense of disenfranchisement, Parameswaran also presents a much less rosy view of Canada. Thus she states that she believes Canadians will be able to generate a sense of national identity by building a "cultural framework" that "does not have to be homogeneous" but that must be "a shared space, a common repertoire." At the same time, she contends that the reason "the browning of Canada" is bound to become a reality is that aboriginal people and racial minorities will no longer accept their "invisible spaces" in the national landscape, adding that they "cannot be forced on to exit ramps because there will not be any" (97). That is, Canada will finally come to terms with its true hybrid face not necessarily because it wants to but because it has no choice.

Parameswaran's tempered optimism about the new multiracial Canada may simply reflect her awareness that racial hybridity remains as much of an intellectual and emotional challenge today as it did in the past. Even writers and scholars who profess to prize hybridity often seem to call into question its very existence. George Elliott Clarke, for one, closes his essay "Canadian Biraciality and Its 'Zebra' Poetics" with the unambiguous declaration: "Our *nation* encompasses *miscegenation*" (2002a, 225, original emphasis).[7] In his piece, he also refers to Canadian writers of mixed African and European ancestry as "Canadian black Métis," yet he ultimately incorporates them exclusively into the black world rather than into a separate category of their own. As he writes, they are "brown Negroes" (225). Clarke also implies that he does not analyze Suzette Mayr's novel *The Widows* because it has "no black characters" (226). This is a curious statement to make in an essay on biraciality, given that Mayr describes her protagonist's mother as "half Mexican, half African, half Chinese, half Kanadian (half mongrel ...)" (1998, 19). Not surprisingly, Mayr has expressed discomfort with Clarke's treatment of mixed-race writers, whose work does not always "fit his thesis about zebra poetics." As she says of his collection of essays *Odysseys Home: Mapping African-Canadian Literature*, "It was odd seeing how we got our own chapter. And got little mention elsewhere" (2004, 446). Indeed, Clarke claims authors like Mayr as part of Afro-Canadian literature yet simultaneously suggests that, because of their hybridity, they are not fully part of the family.

Of course, what Clarke's contradictory responses to Mayr underline is that mixed-race people, including writers, are often figures of suspicion. Because they tend to articulate multiple subjectivities, others are uncertain of their identities and group loyalties. The Lakota writer Elizabeth Cook-Lynn, for instance, attributes most of the ills facing aboriginal literature to its supposedly being dominated by "mixed-bloods," including such luminaries as Paula Gunn Allen and Thomas King (1996, 67). Cook-Lynn's claim that "mixed-blood literature is characterized by excesses of individualism" (69) is dubious since it is rather easy to find mixed-race writers, like Maria Campbell, who are profoundly engaged with the welfare of their communities. Yet Cook-Lynn is probably right to envisage racial hybridity as threatening to racially homogeneous groups. The reality is that all concepts of racial fusion in the Americas, including Riel's, are highly problematic from an aboriginal perspective. After all, Riel left little doubt that the First Nations, like the European immigrants and everyone else, would be subsumed into the new hybrid nationality. He appears to have shared Jean Toomer's sentiment that "race-forms die" (1993, 107), and in his case, there was never much question which groups he had in mind. As Riel declared in the early 1880s, "Je crois que dans un espace de temps relativement court, cette manière de procéder vis-à-vis des sauvages aurait pour effet de les faire disparaître sans secousse et degré par degré," adding that "toute la race sauvage de l'Amérique du Nord ferait place à une race nouvelle[:] la race métisse" (1985, vol. 2, 409). Nevertheless, given the similarities between Riel's concept of *métissage* and Bolívar's middle species ("especie media") (1960, 48), Martí's "mestizo" America (2000, 290), and Vasconcelos's "synthetic race" ("raza síntesis") (1997, 23, 63), it is astonishing that Riel remains unacknowledged in discussions of racial hybridity and continental identity in the Americas, all those deliberations that place "*mestizaje* ... at the root of our America" (Fernández Retamar 1989, 27). His omission is particularly striking because he calls into question the thesis that racial hybridity is somehow restricted to "Nuestra América." However, it becomes even more conspicuous given that, prior to the twentieth century, Riel was one of the rare proponents of racial hybridity and continental identity who was of mixed race. Still, ignored he has been. As far as I know, the only Latin American figure who shows any awareness of Riel's existence is the nineteenth-century Brazilian poet Mathias Carvalho. Unfortunately, Carvalho had so little knowledge of Riel and the northernmost part of the continent that he portrayed the architect of the two North-West conflicts with Canada as a "fearless fighter for Canadian independence" (1997, 16).[8]

In conclusion, Riel's nonpresence in inter-American discourse, like that of subsequent Canadian writers, is not an anomaly but rather a reflection of Canada's lack of profile in the Americas. As well, I would like to stress that this state of affairs is not only, or perhaps even primarily, the consequence of Latin American indifference to Canada, the fact that, as Jorge Luis Borges notes, for Latin Americans, Canada is so distant both culturally and geographically that "it almost doesn't exist" (quoted in Manguel 1998, D9).[9] No less crucial a factor is Canada's noninvolvement in continental affairs, a detachment likely caused by the country's ambivalence about its spatial location. English Canadians, as several scholars have noted, have never embraced the concept of "Americanity" the way that Spanish Americans, Brazilians, and Québécois have (Bahia 2006, 29; Braz 2008, 126–7). Moreover, this lack of continental identity may reflect not so much a desire to prove that "Canadians are not Americans" in the US sense of the term, as the title of a recent book has it (Morrison 2003; see also Bahia 2006, 29), but the general acceptance of US hegemony on the continent. As Carlos Gabriel Argüelles Arredondo contends, the reason that historically Canada has ignored much of the continent is that it accepted that "les États-Unis considéraient l'Amérique latine comme leur aire d'influence exclusive" (2006, 126). Again, the almost universal equation in Canadian discourse of America with the United States evinces that most Canadians do not see themselves as part of the full continent.

Admittedly, there are indications that Canadians may be becoming more engaged with the Americas as a whole. For example, at the eighth international meeting of the Brazilian Association of Canadian Studies, held in the southern state of Rio Grande do Sul in November 2005, the then Canadian ambassador to Brazil, Guillermo Rishchynski, repeatedly stressed that Canada considers Brazil a "strategic partner" ("parceiro estratégico") in world politics. To underscore the critical significance of the relationship between the two countries, he delivered his speech almost exclusively in Portuguese,[10] a critical departure from his not-so-distant predecessors. The existence of works such as Pierre Samson's Brazilian trilogy, Sergio Kokis's writings on his journey from Rio de Janeiro to Montreal, Stephen Henighan's explorations of encounters between Canadians and Latin Americans, and Paul Anderson's monumental novel *Hunger's Brides*, a nearly 1,400-page fictional meditation on the life and writings of Sor Juana Inéz de la Cruz, also suggests that at least some Canadian writers no longer feel the need to justify their interest in the cultures of their own continent. Yet such examples of inter-American transculturation remain largely exceptions. Much more representative is the feeling, bemoaned by Jack Hodgins, that "there's something suspect" about a Canadian writer who acknowledges the influence of Latin American literature (1987, 212). In his celebrated "Conclusion" to Carl Klinck's 1965 *Literary History of Canada*, Northrop Frye asserts that "the Canadian sensibility" has been "profoundly disturbed, not so much by our famous problem of identity, important as that is, as by a series of paradoxes in what confronts that identity. It is less perplexed by the question, 'Who am I?' than by some such riddle as 'Where is here?'" (1965, 826). Continentally speaking, the situation does not appear to have changed fundamentally since then. Gabriel García Márquez once stated: "It bothers me that the people of the United States have appropriated the word America as if *they* were the only Americans. America, in fact, begins at the South Pole and ends at the North Pole. When residents of the United States call themselves Americans, they are telling us they think of themselves as the *only* Americans.[11] Actually, those people are residents of a country without a name" (1983, 67, original emphasis). Along those lines, one could also say that, by virtue of both its invisibility to the other American states and its own lack of identification with the larger land mass where it happens to be situated, Canada remains, at the beginning of the twenty-first century, largely a country without a continent.

NOTES

An earlier, and much shorter, version of this chapter appeared as "North of America: Racial Hybridity and Canada's (Non)Place in Inter-American Discourse," *Comparative American Studies* 3, no. 1 (2005): 79–88.

1 The invisibility of both Brazil and Canada (or at least the English-speaking part) is vividly illustrated in the 700-page collection of essays edited by Barbara Buchenau and Annette Paatz, *Do the Americas Have a Common Literary History?* (2002). Although they include several works on Quebec literature, Buchenau and Paatz do not devote a single essay to English Canada and only one to Brazil – in Spanish!

2 Late in the film, Lord Cigano says that someone has told him the troupe's name should end with a *y*, seemingly unaware that a *y* would not make the word Rolidei any more English than does the *i*.

3 Fernández Retamar contends that this Caucasian "homogeneity" is false when it comes to the United States, which is able to achieve its sense of ethnoracial purity only by deliberately ignoring its own "diversity," its aboriginal and Afro-American populations (1989, 4).

4 Although Riel's spelling, capitalization, and grammar can be rather idiosyncratic, all quotations from his poetry and prose are reproduced as they appear in the text.

5 Nomenclature is a major problem when discussing Riel's work. For instance, he often asserts his affinities with Canada and *les Canadiens*. However, he tends to mean not the whole of Canada and its people but only French-speaking Canadians.

6 One of the most telling ways that contemporary writers and other artists circumvent the matter of Riel's political sympathies toward the United States, and stress his ostensible Canadian patriotism, is by transferring his religious epiphany from Washington to Montreal (Braz 2003, 143).

7 This line does not appear in the chapter of the same title in Clarke's collection of essays *Odysseys Home* (2002b, 232).

8 This is my translation of "o destemido luctador da independencia do Canadá" (Carvalho 1997, 16). At least as it appears in this edition, Carvalho's Portuguese is quite faulty. However, as with Riel's work, I reproduce it as it is presented in the text.

9 Too typically, in his recent collection *Mutual Impressions: Writers from the Americas Reading One Another* (1999), Ilan Stavans does not include a single Canadian author either reading or being read by a Latin American counterpart.

10 I would like to express my gratitude to Ambassador Rishchynski for kindly sending me a copy of his speech.

11 Seemingly tongue-in-cheek, but perhaps not, Richard Rodriguez states: "America (the noun) became our border against all that lay to the south and north – much to the annoyance of Mexicans, for example, or Canadians. 'We are Americans, too,' they said. No you're not, you are Mexicans. And you are Canadians. We are Americans©" (2002, 119).

POSTSLAVERY ROUTES

7

Eyeing the North Star? Figuring Canada in Postslavery Fiction and Drama

MAUREEN MOYNAGH

Lois Parkinson Zamora has argued that recent fiction of the Americas is characterized by a search for a "usable past" and a clear rejection of the "New World myth that Americans are free of the burdens of history because they are free to create their own" (1997, 4). For contemporary African Canadian writers, the particular burdens that come with the need to create a usable past have to do, at least in part, with a peculiar variant of that New World myth, and that is the myth that Canada is free of the history of slavery by virtue of being the "north star," the land of freedom for fugitive slaves. This myth has a long history in Canada, beginning with nineteenth-century Loyalist literature and the Imperial Federationists of the turn of that century (Coleman 2001; Berger 1970). Recent studies of postslavery fiction and of the "Black Atlantic" have effectively colluded in this national variant of the New World myth by stopping at the Canada-United States border.[1] Canada, it seems, is not really part of the "New World" but an oddly displaced bit of Europe, recalling the Canada First Movement vision of a "Britain of the North" (Berger 1966, 4). Stubbornly, contemporary African Canadian writers insist otherwise. In this chapter, I consider a central trope in recent representations of slavery and its legacies in African Canadian fiction and drama, and I argue that the diasporic linkages rehearsed in these texts challenge both Canadian national narratives and national isolation in the hemisphere. I also argue implicitly for the importance of a comparative hemispheric approach to the study of these texts, as well as for the importance of putting Canada back into the Americas in studies such as these.

George Handley contends that "family history is the sine qua non of postslavery narrative" (2000, 3), and this assertion is certainly borne out in the three works I focus on here. Dionne Brand's novel *At the Full and Change of the Moon* (1999) traces several generations of descendants from Marie Ursule, a slave who carries out a mass poisoning among the slaves on a Trinidadian plantation in 1824, having first secured the escape of her infant daughter, Bola. Lawrence Hill's novel *Any Known Blood* (1997) centres on the genealogical activity of Langston Cane V, who researches and writes the story of his paternal family over the course of the novel. George Elliott Clarke's verse drama *Beatrice Chancy* (1999) is less preoccupied with multiple generations than with what one might call the national family and its crimes of incest and parricide as he tells the story of the mixed-race daughter of a white, slave-owning Loyalist in the Annapolis Valley of Nova Scotia in 1801. Not only is genealogy the central trope of the works I consider, but it is central to my method as well. Like Russ Castronovo (1995), I am interested in the genealogy of slavery as "an insurrection of subjugated knowledges" (Foucault 1980, 82), and I argue that it is possible to understand contemporary "postslavery" literature in Canada in these terms. Foucault defines genealogy as "the union of erudite knowledge and local memories which allows us to establish a historical knowledge of struggles and to make use of this knowledge tactically" (83) in the present. The writers I discuss here (and others I do not, such as Lorena Gale, Diana Brathwaite, Paul Fehmiu Brown, and Austin Clarke) are engaged in this tactical use of a knowledge of struggles and have forged that knowledge through their creative mobilization of cultural memory. The genealogical endeavours of Clarke, Hill, and Brand offer "unbroken lines of filiation [that] splinter and branch off to recover obscured, illegitimate bodies and memories" (Castronovo 1995, 24), genealogies that figure Canada by supplementing, in the Derridean sense, both national narratives and transnational linkages.

I want to underscore that my focus on three "Canadian" postslavery texts is not an effort to resurrect some vision of the nation via the construction of a nationalist poetics but an attempt to challenge hegemonic visions of both nation and diaspora. I hope the extent to which these writers both exhibit the patterns at work in neoslave narratives from the US and the Caribbean and draw on those literary traditions will become clear. Certainly, the diasporic history of the slave *narrative*, as well as of slavery, is foundational for Clarke and Hill, and the rewriting of the trope of the "flight north" that pervades Brand's earlier novel, *In Another Place, Not Here* (1997) (see McCallum and Olbey 1999), finds a new articulation in *At the Full and Change of the Moon*. If, as Pamela McCallum and Christian Olbey suggest, "[t]he evocation of the antebellum slave narrative in the form of the neoslave narrative retrieves and redeploys in the contemporary sphere the conventions of a genre initially defined by its capacity to intervene in actual material struggles for social transformation" (166), it is incumbent upon literary critics to trace the contemporary trajectories of struggle that the texts engage. A comparative, diasporic poetics is vital for coming to terms with these "Canadian" texts – here, I am in accord with Handley (2000) and Zamora (1997) – since the history of slavery and its legacies, the "local memories" of which Foucault speaks, are transnational.

To compare transnationally within the Americas is nonetheless to work against the dominant Canada-Europe axis that, until relatively recently, has informed the nation's sense of self and, in large part, its main paradigm of literary analysis. Within the Canadian literary-critical establishment, the US has figured largely as an influence to be fended off in the establishment of a national literary tradition, whereas British literature has been promoted as an example to be followed (Godard 2000; Fee 1992), the assumption being that as Canadian literature "matured" it would become "increasingly native in texture as the New World abandon[ed] the Old World's idiom" (Kertzer 1998, 20). This cultural model, in addition, was meant to "manage" an ethnically diverse population (Godard 2000), although not necessarily by allowing all voices to speak. In their insistence on historical and geographical experiences that exceed the geopolitical boundaries of the Canadian nation, the writers I examine here "worry the nation" (Kertzer 1998) with a "transnational imaginary," "a chronotope, a contact zone ... within which singularly delineated notions of political, social, and cultural identity do not suffice" (Moya and Saldívar 2003, 2). These texts challenge the complacent multiculturalism of the past thirty years with a history of racism and intolerance that the dominant narratives of nation abjure. The vision of Canada as the "north star" lives on in the insistence that racism is an American problem, and it is against the smug intolerance of this vision that the transnational imaginary of Canadian postslavery fiction and drama offers an effective counternarrative.[2]

By way of offering something like a national counternarrative myself, I have ordered my discussion of these three texts chronologically in terms of their figuring of Canada's relationship to the history of slavery in the Americas. Accordingly, I begin with George Elliott Clarke's *Beatrice Chancy*. Against the dominant vision of Canada as the "north star," the land of freedom for blacks escaping slavery in the southern US, Clarke depicts a "Canada" that not only was no secure haven but also practised slavery itself. The play is set in the Annapolis Valley of Nova Scotia at a time when slavery remained legal, as it did in the rest of British North America, until it was officially abolished throughout the British Empire in 1834. Both French and English settlers practised slavery in the colonies that were eventually to become Canada, and if slavery was not to become the economic cornerstone in these northerly colonies that it was elsewhere in the Americas, the existence of a sizable racial underclass, whether slave or "free," nonetheless made for what was effectively a slave society (Mannette 1984; Walker 1992).

This history of slavery is the backdrop for the dramatic action in *Beatrice Chancy*, and in this way, as I have argued elsewhere, Clarke "confronts the national amnesia about slavery with the diasporan linkages the nation prefers to deny or displace to the late twentieth century" (Moynagh 2002, 103–4).[3] That slavery was an intimate part of the formation of the nation is clearly dramatized in this family romance. Beatrice is both slave and daughter, and this ambiguous status serves at once as dramatic impetus and as an allegory about the nation's intimacy with racial and sexual violence. Clarke borrows the sixteenth-century tale of the Cènci family and transplants it to nineteenth-century Nova Scotia, making Francesco Cènci, or Francis Chancy, a slaveholder and Beatrice his mixed-race daughter by a slave mother. Beatrice is raised in her father's household and educated in a Halifax convent where she is sent to "copy / White ladies' ways" (Clarke 1999, 17), in a manner reminiscent of the pattern laid out in Frances Harper's *Iola Leroy* (1892), where Eugene Leroy sends Iola's mother, Marie, north to be educated before he manumits and marries her. Beatrice, however, foils Chancy's plans to marry her off to "some slavery-endorsing Tory / To fat [his] interests in the Assembly" (Clarke 1999, 28); she falls in love with Lead, one of Chancy's other slaves. Until Beatrice spurns his desires by declaring her love for this fellow slave, Chancy indulges in a fantasy facilitated by Beatrice's mixed racial heritage. Beatrice's lighter skin allows

Chancy to pretend that bondage is kinship: "My power isn't viola-
tion, it's love" (27), he dissembles. But Beatrice's desire for Lead
makes impossible her borrowed whiteness, for when Chancy discovers that Beatrice wishes to marry Lead, he punishes her by demoting
her to slave status, declaring that "my daughter can't love some
bull-thighed nigger!" (54) and treating her accordingly, first by lock-
ing her up and then by raping her. As a "mulatta," Beatrice is
subjected both to white-male fantasies and to the rule of sexual
availability that applies to all black women under slavery (Davis
1981; Carby 1987; Spillers 1987). Having slipped from daughter to
slave through her confession, Beatrice is symbolically both of the
national family and its disavowed other. Barred from her tenuous
position as daughter, yet suffering as a daughter, Beatrice embraces
the role of outlaw in order to indict the duplicity of slave societies.
Having no other recourse, she acts on her own behalf and on behalf
of the other slaves by murdering Chancy. She signs her own death
warrant through this act, but she also deals a blow to slavery by
sparking a revolt. As an act of "diva citizenship," in Lauren Berlant's
terms, whereby Beatrice stages "a dramatic coup in a public sphere
in which she does not have privilege" and "[calls] on people to
change the social and institutional practices of citizenship to which
they currently consent" (1997, 223), this insurgent gesture is aimed
at refiguring contemporary national disavowals of racial and sexual
violence. In this way Clarke makes tactical use of a knowledge of
struggles, linking Beatrice's denunciation of the historic slave society
in Nova Scotia to antislavery struggles throughout the Americas and
to contemporary struggles on the part of African Canadians.

As Cary Nelson has argued in a different context, "the effort to
move beyond the limitations imposed by studying national literatures
in isolation might well work less with broad generalizations than
with specific historical conjunctures"; the place to begin, he suggests,
is with "the key sites of internationalisation we have long ignored"
(2002, 9). The history of slavery in the Americas, and in particular
Canada's place in that history, is one such site. Clarke's focus on the
national family is by no means isolationist; he confronts the nation
with its place in that international frame: "Essentially, African slavery
was a hemisphere-long practice, from Québec to Argentina, and the
American Revolution marked only a minor disruption" (1999, 7).
Lawrence Hill opts for a binational family history, Dionne Brand
for one that stretches south from Trinidad to Venezuela, Surinam,

and Curaçao, and then north to the US and Canada. The emergence of both slave narratives and neoslave narratives in conjunction with that international history not only warrants a transnational comparative approach but also renders suspect particular claims to exceptionalism. In laying claim to the geopolitical locus of the north star, Canada has long insisted that when it comes to slavery, it is a place apart.

The north star mythology finds its central avatar in the history of the Underground Railroad, in which Canada is figured as Canaan. In 1855 Samuel Ringgold Ward, fugitive slave and prominent black community leader in Canada West, articulated the vision of Canada smugly embraced in national narratives: "There is no country in the world, so much hated by slaveholders, as Canada; nor is there any country so much beloved and sought for, by the slaves" (1968, 158). According to Robin Winks, Canada appears in these terms in twenty-six of the most widely read slave narratives published in the mid-nineteenth century (1970, 241). More than merely flattering to its conception of itself, the role assigned to Canada in narratives of the Underground Railroad was consistent with its need to validate and defend the border newly constructed between Canada and the United States in the wake of the Revolutionary War. To explain and justify the break between British colonizers in North America, Daniel Coleman argues, Loyalist narratives erected an "allegory of fraternity"[4] that turned on a moral differentiation between Canadian and American "brothers" (2001, 132). One of the key tropes in Loyalist literary figurations of the differences between Canadians and Americans has to do with the protection that the former are thought to have afforded "vulnerable others," either black or Native (144). These figures "instantiate the ethical differences between the upright [Canadian] and the downfallen [American] white brothers" (145). An instance of the way this moralizing discourse corresponded to the trope of the "flight north" is to be found in William Kirby's epic poem The U.E.: A Tale of Upper Canada (1859). Here, an escaped slave contrasts the warm welcome he receives from whites in Canada with the horrors of slavery in Tennessee, neatly confirming "the nobility of the white loyalist's enterprise," as Coleman points out (2001, 145). The narrative of the Underground Railroad, in other words, is about defining the border, and in this project black Canadians become the warrant for a distinctive Canadian citizenship on moral grounds.

In Lawrence Hill's *Any Known Blood*, the transnational imaginary that marks the family history undertaken by narrator-protagonist Langston Cane V offers an effective counter-narrative both to the Loyalist allegory and to what we might think of as the "Heritage Minute" version of the Underground Railway narrative,[5] keeping the border open, as it were, by tracing the cross-border activities of the Cane family. Whereas Clarke repatriates a diasporic narrative in order to expose the nation's intimacy with racial and sexual violence, in Hill's novel the transnational linkages are imbedded not only in the history of fugitive slaves but also in the movement of successive generations of the Cane family back and forth across the Canada-US border, migrations that suggest the always vexed status of blackness within national frameworks in the Americas. Through his characters' multigenerational crossing of the border, Hill revisits the "flight to Canada" trope again and again, suggesting that the quest for Canaan continues, despite myths of nation that depend on Canaan having been achieved.

Handley points out that "an interest in patrimony has been a driving force of slavery and ... of the narratives that have attempted to tell its story" (2000, 145). Hill's novel focuses on what I call a metonymic patrimony by telling the story of the Cane family – the story of the five black sons of two national families. The narrator's genealogical endeavour is metonymic by virtue of supplementing national narratives that turn on the Canaan myth, setting out an alternative vision that adds to and is always already part of those narratives. Not only is the celebratory myth of Canaan subjected to a critical, revisionist eye in this genealogy, but the Loyalist white-washing of national narratives is also similarly overturned, as the Cane family history attests to the presence of those black "brothers" who were written out of the fraternal allegories of national unity once they had served their purpose. If this metonymic patrimony can be said to have an ethical function, then, it is to expose the moral lacunae in the north star narrative rather than to demonstrate the moral supe-riority of white Canadian over white American. Members of each successive generation of the Cane family are drawn north and at least partly disappointed at what they find, and this pattern holds for the memoir of the fugitive slave that is at the heart of the genealogy.

Handley argues that "testimonial language is metonymical because it always points to the experience of others who have not told their stories" (2000, 150). Setting the memoir of Langston Cane I alongside

popular narratives of the Underground Railroad and the genre of
the slave narrative, we can measure the significance of the suggestion
that this testimony implicitly gestures at other stories like his. Significantly, the narrative of Langston Cane I departs from this utopian
vision and from the heroic tenor of many slave narratives. Cane
refuses the Loyalist work ethic directed at black settlers, which emphasized homesteading, sobriety, and churchgoing as a means to self-
reliance and independence, complaining of the black community in
Chatham, "There were too many colored folks, too close together,
each one making sure the other was praying enough. And they were
farming. I didn't care for farming ... The whole thing made me think
of the Virginia plantation where I was born" (Hill 1997, 463). Critical
of what he reads as black submission to white expectations, he
attests, "I was not made for Oakville. I was not made for marriage.
I was not made for church and children and unwavering employment" (473). In Hill's imaginative reconstruction, the slave narrative
takes on elements of the picaresque.[6] The portrait of Langston Cane
I is very much one of a rogue who lives by his wits in a corrupt
society, and his critique of the world around him is not limited to
slavery itself but extends to the homesteading economy to which
black fugitives were directed in nineteenth-century Ontario and its
accompanying ideology of uplift and independence (Law 1988).
Cane's refusal to be shackled by a new racialized economy is the
implicit answer to the narrator's puzzlement over Cane's motivations
to turn back to the South: "It was hard to imagine a fugitive slave
settling comfortably in Oakville and then turning around and heading right back south into slave territory" (Hill 1997, 62). That he
does so in the company of John Brown is not meant to redeem him;
he abandons Brown's failed insurrection early on, escaping to resume
his peripatetic life. The narrator's patrimony is the slave narrative
he finds in the archives at Harpers Ferry, an appropriate resting place
for a narrative that traces transnational connections back and forth
between the US and Canada. Harpers Ferry, after all, is a kind of
nodal point in the struggle against slavery waged on both sides of
the border and indeed across it. The novel ends with the narrator's
return to Canada, literally bringing home this supplementary testimony. The narrator is accompanied by a Cameroonian friend who
has been living illegally in the US and who plans to seek asylum in
Canada. This final flight to the North is still hopeful, but the characters are aware that it is not utopia that awaits them.

The flight north in Dionne Brand's *At the Full and Change of the Moon*, although it encompasses Canada, is better conceived as a journey from the geopolitical "South" to the geopolitical "North." The lines of flight that Brand traces are etched not only by the legacies of slavery but also by the socioeconomic conditions in the contemporary global South that fuel the desire for escape. That Canada is implicated in those contemporary conditions as well as in the history of slavery is made clear in the novel. Although my focus in this chapter is on Brand's figuring of Canada in this novel, Canada is but one of the many places across the Americas and Europe that form the diaspora inhabited by the descendants of the slave-matriarch Marie Ursule. In this context, genealogy becomes a means of figuring the fractured and attenuated connections across the Americas and Europe that are produced by slavery and maintained by successive colonial and neocolonial structures of domination. Of the multiple generations that populate the novel, those late-twentieth-century characters who end up in the North might usefully be seen as "maroons of the macadam," to adapt a phrase from J. Michael Dash (1998, 133), by virtue of their marginal relation to (post)modernity and their efforts to improvise an existence within the framework of globalized capital.

From Toronto, Marie Ursule's great-great-granddaughter Eula writes a letter home to her mother in Trinidad full of longing for what diaspora and the legacies of slavery obscure: "one single line of ancestry ... one line like the one in your palm with all the places where something happened and is remembered" (Brand 1999, 247). Eula continues: "I would like one line full of people who have no reason to forget anything, or forgetting would not help them or matter because the line would be constant, unchangeable" (247). Even as she articulates this desire, Eula implicitly acknowledges that it is impossible, that her people have plenty to forget, that her ancestry is anything but constant. The nostalgia she voices is, moreover, quite literally a dead-end: the mother she writes to in Trinidad is no longer living. Even as Brand rejects nostalgia for what slavery made impossible, like Toni Morrison, Jean Rhys, Gayl Jones, and others, she acknowledges the haunting legacies that must be reckoned with in the present. That the streets of Toronto are "full of human wreckage, breakage and ruin" (241) implies once again that Canada cannot evade complicity in that history. On the contrary, Eula's depiction of Toronto suggests it has been visited by Walter Benjamin's (1940) angel of history: "I am living in a city at the end of the world, Mama. It is rubble. It is where everyone has been swept up, all of it, all of us are debris, things that a land cleaning itself spits up. It is the end of the world here. The office buildings and factory buildings and houses and shops and garages all wreathed in oil and dust and piled on top of themselves. It is as if some pustule erupted from the ground and it is this city. It is bloated and dry at the same time, crumbling with newness, rubbled in glitter" (Brand 1999, 238). Modernity is no escape from decay. The catastrophe that is the history of slavery continues to pile up at our feet as we back into the future. If Eula has come to Canada seeking an escape from haunting memories, she has not found it. In this novel, too, Canada is inescapably bound up with the history of slavery, and the trope of the north star is held out only to be called into question. Brand's project is not only to pick precursors out of the wreckage in the name of community, to para-phrase Zamora (1997, 4), but also – to borrow Brand's (2001) own metaphor – to sketch out a map to the door of no return.

In Brand's novel, genealogy is a means of figuring diaspora, of representing the paradox of a shared history that affords common ground yet is marked by disruptions and displacements that produce a diversity of experience and identity. Thus Brand prints a genealogi-cal table at the front of the novel that is simultaneously a road map to the complicated, submerged, and half-forgotten family ties that emerge in the novel and a record of the disjunctions and interrup-tions that obscure those links. For although Marie Ursule's family tree and the novel itself sketch out the connections between Marie Ursule, her daughter Bola, and all of Bola's children, grandchildren, and great-grandchildren, they also point to the lost events, the for-gotten links: in Brand's words, "the one unrecalled," "the ones left in the sea," "the one who stole her footsteps," "the one who was taken in a hurricane," and so on (1999, "Family Tree"). These off-spring are scattered to Venezuela and Surinam, Amsterdam and New York; they do not know one another – cousins marry without know-ing they are related, they pass one another in the street without recognizing their connection, or they find one another in a US immi-gration detention centre and are compelled to claim kinship because of an uncanny physical resemblance. The reader is left to forge the links on behalf of the characters, to reassemble what Derek Walcott (1981, 4–5) aptly calls the *disjecta membra* of the plantation great house, in the name of countermemory.

Although I have focused here on a common trope in my discussion of these three postslavery texts, I do not want to elide the ways that each positions itself differently in relation to the transnational. Pilar Cuder-Domínguez proposes to categorize each work in relation to the "distinctive black Canadian constituency" that it appears to address: "African-American (Hill), Africadian[7] (Clarke), and Caribbean diasporic (Brand)" (2003, 57). Although this approach accurately captures the dominant emphasis of each work, and offers an important acknowledgment of the extent to which African Canadian literature exhibits a "poly consciousness" (Clarke 1998, 17), this recourse to a nation-based or regionalist paradigm obscures the extent to which even the most evidently nationalist of the three, *Beatrice Chancy*, relies on a transnational history. I would reiterate Diana Brydon's contention that "To be part of the black diaspora in Canada entails working through specific relations to history and place, [including] ambivalently utopic expectations of Canada, [and] ambivalently nostalgic longings for Africa" (quoted in Cuder-Domínguez 2003, 71), and suggest that in the case of postslavery literature this "working through" the "ambivalently utopic expectations of Canada" embedded in the north star mythology involves a multilayered approach to the "transnational imaginary." From a re-evaluation of national narratives through the lens of a hemispheric history, to a binational comparison that suggests, as Rinaldo Walcott puts it, "that it is impossible to make sense of some aspects of Black Canadian history without a serious and sustained consideration of the place of the US in that history" (1999, 73), to a situating of Canada in the African diaspora in a way that renders it minor, one of a number of places in the Americas, these three texts read together offer a series of vantage points from which to consider the nation in relation to a transnational trope. It is not a question of conceiving the transnational as a kind of deterritorialized abstraction hovering somewhere above the earth-bound places where people live; rather, my interest in the transnational imaginary at work in these three African Canadian texts has to do with embedded, place-specific, material, and historical relationships that nonetheless operate across national borders.

If, as I have argued here, we can understand the genealogy of slavery in contemporary African Canadian literature as "an insurrection of subjugated knowledges" (Foucault 1980, 82), then we must also recognize that the "local memories" to which Foucault refers when he defines genealogy are *trans*local. That is, these countermemories are not "local" in the sense of being bound to a specific geographic location so much as they are *located* in a subjugated relation to dominant historical narratives. The three texts I have taken up here might then be understood to offer *petits récits* in relation to the grand narratives of slavery and imperialism. This does not mean we can forget the grand narratives. On the contrary, as Peter Hulme has argued in another context, the *petits récits* are to be understood as "local sentences in the chapter of the [postslavery] world" (1994, 74). A comparative, trans-American approach to the study of post-slavery literature is therefore indispensable. As the "juncture-point where the many cultural tributaries meet," as the "space where the creolisations and assimilations and syncretisms were negotiated," and as "the place of many, continuous displacements," what Stuart Hall has called the *"Présence Americaine"* (1994, 400–1) ought not to be overlooked. This "New World" is replete with the history of these meetings, these negotiations and displacements, including the particular national articulations of this history. The burden of history that is the narrative of the north star, Clarke, Hill, and Brand suggest, has to be weighed in these terms.

NOTES

1 See especially Gilroy (1993) and Handley (2000).
2 Regarding the Canadian myth that racism is a US phenomenon, see Hill (2001), Huggan and Siemerling (2000), and Moynagh (1996).
3 In this earlier essay, I developed some aspects of the argument that follows.
4 A representative selection would include John Richardson, *The Canadian Brothers, or The Prophecy Fulfilled: A Tale of the Late American War* (1840); William Kirby, *The U.E.: A Tale of Upper Canada* (1859); Charles Mair, *Tecumseh, a Drama* (1886); Sarah Curzon, *Laura Secord, The Heroine of 1812: A Drama* (1887); Wilfred Campbell, *The Beautiful Rebel: A Romance of Canada in* 1812 (1909); Hiram A. Cody, *The King's Arrow: A Tale of the United Empire Loyalists* (1922); Ralph Connor, *The Runner: A Romance of the Niagaras* (1929); and Thomas Raddall, *His Majesty's Yankees* (1942).
5 CBC-TV broadcasts minute-long vignettes of significant moments in Canadian history as filler between regular segments. One of these depicts

the arrival of a slave hidden in a coffin transported by white abolitionists
and his reunion with family members already in Canada.

6 For a study of the place of the picaresque mode in slave narratives,
see Nichols (1985).

7 "Africadian" is a word coined by George Elliott Clarke as an alternative
to "African-Nova Scotian," "Afro-Nova Scotian," or "black Nova
Scotian," other possible appellations. A fusion of Africa and Acadia,
this term is evocative of an imagined community; as Clarke himself puts
it, "if Africadians constitute a *state*, let it be called *Africadia*" (1991, 9,
original emphasis).

8

"May I See Some Identification?" Race, Borders, and Identities in *Any Known Blood*

WINFRIED SIEMERLING

> Race isn't about skin colour. It's about social categorization.
> Lawrence Hill

> Every identity is actually an identification come to light.
> Diana Fuss

Our most postidentitarian moments and movements notwithstanding, identities are hardly a matter of the past. New constructions of identities and postidentities are continually wrought by historical subjects, the agents who invent or choose them and who modify, resist, or discard them. "Unused" identities continue to exist as possible scripts, as virtual and often virulent realities until human actors put them into play and through identification use them in practice and performance. One of the important ways of crossing borders of identity is travel, a movement I explore here with respect to "crossing cultures," "frontiers of North American identity,"[1] and identities ascribed or self-ascribed through "race." Identification, a transformative displacement or transposition and a form of cognitive travel, signals the crossing of borders of who we think we are or of who others think or say we are. Under the sign of "race," however, identity, identification, and travel have worked in particularly "arresting" constellations. Through race, identity and identification were tied to pseudo-scientific laws of biology, abetting the enforced displacements and the end of free personal movement in the Middle Passage and in slavery, as well as the impeded mobility across social and economic lines ever after.

Lawrence Hill continues to devise, from a Canadian vantage point, intriguing laboratories for the study of the intricate relations between identification, identity, and race. Hill is an expert on the crossings of (borders of) identities and cultures with respect to race and language as well as on the changing processes of ascription and self-ascription that he calls "the endless dance of adjusting how we see others, how we want to be seen, and how we see ourselves" (2001a, 5). In his first novel, *Some Great Thing* (1992), a black reporter with an interestingly allusive first name, Mahatma Grafton,[2] explores the borders of race together with divisions of language and the state of French in Winnipeg, Manitoba. Hill's second novel, *Any Known Blood* (1997a), crosses borders of racial identity and identification by travelling in time and geography across generations and the Canada-United States border. I concentrate here on this text, together with his *Black Berry, Sweet Juice: On Being Black and White in Canada* (2001a), which is partly "memoir, an examination of my own life through the prism of mixed race," but also "includes comments and observations from the many people I interviewed of black and white ancestry" (13). Not surprisingly, one of its sections is entitled "Crossing Borders."[3]

Identification is an act of recognition with both positive and insidious possibilities, ranging from acceptance and fame to stereotypes and defamation. Identification works from the inside as reflexive self-relation. In Diana Fuss's words, "Identification is the psychical mechanism that produces self-recognition ... It operates as a mark of self-difference, opening up a space for the self to relate to itself as a self, a self that is perpetually other" (1995, 2). Yet this phenomenological and psychological algorithm of cathexis describes only the formal side of variable binding. If "identification is the detour through the other that defines a self," it does not "travel outside history and culture. Identification names the entry of history and culture into the subject, a subject that must bear the traces of each and every encounter with the external world" (2-3).

Literary texts have time and again thematized one such "entry of history and culture into the subject," the moment of racial identification. The entry into race has often been rendered, for instance, from the perspective of a child in biographical or seemingly biographical texts. It appears thus at the beginning of W.E.B. Du Bois's *The Souls of Black Folk* (1903), in the shock of recognition experienced by

James Weldon Johnson's young protagonist in *The Autobiography of an Ex-Colored Man* (1912), and when Zora Neale Hurston's Janie as a child does not recognize her photographic likeness in *Their Eyes Were Watching God* (1937). Another limit of racial identification and recognition is thematized through racial passing, as in, again, *The Autobiography of an Ex-Colored Man*, Nella Larsen's *Passing* (1929), William Faulkner's *Light in August* (1932), Philip Roth's *The Human Stain* (2000), and Henry Louis Gates's portrayal of a long-time *New York Times* literary critic in "The Passing of Anatole Broyard" (1997).[4] Passing highlights "race" as social convention – epitomized in the arbitrariness of the one-drop rule – which here leads to disidentification from unwanted ascriptions. In Anthony Appiah's words: "It is because ascription of racial identities – the process of applying the label to people, including ourselves – is based on more than intentional identification that there can be a gap between what a person ascriptively is and the racial identity he performs: it is this gap that makes passing possible" (Appiah and Gutmann 1996, 79).

Appiah reviews extensive evidence against the existence of factual "race" in the first part of his long essay "Race, Culture, Identity: Misunderstood Connections," entitled "Analysis: Against Races." In the second part of the essay, however, entitled "Synthesis: For Racial Identities," he observes that "the label works despite the absence of an essence ... In fact, we might argue that racial identities could persist even if nobody believed in racial essences, provided both ascription and identification continue" (Appiah and Gutmann 1996, 81–2). He quotes in this context Du Bois's reflection in his 1940 autobiography *Dusk of Dawn*: "But the physical bond is least and the badge of color relatively unimportant save as badge; the real essence of this kinship is its social heritage of slavery; the discrimination and insult; and this heritage binds together not simply the children of Africa, but extends through yellow Asia and into the South Seas. It is this unity that draws me to Africa" (75).

Racial labels for Appiah are socially constructed signifiers that lack an essence yet possess reality in that they have social and psychological effects. With Ian Hacking, Appiah refers to this reality as "dynamic nominalism": "numerous kinds of human beings and human acts come into being hand in hand with our invention of the categories labeling them" (Hacking 1986, 87, quoted in Appiah and Gutmann 1996, 78). As Appiah suggests, such labels can be ascribed from the outside, but they also motivate psychological self-identification: "[They] shape the ways people conceive of themselves and their projects. In particular, the labels can operate to shape ... 'identification': the process through which an individual intentionally shapes her projects – including her plans for her own life and her conception of the good – by reference to available labels, available identities" (78).

Lawrence Hill lays out a similar position in his 2001 *Black Berry, Sweet Juice*, where he refers, like Appiah, to scientific accounts of genetic variation to conclude that there "is no biological difference between black people and white people. One cannot use genetics to explain race" (2001a, 201).[5] Despite this affirmation, however, again like Appiah, he does not negate racial self-identification in response to socially constructed racial realities:

> You can have a white parent and still be considered black, but you can never have a black parent and be considered white. Unless you are so light-skinned and devoid of black facial features that you can pass for white, you don't get to be white in this society if you have black parents. It ain't allowed. You'll be reminded of your "otherness" more times than you can shake a stick at. This is one of the reasons why I self-identify as black. Attempts at pleasant symmetry, as in "half white, half black," trivialize to my eye the meaning of being black. (41–2)

Yet, in addition, Hill, who was born in Canada but whose parents immigrated from the United States in the 1950s, also notes in particular certain differences in this respect between Canada and the United States:

> Canadians are quick to point out what we of mixed race are not – we are not White, and we are not Black – but they don't tell us what we are. This is the quintessential Canada: the True North, Proud, and Vague. What interests me is that, in recent years, it has become possible to define oneself in one's own terms ... Growing up, I was aware that Canada provided me with a little maneuvering space that my American cousins did not have. For example, I didn't have the weight of a legally sanctioned United States school system telling me that I had to attend this particular school because I was black. Unlike my

cousins, I had at least some room to concoct my own identity, declare it, test it out, see how it flew out there in my world. This, I think, is what still defines Canada today for a mixed-race person. There is some wiggle room. (228–9)

Hill's *Any Known Blood* (1997a) unfolds identification in Appiah's sense in considerable complexity, using and transforming to some extent materials and incidents from his own family history. Hill's protagonist, Langston Cane V, tries to work out how to conceive of himself, his projects, and indeed his conception of the good in rela- tion to available labels of race and identity. His identifications at first travel and pass across lines of racial identity; since "passing over" his identity delivers only the ambivalent downside of double consciousness without its potential multiple affirmation, he travels across geographical borders that separate different mappings of available identities, partially in order to disambiguate his identifica- tions. In addition, *Any Known Blood* also explores how identification crosses lines of identity both as ascription of identity by others and as self-identification (or disidentification) from the inside.

Any Known Blood engages issues of racial identification and "mixed race"[6] from the title and the epigraphs on. Gunnar Myrdal's *An American Dilemma* (1944) provides the first epigraph: "Everybody having a known trace of Negro blood in his veins – no matter how far back it was acquired – is classified as a Negro. No amount of white ancestry, except one hundred percent, will permit entrance to the white race." The second epigraph sounds Langston's name and filiation by citing Langston Hughes's poem "Cross" (1926):

My old man died in a fine big house
My ma died in a shack
I wonder where I'm gonna die,
Being neither white nor black?

Whether the cross of being "neither black nor white yet both" – as the title of a text by Werner Sollors (1997) puts it by reversing Hughes's sequence – means crucifixion or distinction remains a complex question in Hill's novel. Langston's surname evokes Jean Toomer's *Cane* (1923) – a text co-opted against Toomer's race-ambivalent will by Alain Locke for the signature Harlem Renaissance anthology *The New Negro* (1925) (see Lindberg 1997) – and calls up Toomer's own pun or misspelling *Cane/Cain* (1988, 145). Hill decides to have none other than Frederick Douglass employ this pun when he meets the protagonist's forebear, Langston Cane I (1997a, 475). Yet the novel's first chapter, which opens with the theme of passing and various conflicted or ambivalent identifications from within and without, also sounds a different note: "I have the rare distinction – a distinction that weighs like a wet life jacket, but that I sometimes float to great advantage – of not appearing to belong to any race, but of seeming like a contender for many" (1). A spirit rebellious both against his black father and against prejudice, Langston Cane V has been playing a "game of multiple racial identities" by identifying himself to others as "part anything people were running down" (2), be it Jewish, Cree, or Zulu. When he does settle on one identity in his application for a position as a government speechwriter, for which "Only racial minorities need apply" (2), he successfully claims the position as Algerian.

Among his motivations seem to be certain joys of passing (which can exist despite the anxieties of discovery),[7] his interest in Canadian officialdom's increasing reliance on racial self-identification, and finally a severe dose of disidentification. Hill's protagonist begins his narrative by relating with a certain relish several episodes in which he passes by self-identifying as a member of another minority, including the already mentioned job application in which he wants "to test my theory that nobody would challenge my claim to racial identity" (1997a, 2).[8] His interest in expanding his freedom of self-definition and self-identification seems particularly motivated, however, by the constraining expectations of his domineering father. He has thus relegated to some psychic limbo a black identity that Langston Cane IV has repeatedly impressed upon him with a long list of family achievements. The pressure is clearly registered: "It has been said that I have come down in the world. Down from an unbroken quartet of forebears, all, like me, named Langston Cane. A most precipitous descent, my father mumbled, when he heard about my latest job" (3). In contrast to his unprincipled speechwriting for a politician whom he despises, "Conviction ruled the lives of my ancestors. They all became doctors, or church ministers. By my age – thirty-eight – they already had their accomplishments noted in the *Afro-American*, the *Oakville Standard*, the *Toronto Times*, or the *Baltimore Sun*" (3).

Passing is for Langston V also a form of resistance to this kind of internalized threat of other-determined identification, a threat that would seem to preclude his own freedom of assent. His reasons for testing this freedom in crossing lines of identification, and his pursuit of the potentials for creative subversion implicit in these crossings, exceed classical motivations. Instead of seeking avoidance of racial oppression outside the family, *mis*identification is driven here by *dis*identification[9] in response to family dynamics – by an aversion, in this case, not to racial identity but to his father's control over his identity through the insistence on racial identity.[10]

This disidentification reveals itself as such at a critical limit that will precipitate its demise. After a particularly painful reminder of the disappointments that his strategies cause an old friend, Langston finds himself almost "unintentionally" leaking a government proposal to abolish human-rights legislation in Ontario. Although he swears upon the memory of Langston Cane I (Hill 1997a, 14) that his sudden action was neither planned nor the "'courageous blow'" (15) reported in the papers, he gets both himself and his minister fired with a doctored speech. Despite the fact that he seeks to downplay the importance of his deed and does not seem interested in taking any credit for an act that, for once, would garner the approval of his father, he certainly *has* written the speech. The moment reveals a decisive identification from within that all of a sudden destabilizes and then derails his habitual disidentification and previous playful passing. The moment indeed changes all shapes and shapings of his future projects in a manner consistent with the logic of identification we have seen Appiah explore with respect to racial labels.

In response to his conflicted (dis)identifications, similarly conflicted "recognitions" mark his last day at the office. A surprise visit by his father creates a double outing: the father learns of his passing, and his boss of his dissimulated race. At the same time, the puzzled minister receives a standing ovation from the Canadian Association of Black Journalists for a passage in the doctored speech that he delivers but fails to understand (Hill 1997a, 17). Langston Cane V thus receives, incognito, recognition for "his" speech and the identification it reveals. At such borders of identity, he decides to travel.

Langston Cane V understands his sacking as chance and challenge. Involuntarily freed from writing speeches for others, he now becomes a writer in search of his own identity and family history. In the process, like all other Langston Canes before him, he crosses the boundary between Canada and the United States.[11] His geographical and generational boundary crossing into the "four family legends" (Hill 1997a, 4) of his namesake ancestors also takes him across different mappings of "mixed race" in Canada and the United States. In this respect, Langston Cane V's experiences resemble very much those in Hill's self-portraiture in *Black Berry, Sweet Juice: On Being Black and White in Canada*:[12]

[M]y own experience of race, including my concept of my own racial identity, is shaded quite differently from that of my parents. They were both born and raised in the United States, and their racial identities were clearly delineated all their lives. The America of their youth and early adulthood was replete with laws that banned interracial marriages and upheld segregation in every domain of public life ... In the United States, there was never any doubt that my father was first and foremost a black man. Or that my mother was a white woman. And there is no question that, had my siblings and I been raised in the United States, we would have been identified – in school, on the street, in community centers, among friends – as black.

But my parents threw their unborn children a curve ball. They came to Toronto right after they married ...

Learning that I wasn't white, however, wasn't the same as learning that I was black. Indeed, for the longest time I didn't learn what I was – only what I wasn't. In this strange and unique society that was Canada, I was allowed to grow up in a sort of racial limbo. People knew what I wasn't – white or black – but they sure couldn't say what I was. (2001a, 4–5)

This borderland of possible identifications is what Langston Cane V also sets out to explore, heading south in search of family roots in Baltimore, where his aunt lives and where two previous Langston Canes were ministers of the African Methodist Episcopal Church.

Juxtaposed with his trip south are flashbacks of his father's crossing north after being an American soldier in the Second World War, which "he later said was enough to make any black soldier hate America" (Hill 1997a, 62). Canada-United States difference with respect to racial difference features prominently in these opposite trajectories of father and son. One of the father's often-told stories concerns a rent refusal that launched his civil-rights career in Canada. From a landlord's reaction to the mixed-race couple at the door, "Langston instantly knew that they would not get the flat ... but Langston sensed that it would come in a distinct way. This wasn't the United States. Nobody would swear at him, or wave a gun. Langston waited for the refusal, Canadian-style" (35). Indeed, racism here comes packaged in (initially) polite formality.

By contrast, whereas his father had travelled north into politeness and ambiguity, his son's trip south is one into disambiguation. Describing his first experiences in Baltimore, several episodes at the beginning of chapter 7 mirror in reverse some of his father's experiences upon arrival in Toronto. Whereas his father failed to find a black neighbourhood in Toronto, Langston Cane V's perception registers immediately segregated geography in Baltimore: "The street switched as quickly as a TV channel" (Hill 1997a, 93). In his apartment search, racism is as prominent as in his father's story, but here it is open (94). And whereas his father confidently discounts the probability of a threatening gun in Toronto, his son expects one from his first encounter with a squeegee punk at a red traffic light in Baltimore; he promptly does walk into a drive-by shooting, and he is mugged to boot. Although the shooting is not aimed at Langston Cane V or directly caused by his race, Hill here clearly marks a different scene.

In his orchestration of these cross-border stories, Hill comments in interesting ways on a pervasive African Canadian theme, the importance of African American culture north of the border. In his essay "Borrowed Blackness," André Alexis, for instance, discusses the presumption of an archetypicality of African American experience, evinced in an interlocutor's opinion that "no experience I might have in Canada could bring me closer to an understanding of real Black experience, that Black Canadians were not Black enough" (1995). George Elliott Clarke, in his by now canonical essay "Contesting a Model Blackness" (1998), is as critical of any notion of a "model blackness" as Alexis, although the impact of African American culture on African Canadian realities seems as ubiquitous as that of the United States in general on Canada. In *Odysseys Home: Mapping African-Canadian Literature*, Clarke quotes Diane Jacobs's "On Becoming a Black Canadian," a poem that both contests the ideology of an insignificant African Canadian experience and confirms some of the catalytic potential of border crossing: "Strangely it was in the U.S.A. / that I truly became a black Canadian. / In an attempt to rebut American Blacks' assumption / that being Canadian was an aberration. / That Canadian Blacks had no history" (1996, 71–2, quoted in Clarke 2002, 41). In Hill's novel, Langston Cane V's disidentified self at first seems to have taken the advice given to Alexis, "that in order to discover my 'Black self' I should move to the United States" (Alexis 1995).[13] Yet Hill's novel as a whole turns in quite different directions. Hill's text, an example of historiographic metafiction that delivers cross-cultural experiences through the writer Langston Cane V (who works on the novel we read) and uses or mentions writings by Langston Canes I-IV, is packed with both actual and imagined aspects of black Canadian history. Searching for his cross-border family roots, Hill's protagonist certainly also presents African American history, and he encounters those positive qualities of African American culture that Clarke describes as prominent in African Canadian perceptions: "For African Canadians, *African America* signifies resistance, vitality, joy, 'nation,' community, grace, art, pride, clout, spirituality, and *soul*" (2002, 39, original emphasis). Yet Hill does not romanticize any such thing as *African America*; his engagement with aspects of African American culture is creative rather than imitative and includes, as we will see, some playful Canadian reappropriation of history as well as negative aspects of *African America*. Significantly, in one incident he has his Canadian border-crossing protagonist, in search of family history and perhaps of a model blackness, become a model himself. Because of his behaviour in the shooting incident, the congregation of the Baltimore African Methodist Episcopal Church perceives him as an exemplary, model community member – an identification so desired by his father and one worthy perhaps of his ancestor Baltimore church ministers, Langston Cane II and III. Yet the narrator finds not only documents about their achievements but also a manuscript by Langston Cane I, a much more ambiguous figure and questionable candidate for identification than the subsequent three Langston Canes, as Langston V has already learned from documents. This crosser of multiple borders is surrounded by family-history rumours: "The link between my ancestor and John Brown" says the narrator, "seemed farfetched, but it had always fascinated me" (Hill 1997a, 11).

With the fictive manuscript of Langston Cane I, Hill (1997a, 429–94) invents a fugitive slave narrative that is reminiscent in some episodes of the *Narrative of the Life of Frederick Douglass, an American Slave, Written by Himself* (1845). Like Douglass, for instance, Langston Cane I thanks his owner for instructing him by interdiction about the forbidden pleasures and activities he will now make sure to seek out (Hill 1997a, 435–6); more important, as we will see, Hill also incorporates some lines from *Life and Times of Frederick Douglass* (1881) in which Douglass recounts his meeting with Brown shortly before the raid on Harpers Ferry. Yet as a border-crossing account, the narrative of Langston Cane I echoes in particular some of those in Benjamin Drew's *The Narratives of Fugitive Slaves in Canada* (1856).

Travelling the Underground Railroad in 1850, Langston Cane I crosses boundaries of legalized racial ascription, first between the southern United States and the North; here, however, he remains under the threat of the 1850 Fugitive Slave Act (Hill 1997a, 443). His further journey takes him across Lake Ontario and into the freedom of "Canaan"/Canada West (436), hidden in the boat of Captain Robert Wilson of Oakville, an actual Underground Railroad conductor re-envisioned by Hill. Yet in a move that perplexes his descendant Langston Cane V, he then doubles back to turn south again: "To escape as he did ... getting into Canada only to turn around nine years later and go back. Why? Could he possibly have joined John Brown's Raid? It was hard to imagine a fugitive slave settling comfortably in Oakville and then turning around and heading right back south into slave territory" (62). One of the reasons for his leaving Oakville, it turns out, is an accusation of bigamy against him. Yet his crossing back into southern slave territory also finds an explanation as a raid on "race." In this border crossing, he travels across boundaries of geographical and legal difference to change the meaning of race not only in his own life but once and for all in North America as well: he is seen last on a wagon with John Brown shortly before the raid on Harpers Ferry.

Without diminishing the historical importance of Brown's actions, Hill's fictive portrayal also echoes less positive contemporary accounts of Brown. When he appears on a fictive recruitment trip in Oakville,[14] Captain Robert Wilson throws him out of his house: "Spittle flew from Brown's lips ... He scared the wits out of my friend, Paul. ... Captain Wilson spoke first ... You're living in a fantasy, and you don't even know it. I believe you are mad" (Hill 1997a, 472). The John Brown portrayed by Hill proves also particularly insensitive to

important United States-Canada differences[15] (Hill thus seems to
extend the critique of a model blackness to a critique of a white,
model resistance to slavery and racism): "'The bondage of men. It
is a blight upon our great nation.' 'Your great nation,' Captain Wilson
said." Reminded by Brown of past slavery in Canada,[16] Wilson asks
him "not to patronize me in my own country and in my own house"
(471). Langston Cane I initially follows Brown nonetheless. He
remains even undeterred when Frederick Douglass shows himself
to be as skeptical as the Canadian captain about the outcome of
Brown's plans and thus denies – like the historical Douglass – Brown's
famous request (which Hill takes from Douglass's *Life and Times*
[part 2, ch. 10]): "When I strike, the bees will begin to swarm, and
I shall want you to help hive them" (476). And although Langston
Cane I joins John Brown during the preparations at the Kennedy Farm
and then in the raid on Harpers Ferry, he will, at the last possible
moment, decide like Douglass. He escapes before it is too late what
Douglass once called the "perfect steel-trap" of Harpers Ferry.[17]

Hill's plot decision is hardly motivated by the need to have the
founder of his family saga survive for it to continue, a man who has
fathered, at this point in the novel, not one but three Langston Canes
II (1997a, 465). Yet his survival and escape allow for his tale to be
told with the effect of heightened authenticity that comes with a
first-person point of view. Such authenticity was one of the most
sought-after qualities in the slave narratives that attested, for predominantly white, northern, abolitionist audiences, to the horrors
of slavery and, in their written form, to the former slaves' capacity
of authorship and literacy, which in many arguments about slavery
stood as the litmus test even of humanity (Gates 1987, 21; 1988,
129–30). In addition, Hill's decision was suggested by available
sources. Fittingly, he draws for the details of the raid on the manuscript of the Pennsylvania-born black Canadian Osborne Perry
Anderson, who survived, like Langston Cane I, the "trap" of Harpers
Ferry.[18] With the entire "masterful" (George Elliott Clarke 2002,
312) journal and slave narrative of Langston Cane I, Hill thus adds
a particularly significant genre to his also genre-wise, border-crossing,
historiographic novel (which includes long epistolary passages and
newspaper accounts), thereby linking it intertextually to the primordial black tradition I have already referenced.[19]

Another significant reason for Hill's choices at this point in the
novel, however, surfaces in his review of a work that appeared one

year after *Any Known Blood*, Russell Banks's *Cloudsplitter* (1998). Banks's novel is a portrayal of John Brown written from the point of view of Brown's son, Owen, who also escaped Harpers Ferry. Both narrators initially follow Brown yet leave the scene at crucial moments (Banks 1998, 744–6; Hill 1997a, 491) and live to tell the tale. Whereas Hill's narrator, like the historical Osborne Perry Anderson, comes to his own conclusions and makes his own decision (Du Bois 2001, 200) – in the case of Langston Cane I, the decision comes earlier than in Anderson's case and as a consequence of a clear rejection of one of Brown's decisions (Hill 1997a, 489) – the Owen Brown conceived by Russell Banks remains caught to the end in a trap, not the one of Harpers Ferry but that of his father's will. Ordered to guard an abandoned school house outside Harpers Ferry to arm insurgent slaves whom he knows won't come, he finally acts against one of his father's instructions: to keep silent about Douglass's refusal to mobilize support for the raid (Banks 1998, 741–2). When his companions decide to disclose this information to the other raiders, Owen neither stops nor joins them. He obeys what he is convinced is the will of his father, who "does not want me to save him" (744). Whereas Hill's Langston Cane moves quickly across boundaries of definition and decision, Banks's Owen Brown remains locked: "For a long while, as if I could not, I did not move" (745). Although he feels for a moment "unexpectedly – free" after having cast aside "the heavy steel manacles and chains" of his father's will, he ponders the freedom of his will and subsequent actions with abiding ambivalence: "But were my actions from then on those of a free man? I cannot say" (746).

Hill's review of *Cloudsplitter* focuses from the beginning on the question of point of view. Comparing Banks's choice to that of William Faulkner in "Barn Burning" (1939), Hill observes that Banks has "chosen to tell the story from the vantage point of the main character's son, Owen," which "brings the reader within intimate reach of ... the gap between a man's public victories and private failures" (1998, 64). And within this question of literary technique emerges for Hill the issue that we have seen to loom large in Langston Cane V's predicaments of identity: the issue of generational position and identification. "What emerges from Owen's first-person account," Hill asserts, "is a sad memoir of how he was unable to create a life for himself under the shadow of a domineering, charismatic father" (64). Although Owen Brown has escaped Harpers Ferry, his identity remains strangely shackled to the internalized will and law of the father. "And what a will John Brown had," Hill writes (64). He concludes his review: "*Cloudsplitter* ... illustrates that people of great accomplishments are not necessarily great people. Banks deftly dramatizes John Brown's commitment to unshackling African-Americans, and at the same time laments that, in the process, he destroyed the lives of those around him" (64).

The consequences of "race" and slavery control the life of Owen Brown as they have controlled that of his father (and of an entire nation headed for civil war). Yet Hill's Langston Cane I, although his identity and freedom would seem to be circumscribed even more tightly because he is black, negotiates a certain freedom nonetheless, despite the realities of racial ascription that dictate many aspects of his life. He not only succeeds in crossing boundaries drawn by North American political and racial geography but also defies the "paternal" authority of John Brown, as well as an identification that would ascribe him the role of victim in the very process of resistance to victimization and American slavery.

Langston Cane V, reading the manuscript of Langston I while in search of his own identity, ponders his affinity with this crosser of multiple borders. He notes a certain self-identification, motivated by what seems to be the indeterminate status of his ancestor with respect to identities and boundaries. If he feels "strangely connected to Langston I," it is because he loves "the fact that he didn't fit in. I love him for his mixture of weakness and dignity" (Hill 1997a, 497). His aunt Millicent (Mill) Cane, however, seems conversant with the pitfalls of romanticizing models: "'Don't make a hero out of him'" (497). Yet she agrees with Langston Cane V's self-identification: "'you are right about him not fitting in. If you ask me, the man had a loose chromosome that skipped a few generations and turned up in you.' She had a point" (497).

Langston Cane V's "not fitting in" – his relationship to boundaries of identity – is intimately connected with the strange "bondage and freedom" of his disidentification. He lives with both a certain freedom and a paternal trap. "My father," he says "has placed so many demands on me – get a doctorate, get a job, hold on to your wife, have children – that I have subconsciously arranged to fail at everyone of them" (Hill 1997a, 331). One more of these demands concerns racial identification, which he sabotages by passing, a choice made possible by his being "neither white nor black," to quote Langston Hughes's words again from Hill's epigraph. With his protagonist's later self-identification as "zebra incorporated" (400), however, Hill reverses the double negative of this phrase.

In his 1994 essay "Zebra: Growing up Black and White in Canada," Hill reveals that his own father used to call him "zebra" (44). Although "Zebra sounds faintly ridiculous," says Hill, he prefers it by far to a term like "mulatto," which "reduces me to half-status – neither Black nor White" (47).[20] Instead of this double negative, Hill arrives at a double affirmation in this essay, after an itinerary across different cultures and with several twists and turns of identification. In a passage later transformed into an episode in his first novel, *Some Great Thing*, he relates his desire during a visit in Niger to distance himself from his white Québécois friends: "Their presence made me feel White. And that summer, with an intensity that I had never anticipated, I wanted to be Black. Welcomed and loved as a brother" (46). People in Niger, however, "appeared to see me as White" (46); and his Québécois friends remain by his side when he is ill. He leaves the hospital, as he says, "a changed man": "I discovered that bringing my White friends into conversation with Africans was more rewarding than hoarding new friendships to the exclusion of the Quebecers. I knew what I was, and I felt it frankly. I was both Black and White, and this was irrevocable, whether other people noticed my colours or not. Years have since passed, but I still feel that way. I'm a man of two races" (47).

Hill relates the possibility of this identification here to his Canadian upbringing: "I didn't grow up under apartheid, or slavery, or racial segregation. I grew up in a country in which I had a say in what I would be. That meant periods of ambiguity. It meant confusion. It meant anxiety. But it also meant the opportunity to come full circle and to decide, years after my father first poked me in the ribs and teasingly called me a zebra, that I truly was both Black and White" (1994, 47). We have also seen, however, that Hill self-identifies as black in his later *Black Berry, Sweet Juice: On Being Black and White in Canada* (2001a, 41–2). "When you are black and white, negotiating racial identity is like going through a revolving door" (41), he writes, and he concludes the book with an emphatic reaffirmation of his black self-identification: "I am black because I say so, because I feel it, and own it. It is not the only thing I am ... But having seen issues of race and identity raise their heads in North America, I know that when the census form comes around, I'll mark myself down as black" (239).[21] That identification, however, will not limit his explorations. These last words of the conclusion come after an "Introduction" in which Hill summarizes the project in *Black Berry* and suggests that his narratives will continue to travel across boundaries and contexts of identity: "Nevertheless, I think the sands of identity are shifting once again in my own heart" (12). Motivated by his mother's family pictures, he announces another "journey," this time to the white side of his family, which would again take him south into the United States. If Hill explores a number of boundaries of identity in *Black Berry*, clearly there are more to come.

Any Known Blood also ends with another crossing of the border. Langston Cane V's return trip home to Canada, his car full of people of different complexion, provokes the "customary" question: "May I see some identification?" (Hill 1997a, 504). The Canadian guard, requesting and receiving border declarations of identity, eventually waves them through with the last words of the novel: "'Have a safe trip home, folks'" (505). The identifications and voyages of this *nostos*, however, are all complex border crossings. For Langston's American lover, Annette, who passes the border without having to show identification, this "would be a trial visit" (504). For Yoyo, the black refugee reporter from Cameroon who had satirized Canadian mores in *Some Great Thing* and who in this novel goes to work on the United States, it is also an undocumented trip. He crosses the border to reconnect with his love interest, introduced also in the previous novel, Hélène Savoie.[22] Langston's aunt Millicent (Mill) Cane returns to Canada to rejoin her childhood friend Aberdeen and her own brother, crossing a line she had drawn with respect to Langston Cane IV's mixed-race marriage.[23] At the border, she (re)claims not only her actual Canadian citizenship but also all other travellers in the car as her family.[24] Her act – in which necessity proves yet again the mother of invention – symbolically and practically has more integrative power than the laws of a country whose official she thus deceives at the border. Her "conducting" on this (rail)road trip permits Annette and Yoyo to cross into Canada and is achieved by her identification of, and with, a "family" that appears to be of many stripes and colours in Hill's description of Mill's earlier, first "adoption" of this family: "There was Yoyo, who was as dark as dark got, and a good deal darker than Mill. There was Annette, who was of a medium complexion, and then there was me – Zebra Incorporated" (400).

Yet even though Hill ends this novel with a border official wishing this group "a safe trip home," he also makes it clear that there is no unproblematic Canadian "national" family (or model) available for homecoming. In an article entitled "Black Like Us,"[25] he writes: "Canada is not nearly as integrated as we like to think" (2000, A13). Instead, as he demonstrates in virtually all his writings, there are stories about black Canadian history and lives to tell. The summary of "Black Like Us" states emphatically: "Let's celebrate our own stories during Black History Month, says Canadian novelist Lawrence Hill, not those from south of the border." Hill himself hardly objects to "American content" per se in the films he discusses in "Black Like Us"; rather, among other things, he objects to the way they are received by Canadian audiences. Reiterating a familiar problematic, Hill worries "that Canadians often develop a second-hand, borrowed impression about what it means to be black in Canada from the American experience" (2000 A13).

In Hill's own stories, as we have seen, identity and identification certainly involve crossing cultures, travel, and the frontiers of North American identity. Partially because he draws on his own experience and family history, these stories also speak about the United States. This does not mean, however, that they are not Canadian stories or that they imitate a "model blackness." They are centrally concerned with important versions of African Canadian experience, whether they deal with Canadian-born characters like Langston Cane V or immigrant experiences like those of previous generations.[26] The story of Harpers Ferry revisited is a prime example. It shows Langston Cane V in the process of searching for and writing part of a family history – certainly an integral part of one's identity – that has much in common with that of Lawrence Hill. In the process, Hill uses a perspective on Harpers Ferry that owes much to the account of the Canadian Osborne Perry Anderson, which has otherwise been routinely relied upon to tell the story as American only, with often nary a note for Canada. Hill reappropriates it as an African Canadian narrative in his multistoried imagining of one major strand of black Canadian history. If Harpers Ferry affords Hill a crossing, he has return fare in his pocket.

NOTES

1 This chapter developed out of a paper I presented at the conference "Crossing Cultures: Travel and the Frontiers of North American Identity" at the Institute for North American Studies, University of Groningen, Netherlands, 19–21 May 2003.

2 Mahatma barely avoids the name "Euripides Homer," proposed by his father, who sees him obviously destined for "some great thing," yet objected to by his mother, whose veto extends to both Greek and "Negro pride names" but fails to include other great race leaders (Hill 1992, 49–50).

3 Hill's other books to date are *Trials and Triumphs: The Story of African-Canadians* (1993) and *Women of Vision: The Story of the Canadian Negro Women's Association, 1951–1976* (1996).

4 For a wide-ranging discussion, see Sollors (1997), particularly the chapter "Passing; or, Sacrificing a Parvenu" (246–84).

5 See Appiah (1986); and Appiah and Gutmann (1996, 69). Hill (2001a, 202) quotes comments by the French geneticist Albert Jacquard about the concept of race:

> The reason why the concept is not valid is well known. If a genetic inheritance is to acquire a certain originality, if it is to distinguish itself significantly from that of neighbouring groups, it has to remain in complete isolation for a very long period ... That kind of isolation can exist in the case of animals, but is barely conceivable for a species as nomadic and as keenly curious as ours ... the proportion of the total genetic diversity of the human species that can be put down to differences between the four traditional "races" is only 7–8 per cent. In the case of differences between nations within these races, it is also only 7–8 per cent, while the remaining 85 per cent is due to differences between groups belonging to the same nation. In other words, the essential differences are not between groups, but contained within them. The concept of race consequently has so little content that the word becomes meaningless and should be eradicated from our vocabulary.

See also Rotman (2003) and Cooper, Kaufman, and Ward (2003) for scientific discussions that take the recent mapping of the human genome into account.

6 Subsequent to his discussion of "race" in Black Berry, Sweet Juice, Hill extends his comments there also to "mixed race," which thus is also under erasure: "If 'race' is in itself a meaningless term, then so is 'mixed race.' I have used the term 'mixed race' all my life, but now see it as an utter absurdity, even as I use it in this book" (2001a, 202).

7 Passing may evoke the "feeling of elation and exultation" that Sollors
  ascribes to "an experience of living as a spy who crosses a significant
  boundary and sees the world anew from a changed vantage point, heightened by the double consciousness of his subterfuge. Thus persons who
  pass may enjoy their roles as tricksters who play, as does [James Weldon
  Johnson's] 'ex-colored man,' a 'capital joke' on society" (1997, 253;
  see also 268).

8 Langston's job, advertised by a fictional "Ontario Ministry of Wellness"
  to "promote employment equity in the public service" (Hill 1997a, 2),
  seems modelled on the actual Ontario Employment Equity Act, introduced
  in the early 1990s under Premier Bob Rae. Hill asks in *Black Berry*:
  "And just how would a person qualify to be considered, say, black? Self-
  definition" (2001a, 209). Hill also observes about the definition of an
  "African Nova Scotian elector," introduced in 2000 under the amended
  Nova Scotia Education Act: "Self-definition is emerging as a key way to
  define one's identity ... In speaking with ... a senior official with the Nova
  Scotia Department of Education, I noted that the government had basically
  concluded a black person was any person who calls himself or herself a
  black person, and I asked whether anyone had considered advancing a
  more specific definition of blackness. 'We weren't going to go down that
  road,' he said wryly" (210). Hill cites a 2001 court decision to similar
  effect with respect to Métis self-identification and comments on the "absurdity of rigid racial categorization" (204) that defined the legal Indian status
  of women by that of their husband under the federal Indian Act until 1985.
  Native women thus lost their legal status when marrying a non-Indian; and
  since status Indians could not vote in federal elections until 1960, "any
  non-Indian woman who married an Indian lost the right to vote" (204–5).

9 Fuss speaks of disidentification with reference to what Judith Butler calls
  disavowed identities: "What at first may appear to be refused identification, Butler proposes, might in some cases more accurately be termed a
  disavowed one – an identification that has already been made and denied
  in the unconscious. A disidentification, in other words, may actually represent 'an identification that one fears to make only because one has already
  made it'" (1995, 7, quoting Butler 1993, 112). Butler also refers to such
  disavowed identities as abject, although I find Julia Kristeva's different
  understanding of the abject particularly useful. In *Powers of Horror: An
  Essay on Abjection*, Kristeva discusses the abject as something that cannot
  be permitted to be constituted as object, which then could be negated and
  pushed into the unconscious; rather, the abject is physically refused by
  the body before it crosses the threshold of thetic constitution (1982, 1–7).

In this sense, Langston's disidentification is a disavowed identity floating between consciousness and the unconscious, but it is not abjection.

10 Relations between father and son suffer from similar pressures in Hill's *Some Great Thing*: "By the time he is a teenager, Mahatma tunes Ben out. Despite the lectures about discrimination on the railway, the struggle to unionize porters, black pride, Martin Luther King and Mohandas K. Gandhi, Mahatma learns little more of these things than how to shut them out" (1992, 46).

11 Hill's decision to write a multigenerational novel in search of identity or, here perhaps better, the possibilities of identification sets his work alongside other recent Canadian novels that chronicle diasporic displacements over several generations and conceive of the unwritten stories of lives lived "elsewhere." One might think, for instance, of Dionne Brand's stunning *At the Full and Change of the Moon* (1999) or of Alistair MacLeod's *No Great Mischief* (1999).

12 There are many similarities but also significant differences between the Lawrence Hill of *Black Berry* and Langston Cane V. Hill's father, "Daniel Grafton Hill III ... son of a minister of the African Methodist Episcopal Church, American soldier during the Second World War, sociologist ... human rights pioneer" (Hill 2001a, 37–8), shares, apart from the profession, all these qualities with Langston Cane IV. The differing generational numbering may be the result of Hill's decision to invent the additional – and as we will see, crucial – Langston Cane I. Yet it also points to a different generational situation that Hill explores in his novel with respect to passing. Langston Cane V's options and predicaments vis-à-vis passing would be closer to those of Hill's children than to his own; in *Black Berry*, he writes: "Passing for white would never have tempted my father, even if his skin had been light enough for him to try. I might have been able to get away with it here and there, but I could never have pulled it off completely. And like my dad [but unlike Langston Cane V], I've never been tempted, either. My children, however, won't have to be tempted. They're going to have a hard enough time asserting their blackness and getting people to believe it" (2001a, 39). In the novel, it is indeed Langston Cane of generation V, not of generation IV, who wants his "race clearly marked" on his trip in the United States and who has to contend with comments like "You're pushing white, son. Pushing awful hard" (Hill 1997a, 123) and "Ain't there enough white churches where you all come from?" (125).

13 Alexis also refers to one of the most cited exchanges on the question of race and nation when he remarks parenthetically: "Of course, the

question whether 'black experience tout court' exists at all is the question. The disagreements between Leopold Senghor and Richard Wright at the first conference on Negritude are a challenge to the idea that a shared race is enough to overcome differences of language, culture and history" (1995). See, for example, Frantz Fanon's "On National Culture" (1963, especially 215–16).

14 In 1858 Brown went to stay with Harriet Tubman at St Catherines, and then to Ingersoll, Hamilton, Chatham, and Toronto (Du Bois 2001, 148–9), and returned briefly in 1859. At the 1858 Chatham meeting, a constitution was read and adopted (154); the Provisional Constitution and Ordinances for the People of the United States was printed later that year in Hamilton (Winks 1997, 268n77).

15 There are factual antecedents for this portrayal. Du Bois quotes (via Martin R. Delany) a member of the 1858 Chatham convention: "One Evening the question came up as to what flag should be used; our English subjects, who had been naturalized, said they would never think of fighting under the hated 'Stars and Stripes' ... But Brown said the old flag was good enough for him ... He declared emphatically that he would not give up the Stars and Stripes" (2001, 152; see also 154).

16 Under John Graves Simcoe, Upper Canada adopted legislation to abolish slavery gradually, although it did not free any slaves. Slavery remained legal in British North America until the emancipation of slaves in the British Empire, legislated in 1833 and effective 1 August 1834 (see Winks 1997, 96–113).

17 Douglass writes in *Life and Times*: "I told him [Brown], and these were my words, that all his arguments, and all his descriptions of the place, convinced me that he was going into a perfect steel-trap, and that once in he would never get out alive; that he would be surrounded at once and escape would be impossible" (1999, part 2, ch. 8).

18 Du Bois calls Anderson's *A Voice from Harpers Ferry* (1861) "The best account of the raid by a participant" (2001, 239); for Hill, it is "most important of all" the books he relied upon for Harpers Ferry ("A Word about History," in Hill 1997a, 508).

19 See also Cuder-Domínguez (2003) for a discussion of other recent African Canadian writing in this context; the article focuses on Hill, George Elliott Clarke's *Beatrice Chancy* (1999), and Dionne Brand's *At the Full and Change of the Moon* (1999). Austin Clarke's Giller Prize-winning *The Polished Hoe* was published in 2002.

20 For discussions of the figure and implications of the "mulatta/o," see, for instance, George Elliott Clarke's "Canadian Biraciality and Its 'Zebra'

Poetics" (2002, 211–37); Sollors's "Excursus on the 'Tragic Mulatto'; or, the Fate of a Stereotype" (1997, 220–45, passim); and Spillers's "Notes on an Alternative Model – Neither/Nor" (2003, 301–18).

21 Excerpts of his book appeared in *Maclean's* under the title: "Black + White … Equals Black" (Hill, 2001b). Decisions about identification influence census results crucially. George Elliott Clarke reports that "43 per cent of African Canadians did not identify themselves as 'Black' in the 1991 Canadian census." According to one source he cites, some Haitians, for instance, identified themselves as French and some Jamaicans as British (2002, 41).

22 Yoyo passes under assumed identities after leaving his home country, while Hélène initially changes her name to Helen to conceal her French Canadian identity in Winnipeg, which she reveals to Yoyo in a code-switching passage (Hill 1992, 67–8).

23 One of the main reasons Mill had opposed Langston Cane IV's mixed-race marriage was a Ku Klux Klan incident (based on an actual event in Oakville in 1930) (Hill 1997a, 512) in which Aberdeen was attacked because he wished to marry a white woman; after this incident, he had left Oakville. Mill was left heartbroken and "convinced that she had lost her best friend because he had been seeing a white woman, and nobody could change her mind" (326). Her nephew's presence and project in Baltimore thus meets an initially cold reception on her part. In *Black Berry*, Hill devotes a chapter to the "emotionally charged issue of black men loving white women" (2001a, 115–49).

24 Rinaldo Walcott points out that Mill's role is central because from a certain point on she provides her support and much of the family documentation; it is thus "through her that Cane V is able to complete his investigation." Walcott sees her decision as the result of having worked through the traumatic experience of the Ku Klux Klan incident and the loss of Aberdeen (2003, 69–70).

25 Hill's title is part of an intertextual web that also includes John Howard's *Black Like Me* (1961), Rinaldo Walcott's *Black Like Who?* (2003), and Hill's review of it, "Black Like Us, Eh?" (1997b). Hill addresses here again the relationship between African Canadian and African American experience and identifies as one of Walcott's main arguments that "part of what makes African-Canadian society unique is the way it plays off black cultures in other countries" (J20). Hill comments on the title:

> It seems ironic but fitting that Rinaldo Walcott's collection of essays about black culture in Canada features cover art and a title taken from the American experience. *Black Like Who?*, which emphasizes

the distinctiveness of the black Canadian experience and urges black
artists in this country to celebrate their identities more profoundly,
draws its title from the American classic *Black Like Me*. Written by the
late John Howard Griffin and published in 1961, *Black Like Me* was a
best-selling autobiographical account of a white American who under-
went a series of medical treatments to change his skin colour tempo-
rarily in order to write a first-person account about American racism.
Borrowing from Griffin's book to create the title *Black Like Who?*
seems to be Walcott's playful way of saying that room remains for new
definitions of the black experience in Canada. (J20)
Walcott discusses other responses to his book, particularly that of George
Elliott Clarke, in his "Introduction to the Second Edition" (2003, 11–23).

26 The author identification at the end of "Black Like Us" thus describes
Any Known Blood as "a historical novel about five generations of a
black family in Canada."

QUEBEC CONNECTIONS

9

Translating in the Multilingual City: Montreal as a City of the Americas

SHERRY SIMON

As the power of national epics wanes, city-dwellers tend to see themselves above all as citizens of the metropolis. The competing and overlapping voices of the city often define a reality at odds with the identity claims of the nation. In particular, North American cities offer an auditory landscape of increasing diversity. In taxis and on street corners conversations are held, sometimes shouted (when they're on cellphones), in all the languages of the world. Languages once confined to the home or to community venues like church basements are suddenly more apparent in the public sphere. The electronic map produced by the Modern Language Association for the United States counts more than 300 languages in use in the United States and almost as many for the single city of New York.[1] There is a visible presence of language too, the profusion of scripts on storefronts, including Chinese, Japanese, Arabic, and Hindi. This multilingualism confirms the intensity of conversations and transactions across languages and nations, the intensity of an increasingly generalized diasporic culture. Cities are spaces of circulation "in the world," according to Alain Médam, characterized by two dynamics: not only a centripetal dynamic of convergence, which brings diversity into cities, but also a centrifugal dynamic of dispersion, which means that cities are nodes in an ever-enlarging network of diasporas (2002, 35).

Multilingualism and translation take on different forms in the cities of the Americas – not only in terms of the patterns discerned by sociolinguists (who speaks which language, where, and why) but also in terms of the values associated with language within the aesthetic traditions and collective imaginaries of the city. Montreal's legendary spatial and linguistic segregation has created a distinctive linguistic consciousness. This means that although Montreal is increasingly a multilingual city – like many others – the doubleness of its two major languages makes for a mix that will be different from that characteristic of other cosmopolitan cities. It contrasts with the multilingualism of Toronto, New York, and Mexico city, where one strong and uncontested language dominates. As an example, one might consider the words with which Doris Sommer begins her collection *Bilingual Games*. Recalling "the barrio of Brooklyn where I learned the fun and the frustrations of bilingual games," she continues:

> Hail to the hood for being the space of encounters and disen-counters, far from any communitarian paradise and close to the messy ground of democratic coexistence. Growing up between streets named after a Dutch Amboy and a Zionist Herzl now seems like an objective correlative for the bifocal vision we developed there. The double focus and double talk made every-thing outside any one of our small apartments look elliptical, pulled between two gravitational points of home and host languages. The ellipses were linked up by a series of *puntos suspendidos* that kept meanings afloat, somehow there but never settled ... For some time now I have appreciated the privilege of spending my formative years in a place where we all fit in, more or less uneasily and with the mutual respect that comes from never presuming to be at the centre. (2003, vii)

Her account of Brooklyn reminds me of my own neighbourhood in Montreal, Mile End, similarly rich in languages, similarly elliptical and decentred in its relation to the dominant culture and to the city as a whole (Simon 1999). But whereas Sommer describes a neigh-bourhood whose multilingualism contrasts with the norm of a monolingual city, Mile End is an added complication in an already linguistically divided city. The internal divisions of Montreal mean that the whole city participates in the kind of double vision that Sommer describes, a space of "encounters and disencounters," of friction and uneasiness. The cities that perhaps today most closely parallel Montreal would be the divided city of Miami (where Spanish is currently the majority language) and the divided towns along the Mexican-US border.

To study languages as they circulate in the city is also to attempt a transversal understanding of languages in North America. The fabric of city life often clashes with national policy and with national self-understandings. Cosmopolitan cities do not reflect their hinterlands and tend to stand in opposition to them. The frame that circumscribes theoretical investigation, as Cynthia Sugars and others powerfully argue in this volume, is decisive for the argument that is being made. The powers of explanation provided by the city may be useful for understanding the diversity of all Western societies – particularly the ways that this diversity is expressed through public language.

Multilingualism is often experienced as a random moment of encounter – a cluster of conversations on the sidewalk, in the bus, in immigrant neighbourhoods, at sites like airports or markets, or at traditional gathering spots like, in Montreal, the belvedere atop Mount Royal. These are moments when the maelstrom of languages can be experienced as euphoria and communion (in the multilinguistic anonymity of the café, in the bustling crowds of the market, in the early morning swirl of costume and colour at the airport) – just as they can be interpreted as a source of disorientation or alienation. But this random buzz of languages, the multilingualism of the street, is no guarantee of citizenship. For nonofficial languages to have a right to expression, they must be translated into the official tongue. Translation, then, is the key to citizenship, to the incorporation of languages into the public sphere. "Citizenship is, first and foremost, engaged with other people in the creation of shared social spaces and in the discourse that such spaces make possible" (Kingwell 2000, 189). There is a long history connecting the idea of public space in the city with the Greek *agora*, a space of conversation where citizenship, governance, and community were intertwined. Public space has come to stand for the combination of material and discursive conditions that make it possible for citizens to participate together in city life. Language, then, is an element of this public space – the very grounds of the possibility of exchange. Whereas the languages of foreigners, of what were known as *barbarians*, were excluded from the Greek *agora*, today's public spaces must include them. But how are these to be integrated into the sphere of citizenship? For such a connection to take place, we need, according to Mary Louise Pratt, "a new public idea about language" (2003, 112) – a renewed recognition of the knowledges that languages carry.

How is multilingualism shaped by the city and given public presence? How is the language consciousness of cities expressed against the horizon of political ideology but also against the backdrop of the imaginative history and creativity of the city? What I propose here are some preliminary moments of inquiry that focus on the idea of *public language* and on *translation*. These reflections are largely speculative yet grounded in the conviction that language has been a neglected element in reflections on diversity in North America. Whereas practical questions of linguistic demographics and language acquisition are given attention, little research is devoted to the symbolic and imaginative functions of language as part of the very fabric of urban experience.

TRANSLATION

This reflection begins with the idea that the language life of cities is to be conceived much more on the model of translation than on that of a simple diversity. The mixture of languages is in fact a pattern of passages, voluntary or forced, through which ideas and styles are reshaped. For Alain Médam, there are three types of tensions in the city: the forces of "co" (consensualities), of "diss" (antagonisms), and of "trans" (which forge new paths through the city). Translation participates in all three of these dynamics – creating consensus, expressing tension, and contributing to the formation of hybrid realities. These forms of translation are to be explored at different levels of the cultural life of the city: informal transactions and practices of everyday life, official communications, and artistic practices (literature, theatre, cinema) that play with language. If the differences of the city are to be negotiated in meaningful spaces of contact, then a politics of broad participation must include a politics of translation. For Michael Cronin, this turn involves seeing "multilingual, multi-ethnic urban space as first and foremost a *translation space*" (2006, 68, original emphasis). He continues:

> In other words, if translation is primarily about a form of interaction with another language and culture (which in turn modify one's own), then it is surely to translation that we must look if we want to think about how global neighbourhoods are to become something other than the site of non-interactive indifference ... Everything, from small local theatres presenting

translations of plays from different migrant languages to new voice recognition and speech synthesis technology producing discreet translations in wireless environments to systematic client education for community interpreting to translation workshops as part of diversity management courses in the workplace, could begin to contribute to a reformation of public space in migrant societies as primarily a translation space. (68)

Cronin's idea of seeing city space as a translation space is crucial. Despite the sensory evidence of multilingual cities, there has been surprisingly little sense of language as a powerful presence in the city. In the explosion of writing about the city that has filled library shelves since the 1980s, authors such as David Harvey, Saskia Sassen, Edward Soja, Allan Blum, and Iain Chambers have turned the question of space and material, cultural history into a rich vein of exploration about city life. Space is more than a set of physically delimiting factors, neither an ideologically neutral and given grid nor a "passive geometry" (Spector 2000, 30) but a productive matrix with palpably concrete and often violent ramifications. This emphasis on space, however, seems to mean that language is neglected. On the other hand, the writings of a committed group of American scholars, proponents of what has been called the new comparative literature, have stimulated reflection on the plurilingualism of the American literary tradition. Joining issues of literature, geography, and translation, Emily Apter, Waichee Dimock, Doris Sommer, Mary Louise Pratt, Domna Stanton, Werner Sollors, Marc Shell, Edwin Gentzler, and David Damrosch have drawn attention to language in the context of the redefinition of national literatures and the issue of world literature. This campaign to restore the visibility of multilingualism in America has both disciplinary and social goals as it seeks to redefine American studies as a contact zone. All draw attention to languages and translation in an explicit effort to undercut the myth of a monolingual America and its harmful social and military consequences. Winfried Siemerling links the evidence that language is "coming to the fore in recent discussions of American literatures with the fact, according to the 2000 U.S. Census, that Latinos have surpassed earlier than expected African Americans as the largest minority in the United States, inherently also modifying the balance between language and race as factors in models of multiculturalism" (2005, 15). He also points to the role of orality and mixed-language vernaculars as strategic elements in the emergence of specific literary identities. "Written orality" is of strategic importance in the African American written tradition, a crucial hinge in Native writing, and central to the intense debates about joual in articulations of North American francophone specificity in Quebec (15). But this attention has not extended into the realm of cities. And thus, for instance, the important issue of the journal *Public Culture* devoted to Johannesburg a few years ago (2004, vol. 16, no. 3) has barely a word on the question of multilingualism in that city.

A focus on translation can, then, make available the language world of cities in a way that accounts for the movement and interactions of conversation. To make sense of the brouhaha of language, of what seems like the shapeless and inchoate wanderings of languages through streets and neighbourhoods, it is necessary to hear these languages in the context of history. This includes the changing social meanings that languages carry within the specific narrative of the city's history. The city is not a background to language; rather, language relations are a shaping presence in the narratives that define the city. Language differences cannot be collapsed into the maelstrom of an undifferentiated multilingualism; they must be understood as part of the interactions of the city. To study the complex, overlapping weave of translations is to identify a field of discreet practices – each with differing stakes and outcomes. Forms of translation are to be explored at different levels of the cultural life of the city: informal transactions and practices of everyday life; public language, including official communications; artistic practices (literature, theatre, cinema); legal negotiations; and so on. These practices can be studied as a key to the interactions among language communities.

Understanding the city as a translation space is also enabled by recent developments in translation studies, which has not only extended the array of objects and practices that fall under its purview but has also sharpened the focus of analysis in telling histories that go beyond individual texts, that sketch out larger frameworks and circulatory logics. Translation is no longer understood as an unequivocally peaceful and friendly activity but seen to participate fully in the fraught politics of the moment. In response to an increasingly violent world, translation studies has recently been ever more attentive to the sometimes complicitous and sometimes activist role of translation in international affairs, to the role of translation in global news reporting, for example, or in situations of violent conflict, as well as in the political and cultural life of migrant and diasporic populations. Translation studies is broadly sustained by the understanding that mediation among languages, as among all cultural forms, necessarily involves displacement. "It is no longer viable to look at circulation as a singular or empty space in which things move," write Dilip Parameshwar Gaonkar and Elizabeth Povinelli (2003, 392). There is a "material culture of circulation" that does more than gatekeeping, that is more than a form of constraining or controlling knowledge insofar as it organizes and shapes passage (392). And thus in literary studies, for instance, a translational perspective has meant an emphasis on transnational and global paradigms of study that emphasize circulation, dissemination, and networks across economic and political inequalities.

Within these histories, the translator has been given new recognition. The materialities of circulation – the places and circumstances of translation, the encounters between individuals, the anchoring of textual matters not only in the politics of book production but also in the social life and cultural interactions of a society – are grounded in a recognition of the materiality of translation events.

COERCION

Translation often occurs as a result of coercion. What remains in the city are traces of former regimes, of prior populations. Naming is an instrument of possession and repossession. Each city has its own paradoxes of naming. In Montreal, street renamings remind us that the modern city is characterized not only by forgetting or "mistranslation" but also by a form of translation more akin to "writing-over." Each new regime brings about its own forms of rewriting and writing-over, sponging-out, and erasure. City streets are renamed as old heroes are disqualified, as new icons are glorified. Sometimes entire cities are covered over in a new language, as though the decor were being changed. This was frequent in the history of Europe – it also occurred in American cities where possession shifted from one colonial power to another.

Naming is a marker of possession. But although many cities in the United States have names of French or Spanish origin, their origins have been largely forgotten or suppressed by the anglicized pronunciation of the names. Language is not only a marker of possession; it is also a marker of time. The old names evaporate into invisibility, only to be rescued by formal attempts at memorialization. Language is engraved into the surfaces of the city, through signs, through inscriptions, through graffiti. And the writing-over of these inscriptions indicates the relentless progression of languages as they come to represent periods in the city's history. Some kinds of English in Montreal have a unique quality of pastness. The trace of an old painted advertisement on a brick wall has the quaint look of a language as ancient as Phoenician. French and Spanish in New Orleans have the same quality of the bygone. The vibrant French-speaking culture of the city, the highly literary culture of the *gens de couleur* in antebellum New Orleans, is now an archive for specialists to research. The successive conquests of the city – first French, then Spanish, again French, and then English – have left a legacy of layered memories, visible today mainly in the form of commodified information aimed at the tourist market. It was the mixture of languages and cultures, however, that accounted for the extraordinarily dynamic cultural life of the city during the nineteenth and early twentieth centuries – for its hybrid cultural forms, particularly the emergence of jazz. In today's New Orleans, the many varieties of language affiliation have given way to the overwhelming racial divide.

The cities of the Americas are by definition colonial cities – products of the colonization by Europe. The link between colonial cities and the coercion of translation is given brilliant focus in the work of Angel Rama. In his *The Lettered City* (trans. 1996), he shows how the cities of the New World were the materialization of an idealized "ordered city," imposed upon the New World landscape. "One could say that the American continent became the experimental field for the formulation of a new Baroque culture. The first methodical application of Baroque ideas was carried out by absolute monarchies in their New World empires, applying rigid principles – abstraction, rationalization, and systematization – and opposing all local expressions of particularity, imagination or invention" (10). The cities indeed were constructed – as symbolic representations – before the countryside was peopled. And thus the Spanish settlers, who had been rural people, were forcibly urbanized. The walled precincts were fortresses "where the spirit of the polis could be distilled, protected, ideologically elaborated, and prepared to undertake the superior civilizing responsibilities that it was destined to fill" (13).

Rama emphasizes the importance of the codified written word in a context where people in Latin America, even people in positions of authority, were "charged with executing orders of obscure logic and distant origin. Local authorities must often have appeared actors in a phantasmagoric shadow play, disconnected from the immediate realities of material life, responding, and appealing for justification, solely to the dictates of the order of signs" (1996, 15). The *letrados*, the class of administrators, became translators, moving not only between Spanish and indigenous languages (obliging the indigenous peoples to learn Spanish) but also between the increasingly distant gap separating spoken and written language. The official missive became a literary genre in its own right.

The importance of letters persisted well into the twentieth century, as Rama illustrates:

Take out a map of a major Latin American city at the beginning of the twentieth century and try to locate the following: the houses inhabited by writers (usually boarding houses in the case of provincial letrados who had come to the national capital for study or employment); the offices of the newspapers (where such writers worked as reporters or at least contributed occasional stories); the government agencies (the post and telegraph office, archives, libraries, ministries, and so on) that constituted their chief source of employment; the universities where they studied a liberal profession (abandoned soon after graduation); the lecture and concert halls (locales of their learned disputations); the cafés where they seemed to spend most of the day (writing, discussing literature, or seeking financial support); the theatres that they attended (to write a review, peddle a script, or pursue an actress); the law offices (where they functioned as clerks or merely chatted about art); the party headquarters (where they practiced their oratory, the most celebrated skill of the day and that which most defined an intellectual); the brothels (that they attended assiduously until the day they were married); the churches (where at least some repented of their sins); and finally the stores selling fine furnishing and objets d'art (imported from Barcelona or Paris). Together these locations signal the outlines of the old city centre, a quadrilateral of about ten blocks on each side, scene of public business and sociability, the places where novelists of the day inevitably plotted the "chance" meetings of their characters. (1996, 114)

Colonial cities are today considered the precursors of the global city, where different languages and cultures meet in the apparent intimacy of the everyday. As a doubly colonized city, one that saw first a French and then a British conquest, Montreal has taken on a particular configuration as a divided city. All cities are in a constant state of redefinition, and city-dwellers have as their task the obligation to continually make new sense of their environment. The definition of community, the "we" of the city, is a temporary victory, always in need of repetition – through multiform activities of mediation. These activities confirm both the uniqueness of cities in relation to each other and the endlessly inventive character of city life.

NEUTRALIZATION

Public displays of written language transmit official conceptions of the linguistic citizen, make assumptions about the capacities of its readers. The written messages delivered by city administrations and transit commissions, by advertising on billboards, and by commercial signage trace out the linguistic portrait of ideal citizens – those who are included in civic conversation. (A sign in a New Zealand park announced in English only that its garbage cans had been poisoned – not caring to add a pictogram for security. Safety instructions in the Berlin metro are written in elaborate paragraphs of German – again, no pictograms.) But against the backdrop of these official missives, cities also allow the proliferation of underground print cultures, the free-for-all culture of posters and stencils, of ads and petitions, that create alternative zones of linguistic citizenship. These indicate linguistic microclimates, zones of neighbourhood conversation, where nonofficial languages can go public.

Public language in Montreal has always been more than information – it has long been a battleground. Signage makes for a tangible target, and for decades signage has aroused unique and longstanding passions in Montreal. The focus on signage deflects attention away from other manifestations of covert translation in cinema, in theatre and opera, in the press, in advertising.[2] These areas remain largely ignored, noticed only on rare occasions when the effects of translation arouse controversy. In the multilingual city, the public soundscape can be both a spark and an irritant. As for Fernando Pessoa writing English poetry in Lisbon or for Régine Robin inhabited by Yiddish in Montreal, private languages can be protection against the aggressive sounds of the city.

The multilingual city nourishes both counterlingual and alingual forms of expression. Atom Egoyan's *En passant*, his contribution to a collection of short films called *Montréal vu par* ... (1991), suggests that the best way out of language competition is to avoid language altogether. He imagines a city where the only form of public communication is the silence of pictograms. *En passant* conjures up a Montreal where language seems to have been abolished and where communication now exists only as a series of ever more demented signs, signals, and pictograms. The soundscape of language, along with its visual representations, can become a message that overshadows semantics. This reduction of language to sign illustrates that, in places where multilingualism complicates and therefore frustrates social interaction, new strategies are devised that can sidestep language altogether. This is the case for the "nodding relationships" (Germain and Rose 2000, 245–6) that arise among neighbours in a city where spontaneous jokes among strangers may well fall flat – for lack of a common language. That the internationalization of Quebec culture has come to rely increasingly on nonlinguistic forms of art (e.g., dance and circus arts like the now globalized Cirque du Soleil) and that its most famous representative on the theatre scene is Robert Lepage, who downplays text in his high-tech and visually imaginative productions, are sure symptoms of the flight from language.

The abandoning of language as the material of art, the dissipation of language consciousness, the abdication of small languages in favour of planetary English – these are signs of the times. Yet, for many, they are precursors to an inevitable loss. Against the double dangers of increased uniformity and extreme atomization, does language interference provide a form of immunization? Tension, competition, and difference are the lifeblood of citizenship.

CIRCULATION

Sociolinguists and linguistic demographers point to some remarkable changes in the language composition of North America. The number of US cities that have a sizable proportion of multilingualism is rising steeply. Not only are US cities increasingly multilingual, but there is also greater mobility of multilingual populations. Although traditional port-of-entry cities like New York and Los Angeles have by far the highest rate of multilingualism, during the 1990s second-language speakers began to sprout up in certain south-eastern and western states, which now have the fastest-growing non-English-speaking populations. For instance, Fayetteville, Arkansas, increased its non-English-speaking population by 368 per cent during the 1990s. Cities like Phoenix, Atlanta, Las Vegas, Seattle, and Denver became secondary magnets for new immigrant groups during the 1990s. Almost one in five Americans say they speak a second language at home. Of these, about 60 per cent speak Spanish, about 20 per cent a European language, and about 15 per cent an Asian language (Frey 2002, 21).

Numbers, however, are not accurate indicators of the actual public presence of language. National language policies, identity politics, and the specific dynamics of cities have a strong bearing. For instance, the recent massive public activism of Latino immigrant communities in the United States regarding immigrant rights has given a strong new visibility to Spanish. This visibility was underlined by a recent audio recording of the Spanish translation of *The Star-Spangled Banner* – an event that became symbolic of the different meanings attributed to translation. President George W. Bush opposed the Spanish version of the anthem (*New York Times*, 29 April 2006), arguing that "people who want to be a citizen of this country ought to learn English, and they ought to learn to sing the national anthem in English." For Bush, the very existence of the Spanish version posed a threat to English. His reaction was paradoxical considering that Bush had used Spanish actively in an attempt to win Spanish-language voters. However, officially, Bush opposed the translation into Spanish as a move away from US citizenship, as a translation arising "out of" Latino citizenship. For Latino activists, on the contrary, the translation of the anthem into Spanish was a move toward increased US citizenship.

Language tensions in Canada are informed by a different bias, with obligatory importance given to the double official languages of French and English. The public presence of French outside Quebec is often exclusively a function of its official status – and therefore related to the presence of federal-government institutions and programs. This leads to paradoxes of visibility. Toronto has become one of the most multicultural and multilingual cities in the world, and Dionne Brand speaks affectionately of her city, Toronto, in her latest novel *What We All Long For*, as a "gathering of voices and longings that summed themselves up into a kind of language, yet indescribable ... Yes, that was the beauty of this city, its polyphonic, murmuring" (2005, 149). It is ironic that in this mix of tongues

French has very little public presence. It is true that a great deal of attention is given to bilingual education in Toronto, and therefore French-language schools are prominent sites in public consciousness. Yet French has little visibility or audibility in the streets. This is because Toronto tends to emphasize ethnicity through spatial, neighbourhood identities: the Greek Danforth, the Portuguese College Street, the Italian St Clair West. Because there is no neighbourhood or ethnic identity related to French in Toronto, it dissolves into the fabric of the city, inaudible next to, for instance, Portuguese. The frame through which francophone identity is shaped is not equivalent to that of immigrant ethnicities.

French in Toronto illustrates the paradox of the "scene" as defined by Alan Blum (2003). He regards the scene as an intensified version of the theatricality of city life – it is some kind of concerted activity (the gay scene, the fashion scene, the singles scene, the art scene), which is both accessible yet hidden, involving restricted access. Language communities would be scenes in this sense – operating at the surfaces of urban life yet retaining an aspect of mystery and of ephemerality.

In a discussion of Mexico City, Nestor Garcia Canclini asks: "What happens when we cannot understand what a city is saying – when it becomes a Babel and when the chaotic polyphony of its voices, its dismembered spaces, and its scattered individual experiences dilute the meaning of the total discourse?" (1995, 748). With this question, he draws attention to the chaotic and uncontrolled aspects of city life, to the fact that the city cannot be encompassed by any single description. The city, he argues, is in fact the totality of the languages spoken within it – "Mixtecan languages from Oaxaca, Mazahuan languages from Hidalgo, Nahuatl from Guerrero, as well as other ethnic groups and the various kinds of Spanish spoken in the various regions of Mexico. One also hears English as well as Spanish spoken with Central American, Argentine and Chilean accents" (748) – and also the totality of the messages that are generated there and carried across the city, the multiple modes of communication, the print and electronic linkages. Canclini's labyrinthine, sprawling, disintegrating megacity is to be explored, he suggests, "not only by what happens within its territory but by the way in which it is traversed by migrants, tourists, messages, and goods from other countries." The city does not just *contain* but is itself *made up of* stories: "journalistic and literary chronicles, photos, radio and television talk, and music that narrates our urban ways" (751).

Canclini is suggesting that it is a question not just of situating languages within the city but also of understanding that the city itself is created and shaped by the languages that circulate within it. These include the Babel of different languages spoken within the city, the languages that traverse the city through electronic signals, the languages of migrants and tourists, and the narratives through which inhabitants speak of and make sense of the city.

Approaching the Babel of languages from a somewhat different angle, Doris Sommer argues for the benefits of language interference, suggesting in fact that the mixed language of bilingual games might become the basis of a new kind of linguistic citizenship. Arguing against the limitations of monoglot culture, Sommer makes the largest possible claims for the interferences, irritations, uncertainties, and surprises of language contact. Playing themselves out in jokes, in conversations, in works of art, in philosophy and psychoanalysis, and in politics, they "interrupt the dangerous dreams of single-minded loyalty," they "flex democratic systems" (2004, 11). Bilingual games improve the "cultural conditions for fair and fulfilling contemporary life" (xi). Sommer sees links between the surprises of daily life, the beneficial effects of estrangement, and the political ideal of citizenship. These notions are deeply embedded in a tradition of thought that highlights the importance of language as an element that complicates communication – rather than reducing it to simple, transparent signs. She explores this tradition, from the Russian formalist Viktor Shklovsky, who defined estrangement as the key to esthetic value, to Sigmund Freud, whose affinity for jokes are at the core of Sommer's project and style, and to Walter Benjamin, who prefers "gnarled dialectical stories" and the "irritating and tangled narrative vehicle of baroque allegory" to the "quick emotional fix of light and heat available from romantic symbols" (51). This is not officially legislated bilingualism but the playful interaction between languages that make "mischief with meaning" (xii) by letting the sound of alternative languages interrupt the singleness that modern states seem to demand.

This suggestion carries risks and cannot be applied equally to any city in the Americas. Sommer's model is New York – a city where the undoubted dominance of English is in no way threatened by interference from Spanish. "I am certainly not in favor of a Tower of Babel that will quake and crumble with the frustrations of incomprehension. Instead, I want to defend code-switching as one of democracy's most effective speech-acts, along with translation and speaking English through heavy accents, because they all slow down communication and labor through the difficulties of understanding and reaching agreement" (Sommer 1998, 298). Negotiating the terms of a new "polyglossic civility" (Cronin 2003, 100) involves a recognition of the different roles that languages play in the very diverse contexts of North American cities – and the changing functions of translation across the contact zones of the continent.

NOTES

1 The map can be seen at http:/www.mla.org/map_single (viewed 18 May 2008).
2 But Marc Shell warns: "It is deceptively easy nowadays in the predominantly anglophone United States to 'celebrate' linguistic diversity. In much the same way it is safe, in a territory where all tigers are believed to be extinct, to celebrate biological diversity. Indeed, the very disappearance of another group's language often provides the dominant group with a sublime platform from which to enjoy it, as well as a tragedian's soapbox on which to bemoan the loss of language diversity. Such decriers can be compared with the imperial Roman grammarians who made anthologies of non-Latin literature gathered from colonial outposts as if to 'preserve' them in imperial translations that 'incorporate and transcend' (sublate) them – as in a jar of assorted 'language preserves'" (2001, 8–9).

10

"Lucky to be so bilingual": Québécois and Chicano/a Literatures in a Comparative Context

MONIKA GIACOPPE

They say "you're lucky to be so bilingual." you wonder:
"what's luck got to do with it?"

Susanne de Lotbinière-Harwood

Inter-American literary studies has long focused primarily on the relations between US and Spanish American literatures. Recently, the Caribbean and English-speaking Canada have begun to receive more substantial attention from scholars in the United States, a positive development indeed – but Quebec still remains somewhat on the sidelines, considered more often in the context of the francophone world than in hemispheric American studies. With this chapter, I propose a more thorough integration of Québécois literature into the field of inter-American studies, specifically through comparison with US Chicano/a writing. The striking parallels between Québécois and Chicano/a literatures have, as yet, received scant notice. Perhaps this is because the scholars in these fields all too often remain artificially divided by departments, disciplines, reading habits, and even habits of mind. Nonetheless, the literatures they study grapple with many common themes and issues, and scholars in either field could benefit from acquainting themselves with work done by their colleagues from across those disciplinary borders.

Although all Latino/a literatures share some common concerns with Québécois literature, the parallels between Québécois and Chicano/a writing are especially compelling. In fact, the very words used to name them provide one of those parallels. But before proceeding further, it may be useful to pause for some explanation of the terms "Québécois/e" and "Chicano/a." The history of naming in French Canada is particularly vexed because the English colonizers who took over former New France in 1763 also took over the name these earlier inhabitants had used for themselves: "Canadien" (in French) became "Canadian" (in English). As Ralph Sarkonak summarizes the problem:

> Lord Durham said of the Canayens that they were "a people with no history, and no literature." Now they had no name to call their own either ... And as if to underscore the secondary, derivative status of these, the descendants of the first inhabitants of the country to consider themselves as Canadians, an awkward appendage was found to isolate them in their regrettable difference: the word *French* was added to *Canadian* in order to mark the difference of language and culture until such time as the name itself was to become redundant by the planned anglicization of the colony's Francophone inhabitants. (1983a, 8)

But the political unrest of the era in Quebec known as the Quiet Revolution generated a desire for a new name, one that would indicate an identity independent of Canada's – and thus one in keeping with the province's aspirations for independent status. The word "Québécois" had long been used to designate the inhabitants of Quebec City. In 1963 the editors of *Parti pris*, a journal described by Lise Gauvin as "separatist, socialist, secularist" (1983, 36), issued a call for the creation of a new "québécois" literature, initiating the use of the term to describe the French-speaking inhabitants of the entire province (Sarkonak 1983a, 11). No longer a hyphenated minority group, the Québécois took a first step toward their goal of becoming *maîtres chez soi* – masters in their own house. This move toward a name affirming a single, unified identity parallels the use of the word "Chicano" – a choice implying a political stance accepted by some, but not all, people of Mexican heritage living in the United States. In *The Hispanic Condition*, Ilan Stavans documents the use of "Chicano" as early as 1947, tracing it to short fiction published by Mario Suárez in the *Arizona Quarterly* (2001, 84). However, the term did not become popularized until the political struggles of the 1960s galvanized a cultural and civil-rights movement that mobilized Chicanos and other Latinos. Chicano activists, inspired by the Black Power movement, formed their own Brown Beret organization in

Los Angeles (94). Québécois activists, whose economic deprivation
was underscored by the findings of the 1963 Royal Commission on
Bilingualism and Biculturalism, likewise saw parallels between the
discrimination they faced and the discrimination confronted by
African Americans.[1] The title of Pierre Vallières's "precocious autobiography," *Nègres blancs d'Amérique* (White Niggers of America)
(1967), is, from this distance, perhaps the most surprising evidence
of that sense of solidarity, reminding readers of the intense anger
and alienation experienced by some French speakers in Quebec
during the Quiet Revolution.

Thus naming itself can be a contentious issue for both Québécois
and Chicano writers because the very question of which language(s)
to use has been a locus of struggle and resistance for literally hundreds of years. If language – and hybrid languages – appears as such
a vital issue in these two literatures, it is because their vocabulary
and syntax bear the traces of historical – and contemporary – battles
for power and identity. Hispanophones in northern Mexico and the
south-western US, like francophones in Quebec, were once powerful
majority cultures whose populations were established as part of a
larger plan to promote Catholicism in the "New World." Of course,
this plan was conceived and executed in different fashions by the
Spanish and French Crowns, leading to very different patterns of
colonization in New France and New Spain. Perhaps because of the
differing patterns of Native settlement, the unwelcoming climate,
and the relatively meager economic gains that were readily available,
the French presence in North America grew comparatively slowly and
peacefully. It contrasts starkly with the military conquest by which
Spain overthrew Native governments throughout the Caribbean,
South and Central America, and what is now the US Southwest over
the course of the sixteenth and seventeenth centuries, conquests during
which Native peoples were "invited" by the infamous "requirement"
to "convert" to Catholicism and declare their allegiance to the
Spanish monarchs. In Canada, instead of dominating by military
force, the French (and, later, Canadien) *coureurs de bois* who participated in the fur trade found it most beneficial to work with, rather
than try to dominate or eliminate, the Native population. In fact,
the *coureurs de bois* often married indigenous women, establishing
family units and, eventually, a new culture, known as the Métis
because of the racial mixing by which they were constituted. As
Monika Kaup comments in an essay comparing Gloria Anzaldúa's

Borderlands/La Frontera (1987) with Maria Campbell's Métis auto-biography, *Halfbreed* (1973), the traders "came neither to settle nor to convert or civilize." Instead, "[r]elations of equality prevailed between Indian tribes and European fur traders, whose survival and economic success depended on the cooperation of Natives" (2002, 197). As permanent settlement for agricultural purposes increased, the nature of this relationship was altered, and the colony's religious and missionary nature grew more pronounced. Under French governance of the region, from 1608 to 1760 immigration was open to Catholics only (Rioux 1980, 36).

But the vagaries of colonialism turned the tables on both the Spanish and the French colonizers: anglophone Protestants who saw their rise to power as proof of the superiority of their "race," religion, and culture displaced the French and Spanish colonial regimes throughout much of North America. Although the phrase "manifest destiny" refers specifically to a nineteenth-century US ideology, white, Anglo-Saxon Protestants on both sides of the US-Canada border invoked remarkably similar rhetoric to justify and explain the "inevitability" of their ascendance. In *Redeemer Nation*, Ernest Lee Tuveson cites a speech given in the United States Senate by "statesman-historian" Albert J. Beveridge, in which Beveridge establishes the role of the United States in world history and affairs by declaring that God has "been preparing the English-speaking and Teutonic peoples" to become "master organizers of the world to establish system where chaos reign[s]." Confident that God's training has readied "Americans" to "administer government among savage and senile peoples," Beveridge declares, with some satisfaction, that "of all our race He has marked the American people as His chosen nation to finally lead in the redemption of the world" (1968, vii). This expectation, albeit tailored to an English audience, is echoed in the infamous report prepared by Lord Durham in the aftermath of the 1837 Rebellion in Lower Canada: "I entertain no doubt of the national character which must be given to Lower Canada; it must be that of the British Empire; it must be that of the great race which must in the lapse of no long period of time be predominant over the whole North American continent" (quoted in See 1986, 56).

Language, then, was not the only marker of perceived difference between the old colonizers and the new. British and Anglo-American attitudes toward French- and Spanish-speaking populations were conditioned by intensely held beliefs about Anglo "superiority" and

Latin "inferiority." We can perhaps better imagine the common issues confronted by French-speaking Canadians and Spanish-speaking "Americans" when we remember that, during this same era, England was pursuing its anti-Catholic colonial designs in Ireland and that the Treaty of Guadalupe-Hidalgo closing the Mexican-American War followed only eleven years after the outbreak of the 1837 Rebellion in Lower Canada.

Thus both cultures have been haunted by a sense of nostalgia, a feeling of exile in what they saw as their own homelands, the very earth to which they were intimately tied. Speaking to this history, Stavans suggests that Chicanos "have experienced a different type of exile than have other Hispanics." In a comment that could just as easily apply to the francophone population of Canada, Stavans continues: "Although Chicanos are at home in the United States, it isn't that they came north, as other Latinos, but that *el norte* came to them" (2001, 80). Or, as Anzaldúa describes in *Borderlands/La Frontera*, following the fall of the Alamo in 1836, "*Tejanos* lost their land and, overnight, became the foreigners" (1987, 6). With the Treaty of Guadalupe-Hidalgo, Mexico lost nearly half its territory to the United States. Stavans declares that "Hispanics, unable to recover from history, are obsessed by memory" (2001, 156) – but surely the same is true of the Québécois, with the provincial licence plate that reads "Je me souviens." The voice of Quebec itself exhorts its people to survive and remember, as in the famous closing pages of Louis Hémon's *Maria Chapdelaine* (1917), also cited as the epigraph to and in the opening dialogue of Félix-Antoine Savard's *Menaud, Maître-draveur* (1937). After an incantatory listing of French-language place names, Quebec declares: "Nous sommes venus il y a trois cents ans, et nous sommes restés ... Autour de nous des étrangers sont venus, qu'il nous plaît d'appeler des barbares: ils ont pris presque tout le pouvoir; ils ont acquis presque tout ... mais au pays de Québec rien n'a change. Rien ne changera, parce que nous sommes un témoinage" (Hémon 1990, 193–4).[2] This voice calls on the people of Quebec to live as their ancestors did, to stay on the land, and to change nothing – to keep faith with the tradition that precedes them but was disrupted by newcomers. Given how much this historical experience resembles that of Chicanos in the United States, it is hardly surprising that the resulting literatures engage many similar concerns.

To some degree, one might consider the literatures themselves to be products of the same earth that fed the peoples of these two cultures, largely agricultural until the past few decades. This attitude has been expressed with singular strength in much Chicano/a writing: "This land was Mexican once, / was Indian always / and is. / And will be again," proclaims Anzaldúa (1987, 3). Similarly, John Phillip Santos invokes the land as his family's only remaining heirloom: "Even if everything else had been lost – photographs, stories, rumors, and suspicions – if nothing at all from the past remained for us, the land remains, as the original book of the family. It was always meant to be handed down" (1999, 10). This attachment to the land, strongly influenced by Native American traditions, may also be discerned in Rudolfo Anaya's classic bildungsroman, *Bless Me, Ultima* (1972). The novel's protagonist, young Antonio Márez, learns from the *curandera* Ultima that "even the plants had a spirit." Out in the hills, he studies her way of walking and finds that, when he imitates her successfully, "[he] was no longer lost in the enormous landscape of hills and sky. [He] was a very important part of the teeming life of the llano and the river" (1989, 36–7).

Of course, although the claiming of a privileged link to the land is a valuable move for budding nationalist movements, it is nevertheless a problematic gesture. After all, Chicanos and Québécois have been both oppressors and oppressed. French and Spanish settlers dispossessed (and intermarried with) Native peoples who had occupied the territory for hundreds, if not thousands, of years. Generations later, Anglo settlers arrived and displaced both Chicanos and Québécois. As several critics have noted, especially in the Chicano context, this history complicates the "natural" relationship to the land that some movement writers and activists have proposed. As José Aranda Jr, warns: "The Chicano/a Movement could never have succeeded in a contest with the American Indian Movement over native sovereignty as a political or moral right" (2005, 18). Similarly, Daniel Cooper Alarcón cautions: "We should also ask who is being excluded when Chicanos stake a claim to the Southwest based on Aztlán, whether that claim is legitimated through myth, history, or genealogy. Obviously Native Americans must be included in these debates, as must the Asian Americans and African Americans living in the region" (1997, 30). Furthermore, Cooper Alarcón observes that "the tendency [in Chicano studies] to focus on the Southwest

minimiz[es] the attention paid to Chicanos who live in other geographic regions" and thus becomes one of several ways that a false
homogeneity has been projected onto Chicanos and Chicanas whose
lives may, in reality, be quite different (8). Although these critiques
are certainly appropriate, it remains true that, especially during the
1960s and 1970s, Chicano and Québécois artists and activists alike
granted the US Southwest and the province of Quebec an elevated
status in their creative and political discourses.

Although an attachment to the land is an important feature of
both Chicano and Québécois writing, one important distinction
between the two literatures is that the early *métissage* between the
coureurs de bois and Native peoples did not so quickly give rise to
a settled population of farmers, as in the US Southwest. Instead,
there was at first a largely mobile population that pushed farther
inland as white settlers occupied growing expanses of Canadian
territory. However, as noted previously, with fixed settlements came
an increased emphasis on developing a community of French-speaking
Catholics capable of serving as a model to the rest of North America
– and in the eyes of the metropole, this model did not involve racial
mixing. Thus Québécois writers would find it difficult even to try to
invoke the same unbroken claim to the land invoked by Anzaldúa
(1987) and Santos (1999). Accordingly, even though the *romans du
terroir* (novels of the land) of the late nineteenth and early twentieth
centuries often do propose a sort of mystical association between
the people and their land, that association owes far less to Native
tradition than to an ideological need to promote the farmer as the
"dépositaire de toutes les vertus de la race," consecrated by daily
labour and isolation from the corrupting power of English (Bouchard
1998, 119).[3]

The initial French settlements lined the St Lawrence River with
seigneuries rather than with centralized, New England-style villages.
Thus the parish took on administrative as well as religious functions,
and the Catholic Church "became the major social institution and
primary force in the formation of a French Canadian identity" (See
1986, 49). French Canada became even more rural after "la Cession,"
known in English as "the Conquest." Katharine O'Sullivan See notes
that "[i]n 1759 the French population was 75% rural; by 1825 this
proportion had increased to 85%" (51). Even as late as 1871, 80 per
cent of the population remained rural, according to Sarkonak (1983b,
278). The lifestyle that connected French Canadians to the land of

their forefathers is celebrated in novels such as Antoine Gérin-Lajoie's *Jean Rivard, le défricheur* (1862), Louis Hémon's *Maria Chapdelaine* (1917), and Lionel Groulx's *Les Rapaillages* (1916). As Earl Fitz writes of *Maria Chapdelaine*, these novels promote "a certain kind of culture for French Canada, one that equates nature (in all its forms) with God and both of these to the supposed moral supremacy of Québec's rural Catholic culture" (1991, 222).

However, the poverty endured on some of these farms, especially with the large families encouraged by the Catholic Church as part of the *revanche des berceaux* (revenge of the cradle), was gruelling. Eventually, it took its toll. Between 1851 and 1900, 500,000 French Canadians crossed the southern border into the United States, where many of them found work in the textile mills of New England. Quebec's rural population began to decline dramatically – by 1911, it had dropped to 52 per cent, and by 1929, 63 per cent of the people lived in urban areas (Sarkonak 1983b, 277–9). This change, of course, gave rise to a new sort of writing in Quebec, exemplified by novels such as Gabrielle Roy's *Bonheur d'occasion* (1945),[4] which offered readers an "urban social realism" (New 1991, 179). A similar split also characterizes Chicano/a literature, which, according to Stavans, has "a couple of clear venues: an urban setting and the itinerant rural life of migrant workers" (2001, 80). Yet some of these urban novels still offer a hopefulness not found in some of the Québécois realist novels; Esperanza, the protagonist of Sandra Cisneros's *The House on Mango Street* (1984) exemplifies this phenomenon. Despite the difficulties posed by racism from outside her family and community, and restrictive gender roles within them, Esperanza still finds elements of solace and creativity in her Chicano background and traditions.

Nevertheless, their Catholic and colonial (and postcolonial) contexts have placed special stresses on Chicana and Québécois women, and gender roles have been a topic of particular interest to many writers of both cultures. Although all women in patriarchal societies face a fundamental imbalance of power, this problem is sometimes exacerbated for women of marginalized social groups. These women may be held responsible for preserving traditional languages and cultural practices at home and for making the home a "refuge" from the hostile world beyond the front door. In the cases of Québécois and Chicana women, the matter was, for a long time, further complicated by an adherence to fairly conservative Catholicism as a means of preserving a distinct cultural and linguistic identity. The old French Canadian saying "la langue, gardienne de la foi" (the [French] language, guardian of the faith) linked language and religious faith – to lose one was to risk losing the other (not to mention your soul). "The traditional guardians of the faith and the language," says Sarkonak, were women. "Theirs was to reproduce and not to reason why. The why was clear: in order to *survive* collectively, as priests told them again and again, from thousands of French-Canadian pulpits" (1983a, 16, original emphasis). In this Catholic context, and with the weight of communal cultural survival on their shoulders, Québécois women were presented with the Virgin Mary as the (impossible) ideal to emulate. Over the course of the 1970s, women writers in Quebec began to verbally defy expectations of a pure, patient, long-suffering femininity, willing to devote itself, body and soul, to the project of preserving French Canada from absorption by their English-speaking neighbours. The mother figure in Anne Hébert's 1975 novel, *Les Enfants du sabbat*, is anything but pure and holy. A practising witch, she offers her own daughter up to her husband for ritual sexual initiation into the cult. More shocking still, the novel closes with this same daughter herself poised on the verge of motherhood – how, the reader cannot know. The girl claims it is a second immaculate conception, whereas the sisters at the convent where she is staying are convinced the baby's father is the devil himself. But the scandal created by Denise Boucher's play *Les Fées ont soif*, when performed in 1978, perhaps exceeds that of *Les Enfants du sabbat*. Denied funding by the Greater Montreal Council of the Arts, the play united a triptych of women on stage: Mary (the wife and mother), Madeleine (the prostitute), and a statue of the Virgin Mary. All three of these women speak their minds, lamenting the limitations and expectations that keep them separated, each in her own unchangeable place.

In *Borderlands/La Frontera*, Anzaldúa recounts the repercussions of these restrictive roles and role models in a Chicano context: "The culture and the Church insist that women are subservient to males ... For a woman of my culture there used to be only three directions she could turn: to the Church as a nun, to the streets as a prostitute, or to the home as a mother" (1987, 17). Yet those unchangeable places have in fact changed considerably over the past few decades, helped along by texts from authors such as Anne Hébert and Denise Boucher (and many others) in French and by writers including Gloria

Anzaldúa, Cherríe Moraga, Helena Viramontes, Sandra Cisneros, and
Lorna Dee Cervantes in English, Spanish, and sometimes a mixture
of both. Like their Québécois counterparts, Chicana authors have
also challenged the models of womanhood most conspicuous within
their culture, namely La Malinche and the Virgin of Guadalupe. The
latter, of course, offers a cultural affirmation for Chicano/a(s) that
Mary herself does not provide for the Québécois. Anzaldúa writes:
"Today, *la Virgen de Guadalupe* is the single most potent religious,
political and cultural image of the Chicano/*mexicano*. She, like my
race, is a synthesis of the old world and the new, of the religion and
culture of the two races in our psyche ... She is the symbol of the
mestizo true to his or her Indian values" (30). Given the drawbacks
of identifying only with the Virgin Mother, however, these women
are also recuperating the memory of La Malinche, or Malintzin,
the infamous translator who not only assisted the conqueror in
his conquest but slept with him, too. The epithets given her, "La
Chingada" and "La Vendida" (literally, the "fucked one" and "the
sell-out"), indicate the degree of blame this individual woman has
been made to bear for the Spanish takeover of Mexico. Furthermore,
Chicanas perceived as displaying insufficient commitment to and
solidarity with La Raza have sometimes also had to endure these
names. Cherríe Moraga describes growing up knowing that "[y]ou
are a traitor to your race if you do not put the man first. The potential accusation of 'traitor' or 'vendida' is what hangs above the heads
and beats in the hearts of most Chicanas seeking to develop our own
autonomous sense of ourselves, particularly through sexuality"
(1983, 103). La Malinche has long been condemned for her supposed
betrayal of her race through sex and language; today, Chicana
women, like Québécois women, are demanding the right to self-
determination in these two essential realms.

In contexts as complicated and politicized as Chicano and Québécois
communities, of course, language becomes weighted with importance
as a means of cultural identification, a marker distinguishing the
dominated from the dominators. Linguistic "purity" becomes a
means of cultural resistance and self-definition. Just as Chicanos in
the United States (and the border region) were belittled by canonical
Mexican figures, including Octavio Paz, for their "degraded" Spanish,
Québécois speakers of French faced "good grammar campaigns"
promoting slogans such as "Bien parler, c'est se respecter" (Homel
1988, 56) and, as mentioned, "la langue, gardienne de la foi." Yet

organizations formed to promote the use of French in Canada and Spanish in the United States implicitly – if not explicitly – encouraged the continuing development (and preservation) of identifiably distinct minority groups. According to Lise Gauvin, the Société du parler français au Canada, founded in 1902, sought "to make the *parler* of French Canada better known, and in its monthly bulletin it complied a glossary of Canadian words, systematically leaving aside any expression accepted by the French Academy. It even proposed encouraging the creation of literary works which would be 'propres à faire du parler français au Canada un langage qui répond à la fois au progrès naturel de l'idiome et au respect de la tradition, aux exigences des conditions sociales nouvelles et au génie de la langue française'" (1983, 35).[5] But this position was not without its opponents. "Il existe une langue française; il n'y a pas de langue canadienne. L'idiome canadienne, ce n'est pas une langue, c'est une corruption," declared Marcel Dugas in *Le Nigog* in 1918.[6]

The intensity of the polemics surrounding the development and "quality" of the French spoken in Quebec bear testimony to an implicit understanding of the connections between political status and the status accorded a person's culture – as evidenced by the perceived quality of that person's language. Thus, when English-speaking Canadians began in the 1860s to demean the French spoken in Canada as nothing more than a "patois," the comments were taken as "une attaque violente contre l'identité même des Canadiens français. S'ils ne parlent qu'un patois, il ne vaut pas la peine de se battre pour conserver ce qui les déclasse, leur langue ne mérite alors aucun statut officiel … Leur culture, leur existence même comme nation, sont remises en cause" (Bouchard 1998, 108).[7] This fear, which motivated so much of the prodigious amount of discussion about language in Quebec during the nineteenth and twentieth centuries, was crystallized in comments made by then candidate for prime minister Pierre Trudeau in 1968, when he declared that "French Canadians" should stop demanding more rights and use those at their disposal to better their "lousy French." They might deserve more rights when they could speak better (quoted in Bouchard 1998, 277). Mexican American activists were quicker to draw explicit links between linguistic heritage and other rights; Stavans describes the National Conference of Spanish-Speaking People, established in 1938, as "one of the earliest Chicano civil rights organizations to equate freedom of speech with freedom of language usage" (2001, 155). But as the above comments on French in Quebec and as the first chapter of Paz's *El laberinto de la soledad* (The Labyrinth of Solitude) (1950) clearly indicate, exactly *which* language one should be "free" to speak is another contentious matter.

Obviously, these language battles have long been, and continue to be, about much more than language. In Quebec, as in some US Latino communities, English has been identified as the language of domination, associated with political and economic power. Crossing the linguistic line has often been viewed as an act of betrayal. As Michèle Lalonde says in her famous 1970 poem/poster, "Speak white": "speak white / c'est une langue riche / pour acheter / mais pour se vendre / mais pour se vendre à perte d'âme / mais pour se vendre" (1992, 149).[8] Nonetheless, starting in the 1960s and '70s, writers (like Lalonde herself) began to claim as their own these "bastardized" languages that incorporated "foreign" (chiefly English) vocabulary and syntax, producing texts in joual in Quebec and in a variety of "Spanglishes" in the United States.[9]

The authors who produce these multilingual texts typically do so not as a way of "selling out" but as testimony to the linguistic and political domination that structures their lives. These multilingual texts are the only way of representing "the fragmentation of identity, and the inability to speak from a unified, noncontradictory subject position," as Lourdes Torres describes. "No existing discourse is satisfactory," she continues, "because each necessitates the repression of different aspects of the self" (1991, 275). This point is especially true for women writers and even more so for the lesbian writers who have achieved significant prominence in both Québécois and Latino/a literatures. Although women are often held responsible for preserving the "authentic" language and culture that maintain the lines of demarcation between ethnic groups, writings by authors including Gloria Anzaldúa, Nicole Brossard, Cherríe Moraga, Susanne de Lotbinière-Harwood, and others frequently (and unapologetically) reject that "responsibility" by crossing borders both generic (fiction, theory, memoir) and linguistic. These women refuse to "choose sides" and demonstrate their loyalty by choosing languages.

In *Re-belle et infidèle: La Traduction comme pratique de ré-écriture au féminin/The Body Bilingual: Translation as a Re-Writing in the Feminine*, her groundbreaking work on feminist translation, de Lotbinière-Harwood relates a disturbing encounter in which she refuses a flyer from an independentist protester. Faced first with the

threat of violence and then with derision, she becomes aware of
the dual nature of her refusal: "No to the piece of paper, No to the
political dream you don't share because it would have you choose
and you refuse to, *'pis j'suis pas moins Québécoise que toi pour ça!'*
even if it is true you're almost incapable of writing a text wholly in
French – so what and why should you" (1991, 80, original emphasis). Her words echo Anzaldúa's earlier declaration: "Until I am free
to write bilingually and to switch codes without having always to
translate, while I still have to speak English or Spanish when I would
rather speak Spanglish, and as long as I have to accommodate the
English speakers rather than having them accommodate me, my
tongue will be illegitimate" (1987, 59). In a 1988 interview of
Anzaldúa that de Lotbinière-Harwood conducted at the International
Feminist Book Fair held in Montreal, shortly after the publication
of *Borderlands/La Frontera*, the Québécois author acknowledges
the immediate relevance of Anzaldúa's work in a Canadian context:
"I think the question of border crossings, borderlands in Quebec – in
Canada actually, which is an officially bi-lingual country, and officially bi-cultural – this idea of borders and border crossings and
what we call here the 'two solitudes' is very much ingrained in us"
(Anzaldúa 1989, 42).

The comment cited above highlights some of the common concerns
shared by Chicano/a(s) and Québécois, but it also draws attention
to some of the very important differences that also merit attention
in any study comparing these two cultures. After all, the United
States is neither officially bilingual nor bicultural, and "English
Only" campaigns rear their heads with unfortunate, if predictable,
regularity. Furthermore, as Sherry Simon points out in "Translating
and Interlingual Creation in the Contact Zone" (1999), the situation
of Quebec (and that of French speakers in Quebec) has changed
dramatically in the past thirty to forty years. Laws protecting the use
of French in work and commercial situations in Quebec have enhanced
the status of that language and provided some level of security for
its survival. Although Spanish continues to grow as an economic
and cultural presence in the United States, many Spanish speakers
have yet to experience the substantial improvement in economic
standing recently enjoyed by much of the Québécois population.

These economic gains reflect crucial changes in the status of French
in Quebec, which, with Bill 101 in 1977, became the province's only
official language. Also known as the Charter of the French Language,

this law "required that all signs on billboards and in stores be in French only. It required that business firms be certified by the newly established Office de la Langue Française as using French as the language of business" and that immigrant children – from other Canadian provinces as well as from overseas – attend francophone schools (See 1986, 151). In 1984 this schooling provision was struck down by Canada's Supreme Court, but the very existence of Bill 101 demonstrates that French speakers in Quebec have achieved a level of power not shared by Spanish speakers in the United States. Furthermore, the school-choice issues raised by Bill 101 bear witness to the contradictory position of Quebec francophones, who form a minority within the larger federation of Canada but a majority within their own province.

Accordingly, Québécois literature, which is a minority literature in Canada, retains the status of a majority literature vis-à-vis the immigrant populations within the province. And another point of divergence between Québécois and Chicano/a literatures is presented by the impact of immigrant literatures, *l'écriture migrante*, in Quebec over the past twenty or so years. Although the heyday of joual writing is over, a new type of hybrid literature is reshaping Québécois letters yet again – and challenging Quebec to rethink not just its own identity but also the very concept of identity. Régine Robin's novel *La Québécoite* (1983) is among the most fascinating examples of such writing, and Robin herself has been outspoken in calling attention to the ways that such texts trouble any attempts to establish a unitary, monolithic Québécois literature or culture.[10] In an article titled "Un Québec pluriel," Robin declares that this migrant literature "inscrit toujours du transitoire, de la dualité, de la double appartenance, de l'inquiétante étrangeté, de la pluralité, de l'hybridité. Elle est, au-delà de la multiplicité des écritures … interrogation sur … les mythes de fondation qui prévalent ici" (1993, 303).[11] When Robin asks, "Qui est Québécois aujourd'hui?" (303), the question is a deeply destabilizing one.

In this respect, the situation of Chicano/a literature stands in sharp contrast. Despite the steady increase in the US Latino population and the growing interest in Latino literature in the United States, Chicano/a writing remains a minority literature in this country. Spanish-speaking Americans (in the US, that is) still exert relatively little influence in defining the national literary canon, and discussions of the relationships between history, literature, and culture that have shaped this nation still tend to focus inordinate attention on New England. As recently as 1991, Ramón Saldívar protested what he saw as the "systematic exclus[ion]" of Chicano/a literature and literary criticism from "the traditional framework of American literature." He also described this exclusion in the present tense: "Works by Mexican-American authors are absent from the American literary histories, the anthologies of American literature, and from the syllabi of courses on American literature. Spanish departments in American universities have also participated in this strategy of exclusion" (1991, 11).

This, of course, is not the only point of divergence between Chicano/a and Québécois literatures and cultures. For, despite their many elements of kinship, these two cultures are distinguished by some fundamental differences. Instead of diminishing our hopes for meaningful comparisons, these differences should further fuel our curiosity. More extended studies comparing Québécois and Chicano/ a literatures and cultures might also usefully incorporate consideration of the Acadians of Canada and the Cadiens (Cajuns) of Louisiana, who have shared the experiences of both privilege and violent dispossession (the Grand Dérangement) yet have managed to maintain unique cultures and traditions in countries where they were initially marginalized, sometimes even unwelcome. The striking historical and linguistic similarities among all three of these groups establish a solid common ground for cross-cultural study, while the important differences in development should help us to achieve a deeper, more nuanced understanding of both literatures and cultures.

NOTES

1 The Commission Report described "a very noticeable disparity in income between Canadians of French and British origin." Specifically, "Canadians of French origin earned about 80 per cent of the average income of those of British origin" (Innis 1973, 82). In Quebec, unilingual anglophones earned more than any other ethnic/linguistic group. Their earnings exceeded even those of bilinguals. Unilingual French speakers earned less than anyone else in the province, except for people of Italian origin. See Innis (1973).

2 "We came here three hundred years ago, and we stayed ... Around us came strangers, whom we are happy to call barbarians: they took nearly all the power; they acquired nearly everything ... but in the country of

Quebec, nothing has changed. Nothing will change, because we are here
to bear witness" (my translation).

3 "depository of all the virtues of the race" (my translation).

4 Roy's novel was translated in 1947 as "The Tin Flute," a title that bears
no relation to its original title, *Bonheur d'occasion* (Second-Hand
Happiness).

5 The translation provided by Gauvin reads: "suitable to making French
in Canada a language that corresponded with the natural progress of the
idiom and the respect for tradition, the needs of new social conditions,
and the spirit of the French language itself." Gauvin cites "La société du
parler français au Canada," *Bulletin de la société du parler français au
Canada* 1, no. 1 (1902): 3.

6 "A French language exists; a French-Canadian language does not exist.
The French-Canadian idiom is not a language, it is a corruption." Both
the original quotation and the translation are from Gauvin (1983, 35).

7 "a violent attack against the very identity of the French Canadians. If
they speak a mere patois, it's not worth fighting to preserve the very
thing that degrades them; their language then merits no official status ...
Their culture, their very existence as a nation are thrown into question"
(my translation).

8 "speak white / it's a rich language / for buying / but to sell yourself /
but to sell yourself and lose your soul / but to sell yourself" (my
translation).

9 Homel defines "joual" as follows: "Take standard Quebec French,
increase the dipthongization, make the grammar remarkably flexible, and
add a healthy dose of Anglicisms – or better, Americanisms. It's this latter
addition that gives *joual* its special savour and creates monumental problems for those brave and foolish souls who try to put a *joual*izing work
into English. For not only does *joual* accept English words into its lexi-
con, it also distorts them once they are inside, in a kind of sabotage
action against a linguistic occupying force" (1988, 56).

10 Translated into English in 1993 as *The Wanderer* by Phyllis Aronoff, this
novel in three parts recounts the experiences of a Jewish woman from
France, a historian, who moves to Montreal. The three parts of the novel
correspond to three entirely different Montreal neighbourhoods and the
life she might possibly create for herself in each of them. The novel is
very much a hybrid text, incorporating substantial use of English and
also testifying to the discomfort of a native French speaker confronted
by "her" language as it is spoken in the markedly different context
of Montreal.

11 "always inscribes the provisional, a sense of duality, of double
belonging, of a troubling strangeness, of plurality, of hybridity. It is,
beyond the multiplicity of the writings ... an interrogation of ...
the myths of foundation that prevail here" (my translation).

11

Louis Dantin's American Life

PATRICIA GODBOUT

In this chapter,[1] I attempt to situate Louis Dantin's work and life trajectory in a North American context.[2] The idea was inspired by an invitation sent out a while ago to comparative-literature critics and scholars to situate certain issues and problematics within the framework of what Winfried Siemerling has dubbed "the new North American studies." One of the advantages of this reconfiguration, according to Siemerling, is that it allows us to escape the synecdoche whereby "America" stands for the United States. "North America is a relational designation that marks it as [the] Northern *part* of a larger entity, which it does not claim to stand for or represent – yet which it could certainly draw on for contextual and differential self-understanding alike" (2005, 1, original emphasis). Louis Dantin's life invites such a reframing by the scholar: first, because this great critic of French Canadian literature and "discoverer" of Émile Nelligan (1879–1941) – the young prodigy who sank into "the black gulf of Dream" before he was twenty and whose poems Dantin can also be credited for saving from oblivion[3] – spent more than half his life in the United States, where he worked for many years as a typographer at Harvard University Press in Boston; and, second, because he himself tried to rethink and redefine America when he gave to two of his volumes of critical essays the programmatic title *Poètes de l'Amérique française* (1928 and 1934).[4] As we shall see, Dantin also became a critic and translator of American literature in the late 1930s and early 1940s.

Louis Dantin, whose real name was Eugène Seers, used many different pseudonyms throughout his life. A few weeks before his death, when taken to a hospice in Boston, he registered under the half-fictitious name of Ferdinand Seers.[5] His turbulent and far from commonplace life began not far from Montreal, in Beauharnois, where he was born in 1865 to a distinguished family that was English in name only.[6] At the age of seventeen, "under the impulse of a mystical fervour," the young Eugène joined the congregation of the Pères du Saint-Sacrement as a novice in Brussels. He then went on to study philosophy at the Gregorian University in Rome, but when he earned his doctorate in philosophy in 1887, his religious faith was already "rather shaken," in contrast with his "natural mysticism." Nevertheless, the following year, according to Réjean Robidoux, he "let himself be ordained to the priesthood" at Saint-Sulpice Church in Paris (in Dantin 1997, 40–1).

His superiors still held him in high regard and entrusted him with sensitive posts within the community, such as master of the novices at the convent in Brussels. The year 1893 marked the beginning of a love affair with a fifteen-year-old girl, Charlotte Beaufaux, whose brother was a novice. The following year, Father Seers left the convent but was forced by the superiors of the religious community and by his father to return to Canada. During the following decade, while he appeared to be living the convent life in Montreal, Dantin learned the art of printing, and he published poetry using various pseudonyms. In 1897 he met Émile Nelligan,[7] a member of the newly formed École littéraire de Montréal. As early as 1901, after Nelligan's confinement, Dantin began to collect his poems with the aim of publishing them. Meanwhile, Dantin was living more and more on the margins of his religious community. In 1902 he met a young woman by the name of Clotilde Lacroix, and they both fled Montreal the following year, before the release in 1904 of *Émile Nelligan et son œuvre*, edited by Dantin. With regard to this publication, Réjean Robidoux writes quite aptly: "This event, which should have been of the utmost importance to these two exceptional beings, the poet and the critic, took place quite removed from each of them, both having been fatefully denied any rejoicing and deprived of all sense of self" (in Dantin 1997, 50).

A son, Joseph Adéodat, was born to Dantin and Clotilde Lacroix in Cambridge in April 1904. After Clotilde left him in 1909, Dantin ended his literary silence when he was invited by Germain Beaulieu, a member of the École littéraire de Montréal with whom he was corresponding, to contribute to the literary journal *Le Terroir*. When one of his poems was published in the journal, he chose to sign it

"Louis Dantin." In a letter to Beaulieu in May 1909, Dantin, who had been living in Boston for six years, wrote: "Tell everyone that Louis Dantin is a regular fellow who has retired to his land near Cape St-Ignace" (quoted in Nadeau 1948, 97).[8]

Dantin, however, did not resume an active literary career until 1920, when he began to submit essays and critical pieces for publication in *La Revue moderne*, then in *L'Avenir du Nord* and *Le Canada*. He began to write critical reviews of works by French Canadian writers such as Paul Morin, Robert Choquette, and Alfred DesRochers. It is interesting to note that these three writers, like many others, all had American connections: Morin taught at Smith College in Northampton, Massachusetts, and at the University of Minnesota between 1910 and 1920, and he also translated Henry Wadsworth Longfellow; DesRochers lived with his family in Rhode Island in 1914–15 shortly after his father passed away; and Choquette was born in Manchester, New Hampshire, and spent his childhood in New England. In fact, it was because of another americanophile, Olivar Asselin, that Dantin began contributing to *La Revue moderne*,[9] and in his correspondence with Dantin, Asselin referred quite regularly to the American books he was reading (Nadeau 1948, 85–90).

Besides his reviews of French Canadian poetry and prose, and his column on American books, which I discuss below, Dantin made a few incursions into other corpora. Two are worthy of note: the first, published on 15 December 1920 in *La Revue moderne*, is a review of an anthology of Haitian poetry,[10] and the second is a review of Lorne Pierce's 1927 anthology, *An Outline of Canadian Literature (French and English)*. The latter "is not only about literature in English," wrote Dantin, because it presents "a complete synthesis of literary creation in our country, as much in the language of Champlain as in the language of Wolfe" (2002, 366). It is interesting to note Dantin's use of the possessive "our" in this review, which was first published in *Le Canada* on 8 May 1928.[11] The use of the possessive reveals an undeniable sense of belonging to the French Canadian literary community. But, at the same time, Dantin had then been living in the United States for twenty-five years, and this certainly contributed to his feeling of not really belonging to any particular group and of not even having any real material existence. In a letter to Olivar Asselin in 1920, he described himself as "an indeterminate and ill-defined being" (quoted in Nadeau 1948, 70–1). Asselin had written to Dantin because he wished to include him in

the *Anthologie des poètes canadiens* (1920) that he was preparing –
and that Dantin himself would later review (Dantin 2002, 134–43).
"You almost made me feel like I was still part of this world," was
the response Asselin received on 13 May 1920 from Dantin, who in
other letters had described himself as "exiled and dead" (128, 131).

In fact, as we shall see, Dantin progressively and almost despite
himself became just as inhabited by America as he himself inhabited
it. Furthermore, this man, who was steeped in European culture,
participated in the awareness that French Canadians were acquiring
of belonging to the American continent. As Jean Morency points
out, like other scholars before him, the 1930s seem to be an important time in this regard. In the introduction to a recent issue of the
international Quebec studies journal *Globe*, devoted to francophone
Americanness, Hans-Jürgen Lüsebrink notes that Americanness
(*l'américanité*) has been a field of research and discussion at the
forefront of Quebec literary studies for the past twenty years (2004,
11). In his article in the same issue of this journal, Morency defines
Americanness in terms of its contrasts with Americanization
(*l'américanisation*): whereas the latter is most often used to mean
subjection to the economic and cultural power of the United States,
Americanness, he says, is associated with "freely chosen influences,
and conscious and voluntary cultural transfers" (2004, 40–1).

Morency also refers to Louis Dantin's Americanness in an article
about a sort of (re)discovery of America by French Canadians during
the 1920s and '30s. He categorizes Dantin with good reason among
the "cultural mediators in Quebec between the two world wars"
(2005, 306). He also includes Choquette among those mediators
who, as previously mentioned, had a direct experience of American
life. Choquette wrote, among other things, a fine book of poems
titled *Metropolitan Museum* (1931), which was illustrated with
magnificent woodcut illustrations by the Canadian artist Edwin
Holgate – who was invited in 1929 to become the eighth member
of the Group of Seven (Pepall 2002, 12). Morency also highlights
the role that DesRochers played as cultural mediator. Throughout
the 1930s, in his correspondence with Dantin[12] and others, DesRochers
often referred to the many American books he was reading. The
Eastern Townships of Quebec, where DesRochers was living at the
beginning of the twentieth century, was still in many ways an extension of New England.[13]

As Morency says, we cannot disregard the importance of the vast migratory movement from French Canada to New England between 1840 and 1930. But what is less often mentioned is that the flow back to Quebec, after a more or less lengthy stay in the United States, was also quite considerable. According to Morency, this to-and-fro movement "contributed to the profound change in the perception of the United States among the working classes and, to a lesser degree, among the social elite" (2005, 301). The reasons that brought Dantin to Boston were personal, of course, but one cannot help ask whether his choice of country of exile was not motivated in part by the wave of immigration to the north-eastern region of the United States. In any case, I think it is significant that it was on American territory that Dantin returned to a literary life and, as it were, once again found his "vocation."

In a chapter of *Intérieurs du Nouveau Monde* entitled "Le poème québécois de l'Amérique," Pierre Nepveu notes that for the many Quebecers who emigrated "to *yankee* country, it did not turn out to be the difficult road to knowledge"[14] that one might have thought it would be. He believes instead that "our most famous emigrants," like Jack Kerouac, were as much victims of the American mirage as they were heroes and that they continue to foster "the double image of expansion and degradation, an image that represents for us an intoxicating yet catastrophic Americanness, both terms feeding off of each other" (1998, 183).

As for Dantin, he did not seem to have let himself be unduly carried away by the intoxicating America to which Nepveu refers. In March 1925, however, in a letter to his son, who had studied at the Massachusetts Institute of Technology and who had left home in 1924 to work in Washington, DC, Dantin wrote (in English) that as a resident of Boston he was taking advantage of the easy access he had to American films. Since real life had ceased to interest him, he explained, he was seeking refuge in the world of dreams (1963, 20).[15]

On a few occasions, in other letters to his son, Dantin describes his work as a typographer for the printing office at Harvard University Press in Cambridge. Dantin held this job from November 1919 until his retirement in March 1938 at the age of seventy-two. He started working at the printing office of the press toward the end of the term of its first director, C.C. Lane.[16] He continued to work there throughout the period that Max Hall, in *Harvard University Press:*

A History (1986, 43), called "the Murdoch Years" (1920–34), under the direction of Harold Murdoch, and also during the beginning of the Dumas Malone administration (1935–43). Dantin, it seems, had adopted a very discreet attitude at work. For example, on 20 April 1937, shortly before his retirement, he wrote to his son: "I know now why they kept me in the shop with so many others dismissed. The boss told me some days ago: it was because *I mind my own business!* I had another pat on the back, very unexpected, from Mr. [David] Pottinger, who is now Associate Director of the Press ... And today Mr. [Dumas] Malone, the *head chief*, was in the shop and wanted to shake my dirty hands in congratulation!" (1963, 40, original emphasis).[17] It also seems, according to Dantin, that the printing-office management realized quite early on that he could do more than correct galley proofs, and he was given work of a more artistic nature (20).

According to Gabriel Nadeau, a doctor who was working at the Rutland sanatorium in Massachusetts and with whom Dantin had corresponded since 1933 (Dantin 2002, 93), living conditions made it difficult for him to keep up his literary activities: "While he arranged the printing type [in his day job as typographer], he composed verse or the plan for an article, which he would then write in the evening. He wrote notes on bits of paper, and took them home with him" (1948, 122). In addition to these writing activities, Dantin, who worked six days a week, shared the basic financial preoccupations of the class of American workers and low-wage earners to which he belonged.

It was probably because he experienced America "day by day," as in the title of Simone de Beauvoir's *L'Amérique au jour le jour* (1948), that Dantin was neither backward-looking nor risk-averse where technological progress was concerned. In his review of Georges Bouchard's *Vieilles choses et vieilles gens* (1926),[18] Dantin reacts to the author's nostalgic comments on "so-called progress." He felt that, on the contrary, industrial inventions "make life easier for the worker and allow him more leisure time. Their vices are not an essential part of them and could disappear with the same impulse for life that produced them. In an even more advanced society, where an interest in beauty has been revived, where there is less rapaciousness and greed, men will reap the benefits of industry without having to pay for it with a part of their soul" (2002, 293).

As early as 1921, in his review of Lionel Groulx's *Chez nos ancêtres* (1920), Dantin declared how illusory it is to want to bring French Canadians back to the days of the feudal land tenants of the eighteenth century. "It is not only the railways and factory chimneys that make this dream illusory," he wrote, "it is a whole world of institutions and ideas that has emerged since then: it is Rousseau, Karl Marx and Auguste Comte; it is a dozen revolutions, each of which has had an effect on us; it is the parliamentary system and feminism … it is the earth that carries us and the water we drink" (2002, 219).

The economic crisis of the 1930s strengthened Dantin's socialist leanings. There are definite hints of this in his correspondence with DesRochers. For example, DesRochers told him in a letter dated 11 November 1932 (Fonds Alfred-DesRochers [FAD]) that he was studying economics by reading, in particular, John Maynard Keynes's *Treatise on Money* (1930) and that he was also very attracted to socialism. Dantin responded that if this were the case, "I wonder if it is necessary to study these other theories so intensively. Once socialism is established, all these theories will collapse and become history" (FAD, letter dated 28 November 1932). Convinced that the days of capitalism were numbered, Dantin brought up the issue once again not long after: "The first thing socialism will do once in power will be to topple the old economics doctrine; so what is the point of learning it so well?" (FAD, letter dated 12 December 1932). In 1934 he wrote that he was interested in the "political and social experiments" that President Franklin D. Roosevelt of the United States had begun the previous year under the New Deal. As an American citizen – which he considered himself to be – he felt that the results of these experiments were "saving us from the brink of stagnation. Saving capitalism through socialism: Now there's a program that may seem absurd, but it may be the last recourse for a capitalism that is in a desperate state and is absolutely incapable of saving itself" (FAD, letter dated 23 June 1934).[19]

In fact, in 1938 Dantin published in the newspaper *Le Jour* a long heartfelt poem called "La complainte du chômeur," in which we picture the contorted grin of a man discouraged by the spectacle of misery:

C'est à rire, si l'on y songe bien,
Qu'il existe parmi les humains

Tant de compétition et tant d'entraves
Pour le privilège d'être esclaves.
Évidemment, c'est encore trop :
Il faut, de gré ou non, déposer ses fardeaux,
Et les puissances, d'autorité,
Nous imposent les jeûnes de la liberté (1962, 54)[20]

Dantin's socialist opinions regarding the poverty of the unemployed apparently caused him some trouble. In a letter to his son on
2 June 1939, he wrote: "I am engaged now in a polemic on the
question of unemployment with a writer in the Montreal newspaper
[Le Jour] to which I contribute myself. This fellow [Édouard Le
Doret] would suppress by a stroke of the pen all the forms of aid
now granted to the unemployed and let them 'shift for themselves.'
Which is, of course, a preposterous idea, and I have been busy telling
him so" (1963, 45).[21]

On 16 April 1940 he wrote to Joseph Adéodat about his abandoning a series of articles entitled "La vie américaine" (American Life),
which he had begun to publish in Le Jour in January of the same
year alternately with a series on American books begun in 1938:

> Reasons: they censured one of my letters in which I was criticizing
> the industrialists and capitalists for their perpetual complaints
> about their "oppression" by the New Deal, which undeniable
> statistics show to be presently enjoying a constantly improving
> and mounting prosperity. This was too much, wrote the Directeur
> [Jean-Charles Harvey], for some of his announcers to stand.
> And as his paper depended on them for its life, he felt obliged
> to cut it out. So I told him I wouldn't stand myself being gagged
> in that outrageous manner and I have gone back exclusively to
> my criticisms of books in which I still find ways and means of
> telling them sound, unwelcome truths. (1963, 51–2)[22]

Dantin also wrote about this on 1 May 1940 in a letter to his
friend Rosaire Dion-Lévesque, a French American poet and translator living in Nashua, New Hampshire, and declared that it was with
"some distaste" that he continued to write for the newspaper. He
added, on 26 June, "I have been reduced to writing insignificant
analyses of works that are for the most part mediocre; and I feel like

Nero playing the flute while Rome is burning!" (Correspondence between Dantin and Dion-Lévesque, 315, 317).[23]

Although it is true that a good number of the American books reviewed by Dantin in *Le Jour* are not of much interest,[24] some titles are noteworthy, like John Steinbeck's *Grapes of Wrath* (1939). More important, these American pieces indicate a shift in perspective for Dantin. He wrote them as someone who had chosen to live in the United States and who wanted to inform French Canadians of certain social, economic, and literary realities that their neighbours to the south were experiencing. Dantin also translated a few poems – by Amy Lowell, Conrad Aiken, and Ogden Nash, among others, reprinted in *Poèmes d'outre-tombe* (1962) – and he reviewed translations of French novels that were released at the start of the Second World War. On 6 December 1941 he wrote a review of "two brand-new novels" by Louis Aragon and Henri Troyat, "which are released in English translation, they say, before their release in their original language" (1941, 7). Dantin played a very unusual role in this case: that of a critic who lived in the United States, who read in English, and who was attempting to give his French Canadian readers an idea of what the "lost" originals might have looked like.[25]

Dantin's own literary work also contains some traces of his "American life." Of course, in many of his tales, the action takes place in the province of Quebec and the characters wrestle with their various problems and moral dilemmas. However, in some texts, it appears that Dantin was beginning to let himself be influenced by American themes and even the narrative style. This is the case especially in his Christmas tale *La comète*, first published in the newspaper *L'Avenir du Nord* on 22 December 1929.[26] It is the story of a banker called Van Dighen who lives with his family in an unidentified city that we presume to be in the United States. "He was a businessman who loved his family, but showed his love for them mainly by earning a lot of money" (1930, 197). On Christmas Eve the banker decides to contract the services of the "Easy Christmas" agency, whose manager explains to him that the agency offers a way of reviving the Christmas Holiday tradition and making it conform "to our era of progressive ways" (195). The agency provides the tree, decorates it, buys the gifts, sends one of its representatives on Christmas Eve to play Santa Claus and distribute the presents to the children, and, once the celebrations are over, cleans the house.

As the manager explains: "The family will be able to enjoy it all without having to lift a finger" (196). The American entrepreneurial approach is put on display here, which consists of offering all the services you can think of and selling the illusion of effortlessness and comfort. Because it is in fact all about illusion, the representatives of the bogus agency are small-time crooks who conspire to fool this well-to-do family.

More important, Afro-Americanness finds its place in Dantin's work, primarily in his semiautobiographical novel *Les enfances de Fanny* (1951). Dantin was involved in the 1920s with a black woman named Frances Fields Johnston, who died in 1924, apparently of complications following surgery. He began writing this novel toward the end of the 1930s, and in a letter to DesRochers dated 10 February 1939 (FAD), he said the novel was half-completed:

> I am writing it mainly for myself (because I have strong doubts that the Canadian public would be ready any day soon for such a book. The subject and the characters would be of no interest to them; the story line would seem too flat or immoral or both; the fact alone that there is nothing Canadian about it will turn them off to begin with). Describing as I know it the life of black Americans in the first third of the twentieth century is a way for me to release personal observations and memories. I have lived for many years in close proximity to black people and I had frequent contacts with them. Therefore, this book *Fanny* may at least have some educational possibility as an exploration into certain parts of the Neo-African jungle.

In *Odysseys Home: Mapping African-Canadian Literature* (2002), George Elliott Clarke describes the racism in *Fanny* – for example, in the narrator's comments about the finer features that Fanny had inherited from her grandmother, who had been her master's favourite slave, but also, and probably even more so, in the "solution" of miscegenation or assimilation suggested by the love relationship between the white-skinned Donat Sylvain and the black woman Fanny Lewis.

Clarke shows that Dantin and other Québécois writers "engage 'race' in ways that re-inscribe romanticized or demonic constructions of the racial Other, even as they interrogate such reductive visions" (2002, 164). According to Clarke, certain texts written by these authors (among whom, surprisingly, he includes the Quebec writer of Haitian origin Dany Laferrière) demonstrate both a liberal openness to the Other – the alien, the exotic – and a nationalist or ethnocentric resistance to this Other (166). For Clarke, the sympathy expressed by the narrator in *Fanny* for the Afro-Americans in the Roxbury neighbourhood in Boston is an example of the superior attitude displayed by Canadians in reaction to racism in the United States (30–1). According to Clarke, Canada is often represented in contrast with the United States as a land of peace and tolerance – a preconceived idea that he clearly intends to challenge.

I believe that in order to fully grasp the importance of Dantin's novel, one has to place it in its historical context. Only then does it become apparent that, despite its serious shortcomings, this piece of writing is unique in the field of French Canadian literature of the period (a field to which the author belonged for lack of any other alternative). Moreover, Dantin was very aware that his novel was not publishable, during his lifetime at least, in French Canada. But this exiled and ostracized man nevertheless committed himself to writing it. According to Gabriel Nadeau, he had at one point considered writing this story in English and sending it to black literary magazines (1968, 78–9), and it is perhaps no coincidence that, before his death, Dantin entrusted "another" American, Dion-Lévesque, with the manuscript. Furthermore, in light of Dantin's marginal position in the field of Canadian literature and the fact that he wrote this work in the United States, it is somewhat difficult to read *Fanny* solely as yet another example of a Québécois text in which Quebec and Canada are unduly portrayed as a land of tolerance and peaceful racial coexistence.

It is also worth mentioning that through one of Fanny's sons, whose name in real life was Stanley Fields Johnston (and who appears as Édouard in the novel), Dantin got to hear about such black Bostonian leaders as William-Monroe Trotter (1872–1934), co-founder of the *Boston Guardian* newspaper (1903), who, according to Nadeau, hired Stanley as his managing editor in 1919 (1968, 17). Incidentally, Stanley's father (and Fanny's husband) was Frederick Douglass Johnston, named after the black abolitionist. Nadeau also notes that the *Neo-African Review* to which Dantin refers in his novel was in fact based on the *Saturday Evening Quill* (1928–30), edited by Eugene Gordon (106–7).[27] As for Stanley, he apparently went on to set up literary magazines of his own, such as the *Popular*

Poetry Magazine (1933), co-founded with the help of Eugene's wife, Edythe-Mae Gordon, herself a writer. Dantin and Stanley Fields Johnston remained in touch with one another long after Fanny's death.[28]

In conclusion, a re-examination of Louis Dantin's "American life" shows that it occupies in fact a larger symbolic space in his writing than one would have believed at first. A more exhaustive study of the question would entail a close examination of his many articles on American life and literature and of his translations into French of American poets.

It is clear that Dantin's American affinities should be considered within a larger context where French Canadian letters as a whole were repositioning themselves with respect to the hegemony of the French model (Morency 2005, 309). There are undeniable traces of this in Dantin's correspondence with DesRochers. For example, in one of the letters, he shares his enthusiasm for Walt Whitman's poetry, which Dion-Lévesque was translating.[29] Dantin particularly admired Whitman's audacity "to express himself and assert the rights of his soul with such splendid freedom" (FAD, letter dated 28 November 1932). In another letter, he claimed without hesitation that Dion-Lévesque's work had become much more refined since he had come into contact with Whitman's genius, instead of "amusing himself" with Paul Valéry's "lovely little pirouettes": "Paul Valéry, next to Whitman, is it not like Mount-Royal next to Mount Etna?" (FAD, letter dated 23 May 1933).

In *Intérieurs du Nouveau Monde*, Pierre Nepveu writes:

> For the Québécois, the encounter with America is by tradition rarely modest, rarely rooted in the immediate. We try too hard to find an opening, a passage, a salvation. We are in too great a hurry to do away with the tightened borders, with our "French soul," with our interiority, which, more often than not, we consider an incurable disease. We are rushing toward the imaginary figure of "America" as we would toward a mirage, where a pure richness of being could be drawn from life's natural sources. Hence the excessive euphoria and, its opposite, catastrophism (America is either divine, or terribly deceiving and certainly infernal), and also the cause of frequent and determined mimetism, which is finally the same as pretending to be USian (*états-unien*). (1998, 165)

Despite his friends' repeated efforts to persuade him, Dantin did not want to return to Quebec. I do not believe that he was pretending to be American. In fact, he had become, at least in part, an American. Dantin's literary contribution has nonetheless been studied almost exclusively within the French Canadian/Québécois context. (Re)situating writers like him in a larger North American context could also act as an incentive to take a closer look – in the study of New England's literary life in the early twentieth century, for instance – at the active presence of Franco-Americans (often dubbed "la Franco-Américanie") who wrote and published in French and English in places like Worcester (Massachusetts), Lewiston (Maine), or Nashua (New Hampshire) and whose literary and life trajectories intersected at numerous points with those of various other individuals and communities. Dantin's "American life" is a case in point.

NOTES

1 This chapter was translated from the French by Christine Famula, including the various quotations (unless otherwise noted).

2 Louis Dantin (1865–1945) wrote poems, traditional tales, short stories, and a novel, as well as numerous critical essays, which were initially published in various journals, then grouped together in books in the 1930s, and recently published in a two-volume critical edition (Dantin 2002).

3 In 1904 Dantin prepared the first edition of Nelligan's poems and wrote the preface, which remains famous to this day. A critical edition of this book of Nelligan's poems, which contains Dantin's preface, was prepared by Réjean Robidoux under the title *Émile Nelligan et son œuvre* (Dantin 1997). "Foundered, alas! in the black gulf of Dream!" are the last words of the poem "The Ship of Gold" ("Le Vaisseau d'or"), translated by A.J.M. Smith (1970, 42). Nelligan's poetry, "which so many readers have adopted in the past century," figures among the top "five or six" Quebec classics, according to Robert Melançon (2004, 57).

4 *Amérique française* was also the title of a Quebec literary journal (1941–55).

5 See Réjean Robidoux's chronology in Dantin (1997, 55).

6 Dantin wrote about this to Quebec poet Alfred DesRochers in the postscript to a letter dated 1 August 1929: "My first Canadian ancestor was a soldier in Wolfe's army. Having 'conquered' Canada, he settled there and married a Frenchwoman, who taught their sons to call her 'maman.' The sons married other Frenchwomen and, in less than a century, the

language of Shakespeare, the memory of Albion and British phlegm had disappeared to the point where my grandfather fought with Chénier in 1837" (Fonds Alfred-DesRochers [FAD]).

7 See Yvette Francoli's chronology in Dantin (2002, 84). According to Réjean Robidoux, this meeting took place in 1896 (see Dantin 1997, 44).

8 An important article on Dantin's use of pseudonyms is Hébert (2004).

9 Born in the Charlevoix region of Quebec, the journalist and essayist Olivar Asselin (1874–1937) received a classical education at the Séminaire de Rimouski before emigrating to Massachusetts with his family in 1892. In 1895 he was an editor for the newspapers the *National* in Lowell and the *Jean-Baptiste* in Pawtucket, and from 1896 to 1898, he was an editorial assistant for *La Tribune* newspaper in Woonsocket. A volunteer in the Spanish-American War, he was demobilized in 1899 and returned to Montreal, where he contributed to various newspapers, including *Les Débats* (see Pelletier-Baillargeon 1996 and 2001).

10 *Anthologie haïtienne des poètes contemporains (1904–1920) comprenant les poètes qui ont continué ou commencé d'écrire après 1904* (Port-au-Prince, Haiti: Aug. A. Héraux, 1920). Dantin's review was published again in Dantin (1928, 222–46; 2002, 144–58).

11 This review was published again in Dantin (1931, 47–54; 2002, 366–71).

12 In collaboration with Richard Giguère, I am presently working on a critical edition of this correspondence (1928–39). See also Giguère (1996).

13 See Kesteman, Southam, and Saint-Pierre (1998) and Godbout (1996).

14 Winfried Siemerling observes accurately that with *Intérieurs du Nouveau Monde*, Pierre Nepveu "has shifted to North American perspectives and concerns of a wider 'Américanité' that reaches into Latin America" (2005, 9).

15 As it happens, Dantin wrote a book of traditional tales and short stories called *La Vie en rêve* (1930).

16 Under the Lane administration, Harvard University Press moved to Randall Hall, "an unusual red-brick structure on Divinity Avenue at the corner of Kirkland Street, about a block from Harvard Yard. This was to be the home of Harvard University Press for sixteen years and of the printing operation for nearly half a century. Today William James Hall stands on the site" (Hall 1986, 33).

17 Malone's arrival as director of Harvard University Press caused some upheaval at the printing office ("a big shake-up," Dantin wrote to his son on 26 January 1936). Dantin said he preferred Malone's "intelligent management" to the old "disordered hodge-podge" that had previously existed (1963, 37).

18 The editor Louis Carrier translated this book under the pseudonym Alan Hunt Holley and published it in 1928 under the title *Other Days, Other Ways: Silhouettes of the Past in French Canada* with twenty-three woodcut illustrations by Edwin Holgate.

19 In his book, Gabriel Nadeau also refers to Dantin's interest in communism, a bias he attributes to the "vicissitudes of his existence" (1948, 112).

20 "It's pitiful / to think that human beings / compete and strive so hard / for the privilege of being slaves. / But even this / is too much to ask for. / Now we have to lay down our tools / while the powers that be / inflict on us the fasts of freedom." Just before the Second World War, the end of which he did not see since he died in January 1945, Dantin anticipated in this poem the irony of an imminent "solution" to unemployment: "Étrange : si demain s'abattait la guerre, / Le chômage disparaîtrait de la terre" ("How strange: if war broke out tomorrow / Unemployment would be wiped off the face of the earth") (1962, 54). We cannot help comparing this to the poems of his contemporary Émile Coderre, alias Jean Narrache, which were written in the popular jargon that Dantin also liked to use at times. An example of this can be found in Narrache's poem "Les économistes" (1932): "Notr' misèr' ça dépend d'nos vices, / de notr' paresse et d'nos défauts, / à c'que dis'nt les économistes / qui parl'nt à travers leur chapeau" ("Our misery stems from our vices / Our lazyness, our shortcomings / If you listen to the economists / Talking through their hats") (1993, 74). The foregoing translations into English are by John Peter Weldon.

21 See, among others, Dantin's article "Chômage et paresse" (1939). Jean-Charles Harvey was the director and founder of the newspaper *Le Jour*, described on its masthead as "political, literary and artistic."

22 This letter was written in English by Dantin.

23 According to the Roman historian Tacitus and others, Nero actually played the lyre while a fire destroyed much of Rome in AD 64.

24 According to Yvette Francoli (2002, 58–9), Dantin published a total of approximately 150 articles on American literature and current events in *Le Jour* and other publications. He had wanted to group these articles in a volume like he had done with his reviews of French Canadian literature.

25 Aragon's novel *Les voyageurs de l'impériale*, which Dantin read under the title *The Century Was Young*, an English translation by Hannah Josephson (who a few years later translated Gabrielle Roy), was indeed first published in New York (by Duell, Sloan and Pearce) toward the end of 1941. The publication of the French edition lagged far behind because, despite the fact that the Germans had authorized it, the Vichy government

was opposed to the book's release. According to the colophon of
Les voyageurs de l'impériale, the publication date was 18 December
1942. Troyat's novel *Judith Madrier* was published in Paris by Les
Éditions Plon in 1940.

26 *La comète* was reprinted in Dantin (1930, 193–219; 1936, 75–98).

27 "First published in June 1928 in Boston, the *Saturday Evening Quill* was
a literary magazine edited by Eugene Gordon. The publication was a
product of the Boston Quill Club, a literary salon of black intellectuals"
(Wintz and Finkelman 2004, 1084).

28 Gabriel Nadeau's *Dantin et l'Universal Bureau* (1968) was to be the first
part of a trilogy entitled *Dantin parmi les nègres*. The next two works
announced in the preface to *Dantin et l'Universal Bureau – Un amour de
Dantin* and *Dantin dans Roxbury* – were never published. The *Universal
Bureau* was a matrimonial review published by Stanley Fields Johnston
in Boston from 1921 to 1929. It is through this multilingual review
that Dantin met Fanny, after having placed an ad expressing his wish
to correspond with a "Colored or Mulatto lady" (Nadeau 1968, 54),
to which this widow and mother of five responded.

29 Dantin wrote the preface to Dion-Lévesque's *Walt Whitman: Ses meilleures
pages traduites de l'anglais par Rosaire Dion-Lévesque* (1933). The preface
has been republished in Dantin (2002, 655–9).

12

Transculturation and National Identity in the Novel *Rojo, amarillo y verde* by Alejandro Saravia

HUGH HAZELTON

PROLOGUE:
CANADIAN LITERATURE IN LATIN AMERICA
AND VICE VERSA

Canada and Latin America have a long and complex literary relationship that includes both parallel historic, artistic, and cultural currents and a remarkable number of authors who have written about their mutual regions. Much of the initial interest in English Canadian and Quebec literature in Latin America was due to the publication of anthologies, translations, fiction, and poetry by Canadians living in the area, as well as by Latino-Canadian writers who settled in Canada. The earliest known anthology of Canadian writing published in Brazil, for instance, was a selection of Quebec poetry edited by Jean Désy, a Canadian diplomat, and published in French in São Paulo in 1943 (Peterson and Bernd 1992, 7–8) – reflecting an interest to be echoed years later by P.K. Page in her *Brazilian Journal* (1989). Manuel Betanzos Santos, a Galician poet, critic, and journalist who settled in Montreal in 1959, founded the trilingual literary review *Boreal*, which would appear intermittently for the next quarter-century and which circulated in both Canada and the Americas. Betanzos also read at cafés in the city with English- and French-speaking writers, and he published a selection of Canadian and Quebec poetry in the Argentine literary review *Cormorán y Delfín* in 1969, as well as a short anthology of Canadian writers in Mexico a few years later (Betanzos Santos 1989, 147, 155) and a key article giving an overview of contemporary Quebec and Canadian poetry in the *Revista de la Universidad Complutense* in Madrid in 1974.

At the other end of the Americas, the Montreal poet Lake Sagaris took up permanent residence in Santiago, Chile, in 1981, where she worked as a translator and as a journalist in both English and Spanish. In 1986 she translated and published a lengthy anthology of twelve contemporary Canadian poets, *Un pájaro es un poema*, which was published in Santiago by Pehuén Editores with assistance from Casa Canadá, a cultural arm of the Canadian Embassy in Chile. Sagaris's own poetic work includes *Medusa's Children*, a historical and cultural comparison of the islands of Newfoundland and Chiloé, the latter located at the northern end of the Chilean archipelago.

The first major Canadian novel to have an impact in Latin America was Malcolm Lowry's *Under the Volcano* (*Bajo el volcán*), which caused a considerable stir in Mexican letters, in the tradition of several other major works about Mexico written by foreigners, such as D.H. Lawrence's *The Plumed Serpent*, the short stories of Katherine Anne Porter, and the novels of B. Traven.[1] Most Mexican critics, however, consider Lowry a British author who simply ended up in Canada, and their opinions of the novel and its relevance to Mexican culture vary widely, from the deeply appreciative (Lara Zavala 2002) to the dismissive (Moussong 1994).

As Canadian and Quebec literature grew more popular in the last quarter of the twentieth century, numerous works by well-known Canadian authors were translated into Spanish and published in Spain. There have also been a number of anthologies of Canadian work published in Latin America, including *Vozes do Quebec: Antologia* (1991), edited by Zilá Bernd and Joseph Melançon; *Literatura francófona II: América* (1996), edited and translated by Laura López Morales, which includes a large selection of Québécois authors; and *¿Dónde es aquí? 25 cuentos canadienses* (2002), edited by Claudia Lucotti, a selection of contemporary English Canadian short stories. In a complementary fashion, the Quebec publishing house L'instant même has brought out an anthology of Mexican short stories, edited and translated by Louis Jolicoeur (1993). Les Éditions les Allusifs has also translated and published some fifteen novels by Latin American authors, including works by new and highly regarded writers such as Roberto Bolaño from Chile and Horacio Castellanos Moya from El Salvador.

The most active Canadian publisher in Latin America, however, has been Les Écrits des Forges, which has brought out sixty translations of poetry from Spanish over the past decade. More than fifty of these books are by Mexican authors, ranging from the high-profile (Jaime Sabines, Elsa Cross, Homero Aridjis) to the newly published, but there are also books by Colombian, Venezuelan, Uruguayan, and Argentine authors (including Juan Gelman). The majority of works have been published in bilingual format, and Nicole and Émile Martel have translated over thirty of them. In tandem, Les Écrits des Forges has also brought out some forty bilingual French-Spanish translations of works by Québécois poets, ranging from Hector de Saint-Denys Garneau to Yolande Villemaire. All of these translations, now totalling one hundred works, are distributed in Mexico and some other parts of Latin America, as well as in Canada and France (Bellemare 2004). The size of the exchange, the range of authors involved, and the extensive, unprecedented involvement of a Canadian publisher in Latin American poetry have caused the initiative to have a major literary impact, especially in Mexico.

Canadian studies programs have grown steadily throughout Latin America over the past quarter-century and have had a major impact not only on cultural and literary exchanges but also on the development of a comparativist dynamic and framework. Almost forty institutions and universities are members of Canadian studies programs in Argentina, Brazil, Venezuela, Mexico, and Cuba. The Brazilian association publishes the review *Interfaces Brasil/Canadá*, which includes comparative articles, as does the Mexican *Revista Mexicana de Estudios Canadienses*. These publications have served as the basis for comparativist research that runs to well over forty books and theses in Brazil alone. *Confluences littéraires Brésil-Québec: Les bases d'une comparaison* (1992), a collection of essays compiled by Michel Peterson and Zilá Bernd, laid the basis for a theoretical comparativist structure for studying Brazilian and Quebec literatures. At the same time, Canadian literary reviews such as *Dérives, Vice Versa, Ruptures,* and *Canadian Fiction Magazine* have been highly instrumental in the translation and diffusion of Latin American literature to the English Canadian and Quebec public.

A key element in the exchange and comparison between Latin American and Canadian and Quebec letters has been the growing body of writing produced by Latin Americans who have settled in Canada. Many of these authors, such as the Salvadoran writer Alfonso Quijada Urías and the Argentine novelist Pablo Urbanyi, are recognized figures in their homelands; as they continue to publish work that now often includes Canadian references and themes, their home audiences acquire a new perspective on Canadian culture. Other Canadian writers of Latin American origin, such as the Brazilian novelist Sergio Kokis, the Uruguayan writer Gloria Escomel, and the Mexican novelist Gilberto Flores Patiño, all of whom are well known in Quebec, either write or publish their work exclusively in one of Canada's official languages, although their themes are frequently Latin American. A number of Latino-Canadian writers, including Chilean authors Jorge Etcheverry and Naín Nómez, also work in literary criticism and have been important figures in establishing points of comparison between Canadian and Quebec cultures and those of Latin America in forums and reviews in both Canada and Latin America. Through their experience of living and writing in Canada, Latino-Canadian writers have been influential in discovering the multiple potential points of comparison between the literatures of their native countries and those of Canada and Quebec, whether it be the common immigrant experience (in the Southern Cone, for example), the effect of avant-garde movements (Brazil and Chile), indigenous writing (the Andean countries and Mesoamerica), bilingual cultural spheres (Paraguay, Bolivia, Peru, and Puerto Rico), *métissage* (Brazil), vernacular literature (Argentina), or the (re)definition of national identity.

One work of Hispanic Canadian literature in particular, the novel *Rojo, amarillo y verde* (Red, Yellow and Green), by the Bolivian Canadian author Alejandro Saravia, stands out as emblematic of the position of Canada within Latin America and of Latin America within Canada. This work, which takes place through narration and flashbacks in both La Paz and Montreal, knits the two cities together through their inherent multilingualism and multiculturalism: the polyglot indigenous character of La Paz (with its mixture of Aymara, Quechua, and other languages), its suffering and cultural plurality overlaid with Spanish, and the linguistic and multi-ethnic Babel of modern Montreal, in which immigrants from dozens of different countries participate in a fertile mélange of experience that includes Spanish speakers from all over Latin America in the "polyglossic civility" mentioned in Sherry Simon's chapter on "Translating in the Multilingual City" in the present collection.[2] The narrator's Bolivian experience haunts him as a constant presence in Montreal, while his years in Canada provide him with the framework for re-evaluating his life in Bolivia. Despite the vast differences between the two countries, one of which is essentially an indigenous nation ruled by a mestizo and white minority – the mestizo here identifying with the dominant class rather than representing the oppressed majority, as in many other Latin American nations – and the other of which is a bilingual nation where the descendants of immigrants from all parts of the world vastly outnumber those of its aboriginal peoples, both nations are fundamentally American in the sense of being multi-ethnic societies of coexistence and fusion.

TRANSCULTURATION AND NATIONAL IDENTITY IN ALEJANDRO SARAVIA'S *ROJO, AMARILLO Y VERDE*

Born in Cochabamba, the third-largest city in Bolivia, in 1962, Alejandro Saravia is one of the new generation of Latin American writers in Canada. His literary output spans a variety of genres, including articles, five published collections of poetry, a novel, and short stories. Throughout his work, however, certain characteristics are present, particularly a complete disillusion with the official history of his homeland, a fascination with language and the intersection of linguistic groups within a single national unity, and a constant feeling of loss, both of his previous cultural sphere and of individuals. Saravia arrived in Canada in 1986, settling first in Toronto and later in Montreal. He is fluently trilingual and now works as a journalist for the Spanish-speaking branch of Radio-Canada International.

Rojo, amarillo y verde is at once an unremitting deconstruction of Bolivian identity and a voice of hope for a new cosmopolitanism. Thus the concept of transculturation, the process of cultural transformation through the influx of new cultural elements and the alteration or disappearance of existing ones, is a key element of the work. The concept was created by the Cuban sociologist and anthropologist Fernando Ortiz, who used it in his monumental study *Contrapunteo cubano del tabaco y el azúcar* (*Cuban Counterpoint: Tobacco and Sugar*), first published in 1940. Ortiz found the term particularly well suited to describing the history of Cuba and other parts of the Americas that had been settled by waves of peoples from a variety of cultures and civilizations that often had little or nothing to do with one another, such as the Ciboneys, the Taínos, the Spanish, the African slaves, and the later Chinese and European immigrants to the island (Ortiz 1963, 101). Bronislaw Malinowski, in his introduction to Ortiz's study, points out that the term was much more accurate than that of "acculturation," which was used in the United States to speak of other cultures gradually accepting a monolithic norm. In the transculturation process, the new culture and the old or "original" one eventually fuse, thus creating a syncretic synthesis of both, as well as of older levels of the palimpsest (Malinowski 1963, xii-xiii). Saravia's novel critiques the rigid, inflexible patterns or traditions that the transculturation process has settled into in his native Bolivia, where an indigenous majority is ruthlessly exploited and repressed by a mestizo and white minority, and he describes the new cosmopolitan reality arising in focal points of world immigration such as Montreal, where transculturation is proceeding largely nonviolently and at a vastly accelerated pace.

The novel is intricately structured and works like a Möbius strip, beginning and ending with the same scene. It is divided into a series of distinct but interrelated episodes and observations, some a few lines in length and others a dozen pages long, which are separated from one another by a few blank spaces. The absence of titles or chapter numbers or any other titling of the sections increases the momentum and gives an underlying cohesiveness to the fragmentary nature of many of the scenes. At times the book circles back to a previous point, commenting on it anew; at others the writer/protagonist and his proofreading alter ego, The Scribe, discuss and even alter the direction the story is taking. The structural aesthetic is essentially postmodern, opening up the text to reader interpretation and participation and letting certain characters, such as the prostitute María, decide whether they want to stay in the book or not. It is only upon finishing the novel that the reader can go back and reorganize the various sections, plotting them out linearly as a consecutive story. One of the sections, written from the point of view of a wounded dog, ends with a two-page break, which itself constitutes a wordless text, an open space in which – according to the author – the reader can integrate him or herself into the manuscript (Saravia 2003, 121–3), inhabiting an expanse of snow and silence (Saravia 2005). There is also a good deal of deconstructive linguistic word play, including comic deformations of military titles in order to poke fun at the protagonist Alfredo Cutipa's late oppressors in the "glorious Volibian Armed Farces"[3] (2003, 113), among them "Colononel Bánzer" and the "Gonorreal García Meza," whose most important

Cabinet member is a certain Johnny Walker (64). Alfredo's musings occasionally break into concrete or sound poetry as well, as when he explores the "infintepossibilitiesofforgetting" and then repeats the word "olvido" (forgetting) for five lines straight, ending the final line with the syllable "lor" – thus transforming the last "olvido" into "dolor" (pain) (51). At the end of the novel, there is a short list of notes and a collection of poems that Alfredo once sent to his Kurdish girlfriend but that was returned to him ten years later by Canada Post, with the note "Le Kurdistan n'existe pas comme pays" (207). All of these satirical, carnivalesque techniques create an open-ended imaginary space conducive to the radical critique of nationalism and the deconstruction of militarism that accompany them.

Alfredo has lived through a terrifying year as a conscript in the Bolivian army during the 1980 coup d'état, after which he moved to Canada. Even there, however, thirteen years later, he is still so obsessed with his experiences in the army that he decides to set them down on paper so he can succeed in understanding and perhaps in freeing himself from them. As he writes, he hallucinates the presence of several important characters from his past, including his dead girlfriend, Amelia, and a rebellious Indian conscript, The Boxer, whom he and his comrades found in their barracks with his rifle in his hands and half his face blown off. The military authorities say it was a suicide, but Alfredo and other soldiers examine the magazine of the dead man's rifle and find that it is full. As he writes, Alfredo gradually comes to the conclusion that Bolivia is an artificial construct imposed by force on a group of indigenous peoples or nations that has impeded their natural development ever since the Conquest, "a country fractured into different societies, languages, and simultaneous historical times" (Saravia 2003, 26). The only lasting relationship that the native Quechua and Aymara speakers (the descendants of the Inca and Tiahuanaco peoples, respectively), as well as the Guaraní and other indigenous groups, have with the European (and mestizo) national structure that has been grafted onto them is characterized by the latter's violent domination, and, in this sense, Bolivia has been a failure as a nation, home to "a population that furiously tried to hide its Indian fingernails, its Indian names, its collective memory of mestizos perpetually ashamed of the blood running through their veins" (18). "Bolivia is an imaginary homeland: a territory that doesn't exist beyond a contradictory geography ... It's the collective ways of imagining ourselves and of dying that unite us" (39). Such a stand, however, involves rejecting the entire official historiography of the country and replacing it with a new interpretation – a lonely and difficult task, especially given the fierce opposition of those who have created and upheld the established order.

In the opening and closing scenes of *Rojo, amarillo y verde*, Alfredo runs through the cars of the St-Michel-Côte-des-Neiges line of the Montreal metro shouting flirtatious compliments in Quechua either out of sheer frustration or else in the hope that some woman will understand him. Immigrant passengers from a multitude of countries prick up their ears (Saravia 2003, 201). He imagines (or perhaps it is real) that a woman passenger asks him:

> "Are you from Cuzco?" A laugh. "No, no, I'm a mutt" [meaning he's not from the Quechua heartland; Cuzco was the Incan capital]. "But even mongrels have a homeland, don't they?" "No, ma'am, I'm Bolivian" … To be Bolivian was to have a wound that never healed. (9–10)[4]

Indeed, Alfredo's obsession with his native country reaches such a point that he dreams that he makes love to the motherland, who tells him she will be whatever he wants, that "there are as many motherlands as there are Bolivians" (46), and then asks him, "Are you positive that I'm … a woman?" (47), upon which his groping fingers find that she isn't, and he wakes up.

As a soldier, Alfredo has been assigned to the garrison guarding El Alto, the country's main air base, built atop the Altiplano just above La Paz. After the coup d'état, El Alto becomes the point of departure for bombing runs against the civilian population, and Alfredo is forced to carry out searches and raids on churches and homes; at one point he is disciplined for insubordination for refusing an officer's orders to take part in a gang rape of a woman trying to get home after curfew – and who turns out to be The Boxer's girlfriend. Writing in Montreal years later, he asks himself why he never mutinied, why he didn't assassinate General García Meza when his unit escorted him down to La Paz from the base (even though it would have implicated him in the circle of violence), and most of all, why he remained silent when the army covered up The Boxer's murder. In a highly poetic passage that uses the words "laugh" and "laughter" as a type of mantra, he finds escape from his guilt, remorse, and disorientation by mocking his oppressor: "I laugh at their symbols ... at their love of coats of arms and cockades. I laugh at the words of their anthems. I laugh at the admirals of inland waters and rubber ducks, at the rear guard generals, at the colonels in their slippers, at the dipsomaniac captains ... I laugh at history. I laugh out loud, laugh until the high command becomes bewildered, laugh as hard as I can until laughter scares away the tears and makes death a little less death" (Saravia 2003, 174–5).

It is as he writes his memoirs in Montreal that Alfredo finally finds a strange completion to his destiny in the form of a Kurdish woman, who is initially attracted to him because of his socks, which happen to be the colours of the Bolivian flag. It seems the Kurdish national colours – red, yellow, and green – are the same as those of the Bolivian flag, from which Saravia's novel takes its name. The woman, who later becomes Alfredo's lover, is an urban guerrilla working with the Kurdistan Workers' Party (PKK) for the establishment of an independent Kurdish homeland. Her greatest dream, the object of her life's struggle, is to have a country, while Alfredo's goal is to rid himself of one – and, as a final irony, her name is Bolivia.[5] In an imagined legal proclamation, Alfredo revokes the name of his country and officially bestows it upon his Kurdish lover, declaring that "the concept of what is called a nation will now be secondary to the primary human manifestation of affection, by designating that 'Bolivia' be the name of a physical person" (Saravia 2003, 134); the nation is henceforth to be known (at least in the novel) as "volibia," without a capital letter ("b" and "v" have the same sound in Spanish). Yet the struggle for nationhood of the woman Bolivia is as fraught with problems as is Alfredo's deconstruction: the Kurds begin marketing copies of Alfredo's tricoloured socks and then branch out into an array of tricoloured clothing, which they produce in maquiladoras in Mexico and sell to Kurdish nationalists in order to buy arms – engendering a split between the socialist and capitalist wings of the movement. In an implicit critique of revolutionary violence, Bolivia accepts the assignment of parking a bomb-rigged car next to a building in Turkey – and then finds that she has been tricked into blowing up scores of people belonging to her own party. "For the first time," she tells Alfredo, "I saw the Turks themselves weeping for their dead," just as her own people have done (186).

But perhaps it is the goal of a national identity that is itself the problem: the nation Bolivia has failed, and the Kurds have struggled for three thousand years without creating their own national state.

The spontaneous, multi-ethnic – and translinguistic – process of transculturation that Alfredo finds going on all around him in Montreal seems to be the antidote to the failed search for national identity. Alfredo's running call in the metro in the opening and closing scenes of the novel takes place on the line that runs through the heart of the immigrant district and affects everyone on the train, from Sri Lankan Tamils to Indian students of Sanskrit, Africans from Gabon, and Moroccans from Marrakech, as they try to decipher his speech. He also integrates words and phrases from French, English, Quechua, and Aymara directly into the text. Indeed, Alfredo himself lives near the Jean-Talon market, where he exults in the vegetable stalls, describing the daily transcultural culinary gathering in terms that recall the Brazilian Antropófago artistic movement of the 1920s: "in a quiet way, immigrants from every language and latitude have set themselves the task of gradually integrating native-born Canadians into the spontaneous cosmopolitanism of Montreal ... Many unions – of the flesh and even of the spirit – had slowly matured among Chinese lettuce, Vietnamese herbs, curry from the Punjab and delicate rice noodles from the Philippines. Women and men who came to this island [Montreal] from strange regions of the planet ended up devouring each other on the kitchen table ... Vivent les papilles libres!, vive le Québec ivre!" (Saravia 2003, 129–30).

By the end of the novel, Alfredo has come full circle from his obsession with Bolivian nationalism to a refocusing on the individual. Writing the novel has served as a catharsis, freeing him from his past and from the guilt and anger it elicited from him. His visions and hallucinations of The Boxer have become so commonplace that he shrugs when he finds the man's half-destroyed head staring at him from inside his refrigerator. He himself, like The Boxer, loses an eye in a beating at the hands of suspicious Kurds; the socket, covered with a patch, becomes transformed into a personal movie theatre for him, in which he watches films of his former life. As his past is banalized and loses its power over him, he turns to the individual element of life, writing to his Kurdish girlfriend Bolivia (in French since she speaks no Spanish): "C'est une histoire pour nous seuls car maintenant je le sais!, ma patrie, ma terre, mes mots c'est toi, c'est ta voix, tes bras, tes paroles" (Saravia 2003, 199–200). The two of them have initiated their own process of transculturation between each other: a spontaneous coming together that is driven by love and desire, unlike the artificial nationalisms of their past. As Alfredo runs through the cars of the metro at the end of the novel, he tells himself: "You're from Kurdistan, Cochabamba, and Montreal. You're African, Arab, and Vietnamese. You're everything and nothing. You're a language, a voice, a question that will never find an answer ¡Chunquituy palomitay ... kolila! *Montréal est la première ville nord-américaine avec la plus grande population trilingue*" (201).

NOTES

1 For an extensive discussion of the work of English-speaking authors as both part and offshoot of Mexican culture, see Drewey Wayne Gunn, *Escritores norteamericanos y británicos en México* (1992).
2 The Spanish-speaking population of the United States, which now numbers well over 40 million, is to a great extent composed of large blocks of different nationalities, such as Chicanos, Puerto Ricans, Dominicans, and Salvadorans, each of which has its own particular culture and literary traditions; see http://www.census.gov/popest/national/asrh (viewed 10 August 2006). The Hispanic population of Canada is just over 335,000 (or less than 1 per cent of that of the US); see http://www12. statcan.ca/english/census06/datatopics/RetrieveProductTable.cfm (viewed 21 June 2009). Although it contains appreciable numbers of some nationalities, such as Chileans and Salvadorans, Canada's small size is less conducive to fractionalization according to national groups and actually promotes interaction among immigrants from the various countries of Latin America. A Spanish-language or multilingual poetry reading in a Canadian city, for example, is likely to include people from a variety of nationalities, whereas a reading in the United States often (but not exclusively) draws on writers from a specific national or cultural group.
3 All translations of passages from the novel *Rojo, Amarillo y verde* are mine.
4 An interesting parallel exists here with Francine Noël's novel *La Conjuration des bâtards* (1999), which Catherine Khordoc analyzes in her chapter "Looking beyond the Elephant" in the present collection. Khordoc notes that "the word *bâtard* [is] an alternative to those [words] that ... refer to an individual of mixed origins (hybrid, métis, creole); hence a *bâtard* is not simply one who is born of an illegitimate union – which of course is how the colonization of the Americas could be viewed – but is also an animal that is not of pure race." Alfredo also refers to himself as a "mutt" and a "mongrel," but his rejection of the traditional mestizo alliance with the governing class has left him stateless, unable to

identify any longer with the artificial construct of Bolivia. It is worth
noting that Alfredo has chosen to accept conscription as a common soldier, a decision he has made because of his desire to experience the reality
of the common people of Bolivia and express his solidarity with them.
Most middle- and upper-class Bolivians are able to avoid conscription
through influence or payoffs; the few who go into the army do so as offi-
cers. Alfredo's idealistic choice, of course, turns into a nightmare after the
coup d'état, and he is finally forced to flee his country, alienated from the
ruling class and unable to become a member of the indigenous majority.

5 Part of the preceding analysis also appears in chapter 7 of my 2007
volume *Latinocanadá: A Critical Study of Ten Latin American Writers
of Canada.*

13

Looking beyond the Elephant: The Mexican Connection in Francine Noël's *La Conjuration des bâtards*

CATHERINE KHORDOC

The fiction of Montreal writer Francine Noël is generally regarded as being unapologetically nationalistic. In all of her works, Quebec's status as a nation is taken for granted, its official political independence but a detail that remains to be worked out. *Maryse*, the first novel of a tetralogy that includes her *La Conjuration des bâtards*, intertwines the coming of age of a young, independent, liberated woman studying French and Québécois literature with the coming of age of Quebec as a nation. However, Noël's representation of the Québécois is not that of a homogeneous people speaking one language, as is the case in some post-Quiet Revolution texts. In *Babel, prise deux ou Nous avons tous découvert l'Amérique*,[1] Noël explores the increasingly multicultural and multilingual character of Montreal and how this plurality is to be reconciled with Quebec's aspirations to nationhood. The fact that the main character recognizes that she inhabits a new "Babel," where diversity is not only tolerated but also celebrated, reminds us that it is no longer accurate (and perhaps it never was) to describe Québécois literature and culture simply in terms of French, Catholic roots. Although Noël's representations of Québécois society are indeed quite innovative and mark important stages within Quebec's literary history, her *La Conjuration des bâtards* makes a bolder statement by taking Québécois literature out of Quebec.

There is no intent to suggest here that Noël is the first author to do so. Hubert Aquin and Jacques Godbout are only two examples, among others, of prominent Québécois authors who have set their novels in Switzerland and the United States, but Noël, who sets *La Conjuration* in Mexico, does so in a way that suggests not how Mexico and Quebec differ but, on the contrary, how the two are part of one continent sharing a similar colonial past and a very large, dominating neighbour. Noël's novels, as well as her play, *Chandeleur*, illustrate that Québécois culture is not an island in the middle of the vast North American continent. In spite of the language that distinguishes it from Canada and the United States, Quebec's culture is shaped by its geocultural context and cannot conceal some of its characteristics that make it "American" in the continental or hemispheric sense of the word. Noël's fictional writing is a very apt illustration of literature that can be read at once as affirming Quebec's status as a nation and as situating it within the context of North America, in a position parallel to that of other established nations on this continent, such as Mexico. This hemispheric approach to Noël's work – which could also be used to analyze other Québécois works, such as *Copies conformes* (1989) by Monique LaRue and *Frontières, ou tableaux d'Amérique* (1995) by Noël Audet – removes any ambiguity that might exist with regard to Quebec's de facto national status: Quebec remains only in the legal sense a province of Canada, but it is a nation in its own right within the Americas in all other senses. It would be reasonable to affirm that Quebec is part of "Canada's Americas," in the way that the United States or Mexico are.

Thus, although Noël's works unequivocally affirm Quebec's claim to nationhood, they also include a significant range of references, themes, and narrative techniques that contribute to the notion that Quebec's culture is pervasively American. Interestingly, it is one of her more recent novels that evokes Quebec's links to the American continent most clearly, suggesting an evolution in her conceptualization of culture in Quebec. Pierre Nepveu, an eminent Québécois literary critic, has highlighted a broader trend that parallels this evolution in his principal studies, *L'écologie du réel* (1988) and *Intérieurs du Nouveau Monde* (1998). In the former, in which he examines Québécois authors, he proclaims the end of Québécois literature in the sense that this label "no longer encompasses anything essential or substantial."[2] A comparative study of the literatures of Quebec and the Americas, the latter work affirms the growing awareness that Québécois literature cannot be read in a vacuum, that it must be comprehended in its larger context. As Winfried Siemerling points out in one of the rare discussions in English of Nepveu's work, Nepveu revisits Quebec's literary project – which, since the 1960s, has sought to articulate Quebec's national identity – "from a horizon that is no longer defined by the concept of nationalism" (2005, 28). In a sense, Noël's work is a literary reflection of this development, from the nationalistic and postcolonialist preoccupations portrayed in *Maryse* to the increasingly "American" considerations found in *La Conjuration des bâtards*. It might be said that it is only once the postcolonial – or perhaps I should say "postnational" – question has been addressed, where Quebec's national identity and status are no longer ambiguous or uncertain, that Québécois writers such as Noël are able to explore and appreciate Quebec's "Americanness."

The preoccupation with America is not a particularly new phenomenon in Québécois literature and criticism. The United States has in fact been represented in many of Quebec's literary movements. In the archetypal *roman du terroir*, which celebrated the relationship between man and his land, the US was not entirely absent, but when this country was represented, it was generally in negative terms of alterity, a force that needed to be resisted, for it lured away impoverished *habitants* with the promise of factory jobs that were considered secure and well paying but that ultimately led to the loss of language and the abandonment of the Catholic faith – and hence to assimilation. If by the 1980s the United States is not viewed as such a menace but rather as a destination for some Québécois characters, it is nonetheless very much a foreign and somewhat suspicious country that has virtually nothing in common with Quebec. More important, however, when the notion of "America" or of *américanité* is examined in Québécois literature, it is almost always limited to the United States.[3] Nonetheless, as Yvan Lamonde and Gérard Bouchard stress in the introduction to their volume *Québécois et Américains: La culture québécoise aux XIXe et XXe siècles* (1995), it is the entire continent as a cultural space that constitutes the backdrop for their studies. The term *américanité* is often used without necessarily being clearly defined, but perhaps because it is assumed that we understand what it means, it is too easily taken to relate simply to the United States. Lamonde and Bouchard define *américanité* as "les nouvelles formes culturelles qui se sont mises en place depuis le XVIIe siècle à la suite des transferts migratoires de l'Europe vers les Amériques et qui reflètent la somme des ruptures, des processus de différenciation (par invention, adaptation) et des projets de recommencement collectif caractéristiques de plusieurs collectivités neuves" (1995, 8).

The originality of *La Conjuration des bâtards*, then, is that it integrates aspects of Mexican and Québécois cultures, recognizing and exploring commonalities between the two and thereby creating a text that must be considered simultaneously Québécois and American, in the continental sense. In his defence of the specific field of Canadian literary studies over a hemispheric approach to Canadian literature, Herb Wyile recalls an image that Pierre Trudeau once used, explaining that it is difficult for the mouse who sleeps next to an elephant to look beyond the elephant.[4] But it is in fact by looking beyond the elephant that is the United States that Francine Noël finds another culture with which Quebec shares history, a religious tradition, a postcolonial past, marginalization within North America – at the levels of language, culture, and economics – and possibly future complicity. Furthermore, on the one hand, this American perspective that Noël adopts reflects Quebec's cultural independence from France, its colonial *mère patrie*, recognizing that nations can share other kinds of ties than those forged through colonialism, and, on the other hand, it affirms Quebec's de facto independence from Canada, illustrating that Quebec can bypass Canada altogether and develop links with other nations such as Mexico so as to assert its own national status.[5]

All of Noël's works contain elements evoking other cultures of North and South America. For example, there are always characters whose origins are either Mexican or South American. The Spanish language is also present throughout, either through allusions or literally, as words in Spanish are interwoven into the French dialogues and narratives. Maryse's children, for example, speak both languages fluently, and they exasperate their mother by insisting on speaking Spanish when they are in Montreal for fear of losing their second language. Mythological and historical references also serve as a reminder that Quebec's history is not isolated from that of other American states. The Mexican mythical figure of La Malinche, for instance, is evoked both in Noël's play, *Chandeleur*, and in the novel *Babel, prise deux*. Fluent in Aztec and Mayan languages as well as Spanish, La Malinche served as a translator for Hernán Cortés. Because of her collaboration with the conquistadors (something that is well documented, in contrast to more legendary aspects of her legacy), she is considered in Mexico to have betrayed indigenous values. But for Tzvetan Todorov, the title of whose book *La Conquête de l'Amérique* is echoed in the title of Noël's novel *Nous avons tous découvert l'Amérique*, La Malinche is perhaps "le premier exemple, et par là même le symbole, du métissage des cultures; elle annonce par là l'État moderne du Mexique et, au-delà, notre état présent à tous, puisque, à défaut d'être toujours bilingues, nous sommes inévitablement bi- ou tri-culturels. La Malinche glorifie le mélange au détriment de la pureté (aztèque ou espagnole), et le rôle de l'intermédiaire" (1982, 107). This mythical character may suggest various interpretations and themes of betrayal, acculturation, or *métissage*, but of interest for us here is that she is evoked in *Québécois* texts. Although it would be interesting to explore the symbolism that La Malinche might have specifically for Québécois culture, we must first recognize that the simple fact of inscribing a Mexican myth in a work of Québécois literature creates a hybrid effect and suggests the possible parallels between different cultures of the so-called New World.[6] Contemporary Latino culture is also present in Noël's works through numerous references to well-known Latin American writers such as Gabriel García Márquez, Julio Cortázar, and Mario Vargas Llosa, mentioned alongside "classic" Québécois authors such as Gabrielle Roy, Anne Hébert, and Jacques Ferron. Such cultural borrowings also constitute a transcultural element in Noël's work since, as Québécois readers become increasingly familiar with Latin American culture and as it is weaved into Québécois culture, it becomes part of Québécois culture. As André Lamontagne notes: "L'ouverture à d'autres littératures, comme on le sait, modifie le champ intertextuel du roman québécois, et la culture hispanique occupe une place importante dans l'œuvre de Francine Noël, témoignant ainsi de sa popularité croissante au Québec" (2004, 104). It is not only the intertextual network that is modified, however, but also Québécois literature and culture in general as they evolve through contact and interaction with other literatures.

Nonetheless, Noël's *La Conjuration des bâtards* merits particular attention. Whereas the first two parts, as well as the final instalment of what is now a tetralogy, are set in Montreal, the third part situates Noël's characters in Mexico. In *La Conjuration des bâtards*, Maryse and her family live in Mexico City, spending extended periods of time in Montreal and thereby maintaining close ties with their Montreal friends, who are like family to them. But a large, international, interdisciplinary conference as well as the tragic events toward the end of the novel lead even the more rooted Montrealers to make a trip to Mexico, such that the whole "clan" eventually intermingles with Mexican culture to varying degrees. Although Noël's other texts hint at the possible links between Quebec and Mexico, *La Conjuration* makes them, at one level, quite explicit, but she also creates a complex network of references and allusions by playing with languages, form, and narrative strategies, by questioning the reliability of history, and by emphasizing history's narrative functions, thus inviting the reader not only to appreciate the affinities between Québécois and Mexican cultures but also to reconsider what the label "Québécois culture" signifies. Here, I focus my attention on two narrative techniques used in this novel that illustrate the extent to which it incorporates aspects of Mexican culture and aesthetics, thus contributing to its transcultural character. They are magical realism and historical metafiction.

Magical realism is a technique employed throughout the Maryse tetralogy, becoming increasingly manifest with each novel. That magical realism is most prominent in the third instalment is not surprising given its Mexican setting and its central theme of hybridity, or *métissage*. Magical realism is by definition a hybrid technique, as it consists of the introduction of elements that are magical or fantastic within a narrative context that seems otherwise "realistic." As Wendy B. Faris puts it, "magical realism combines realism and the fantastic in such a way that magical elements grow organically out of the reality portrayed" (1995, 163). Furthermore, as Faris explains, although the precursor of Latin American fiction usually identified as magical realist is European realism, the "magical supplement to realism may have flourished in Latin America ... because in dismantling the imported code of realism 'proper' it enabled *a broader transculturation* process to take place, a process within which postcolonial Latin American literature established its identity" (165, my emphasis). David Mikics considers magical realism to be a trait that is part of a "larger strategy of cultural mixing – a creolizing or transculturation – that is central to much of what Vera Kutzinski has called 'New World writing'" (1995, 372). If, however, magical realism is indeed most often associated with Latin American literature, it is rarely associated with Québécois literature. This technique is not employed very frequently by Québécois authors; when they do, not only do their works display a degree of originality, but they also manifest hybrid or transcultural qualities.[7]

As far as *La Conjuration des bâtards* is concerned, the use of magical realism is extensive. There are archangels who announce births and deaths, a language genie who attempts to influence Maryse's language in her writing, and a devil who runs an underground bar that has outlets in Montreal and Mexico City, among other places. The patrons of this bar can communicate with each other even if they are in different locations, and among them are dead characters as well as historical figures such as Jesus, René Levesque, and Bertrand Russell, who strike up conversations with some of the novel's "living" fictional characters.

In the first apparition of the archangel Gabrielle (note the feminine form of the name; this archangel is indeed female) in *La Conjuration*,[8] she appears as the reflection of a secondary character, Tristan, a young man in his early twenties. When he notices that his own reflection has become a female figure with large bluish wings, he is understandably taken aback and believes he is hallucinating. The archangel's reply is indeed amusing, although ambiguous: "Tu n'hallucines pas ... Je suis réelle, aussi réelle que ce rideau de poly-ester et rayonne que je tiens dans ma main droite" (Noël 1999a, 82). The ambiguity of this response stems from the fact that the concept of what is "real" is problematic in a work of fiction (there is no archangel, there is no polyester curtain, there is no Tristan – in fact, they are of course just words); at the same time, the ambiguity evokes one of the defining traits of magical realism: "Both the uncanny and magical realism narrate fantastic events not merely alongside real ones, but *as if they were real*. What seems most strange turns out to be secretly familiar" (Mikics 1995, 372–3; my emphasis). The focus on "being real" in the archangel's response is perhaps an allusion to the definition of magical realism, but at the very least it forces the reader to be fully aware of the fact that interwoven into the realistic traits of this novel are surreal or fantastic elements that are not considered extraordinary within the narrative framework. This realization requires more than a mere "suspension of disbelief"; rather, it is in the tension created between belief and incredulity that the reader can fully partake in the creative reading demanded by such works of literature.

In another example, this time featuring the Diable Vert and his underground bar that transcends time and space, the conventional lines separating reality and magic are blurred once again. The Diable Vert is riding the Mexico City subway pretending to be blind in order to train his dog who longs to become a guide dog for the blind. But Gabriel and Lilith, having previously been acquainted with this Green Devil,[9] recognize him easily, although they notice that the other passengers seem to sense something is wrong as they distance themselves from him: "Et l'aveugle est bizarre: ce n'est pas son teint blafard ni ses traits, qui ne sont pas mexicains, ni les larges bretelles qui lui strient la pansent, on ne sait pas, il a quelque chose d'irréel" (Noël 1999a, 148). It is ironic that the anonymous riders of the subway, who have no reason to believe there is something afoot in this scene, nonetheless intuit that this blind man is not quite real,[10] whereas the two characters who do know his "real" identity do not seem at all perturbed by it. Moreover, this incident alludes to the relationship between postcolonialism and magical realism. The Diable Vert, accused of being lazy by Lilith, declares that he is a "minor" devil who has survived "deux siècles d'athéisme européen" (169), lending a nonconventional meaning to the word "atheism," which here alludes to European skepticism regarding the supernatural.

Because the use of magical realism is not very common in Québécois literature, its presence in Noël's works can be perceived as an instance of intertextuality. Although magical realism is important and must be studied for its own sake, it plays another role in Noël's texts by evoking the writings of Latin American authors such as Alejo Carpentier and Gabriel García Márquez. The use of magical realism in *La Conjuration des bâtards* as a form of intertextuality is significant because the reader who is not only aware of the technique in and of itself but also recognizes it as a characteristic trait of Latin American fiction that subverts traditional realist fiction will comprehend more fully the innovation of this novel at many levels. As Lamontagne points out, "l'intertextualité du roman québécois contemporain reflète l'évolution de la société dont elle est le produit: par son intonation diégétique récemment acquise, elle traduit un changement dans le statut de la lecture et de l'érudition, qui ne sont plus vues comme affectation étrangère; par sa diversification, elle témoigne d'une ouverture et d'une vision plus complexe de l'autre, qui n'est plus uniquement l'Anglais ou le Français" (2004, 14–15).

I would add that the use of magical realism constitutes a type of intertextuality through which a literary form, if not a *genre*, is suggested rather than a particular work or author, from which two considerations must follow. First, this work of Noël's illustrates how Québécois literature can be integrated with other literatures of the

Americas and also that a transnational approach is relevant in order to avoid the pitfalls of a more traditional national perspective or, as Josias Semujanga warns, to avoid hitting the wall that prevents us from appreciating "un phénomène en mouvement continuel traversant les cultures connues de l'artiste ou de l'écrivain" (2004, 8). Second, the appropriation of magical realism, a technique often used in modern Latin American fiction and, in general, in postcolonial literature, is a further instance of the hybridization or the transculturation taking place in this novel. It also situates Québécois literature within the context of New World or postcolonial literature, at least to a certain extent.

Magical realist fiction is also inextricably linked to historical metafiction. As Faris explains, "we witness an idiosyncratic recreation of historical events, but events grounded firmly in historical realities – often alternate versions of officially sanctioned accounts" (1995, 170). Although I hesitate to strictly categorize *La Conjuration* as magical realist fiction, it does bear some of its characteristics, including the retelling of historical events. But unlike Gabriel García Márquez, who focuses on a local example by telling the history of the fictional town of Macondo in his novel *One Hundred Years of Solitude* (1967) in order to retell the history of Latin America, Noël broadens the historical scope to include events relating to the Americas, including Christopher Columbus's discovery of the continent in 1492, in order to show how Quebec's history is inextricably linked to that of the Americas in general. According to Mikics, "magical realist writing often stems from a place and time in which different cultures or historical periods inhabit a single cultural space" (1995, 373). Noël's innovation, in this respect, is that the cultural space represented is very broad, encompassing all of North America, in which different cultures and languages indeed cohabit on one continent, but by retelling certain episodes of their histories, she contests the paradigm of a national history, revealing a certain common heritage among the countries sharing a continent.

The historical discourse in *La Conjuration* often takes playful forms – literally – as in the opening scene, in which the children in the Montreal neighbourhood where many of the characters live are re-enacting the 1492 conquest of Granada, playing the roles of Columbus, Ferdinand II of Aragon, and Isabella I of Castile, among others. An amusing effect is created when the children are determined to get the historical details right, mainly by consulting their elders, namely the ones who "invented" the game a decade before (in *Myriam première*, the second part of the tetralogy) and who are now young adults: "Il connaît la vraie version de l'histoire qui viendrait, à ce qu'on dit, de l'autre côté de la ruelle" (Noël 1999a, 12–13). At the same time, the historical discourse is intertwined with some of the everyday concerns of the children. Thus "Ferdinand" is in a hurry to get on with the conquest because he has a hockey game at five o'clock (16). This scene, which constitutes a sort of prologue, sets up the historical scope of the novel since the conquest of Granada is a crucial event leading to Columbus's departure for America, but it also sets the tone, as the children are critical of the Catholic take-over and the intolerance demonstrated toward Jews and Muslims in the fifteenth century, thereby revealing a bias in favour of heterogeneity and plurality. Furthermore, through this playful opening, Noël also suggests that historical narratives must be questioned and that history in Quebec must be situated in a larger context than the colonization of New France and its conquest on the Plains of Abraham.

History also forms the basis upon which stories or tales are told to Maryse's children and their friends. The "fairytales" they listen to include yet another rendition of the conquest of Granada as well as other historical stories included in *La Saga des Survivants*, which is the title of the book on which François Ladouceur – one of Maryse's best friends and Myriam's father – is writing. When a young Mexican girl, a friend of Maryse's children, expresses her amazement that all of her Québécois friends know the story of Granada, Myriam[11] explains: "qu'on soit de Montréal ou de Mexico, 1492 est une date décisive pour tout l'Occident. C'est l'année où les gens d'ici voient arriver leurs premiers découvreurs blancs et barbus dans l'équipage de Christophe Colomb. L'Amérique deviendra bientôt le grenier d'une Europe affamée, cupide, inquisitoriale" (Noël 1999a, 215). Clearly, this statement underscores the importance for Quebec of knowing its history – that is, a history that does not simply begin with Samuel de Champlain's discovery of the St Lawrence River but rather with that of the continent. But by using more or less traditional storytelling techniques, Myriam and François manage to captivate the children and generate an interest in history. Adult readers are perhaps similarly drawn in by these history lessons disguised as fairytales and adventure stories.

La Saga des Survivants tells semifictitious, semihistorical stories of displaced, exiled peoples of diverse origins and periods. François

tests out his stories by telling them to the children before writing
them, and his own daughter, Myriam, as a young adult, continues
the tradition with Maryse's children. The two stages of the creation
of this historical fiction remind us of the importance of the oral history that precedes its written form. Maryse's children, who are quite
precocious intellectually, complain that Myriam is embellishing the
stories, making it impossible to distinguish truth from fiction. Not
only is it her privilege as a storyteller to diverge from the "truth,"
she declares, but it is also her duty, as one must show a certain degree
of sensitivity when telling historical stories. Although the distinction
between story and history (both rendered in French as *histoire*) is
blurred quite explicitly in this novel, both types of discourse are
discernible, suggesting that both are necessary to each other. This
perspective is valid not only for *La Saga des Survivants* but also for
the work we are currently reading: *La Conjuration des bâtards* is
indeed a story, a work of fiction, but by interweaving the novel with
historical events that are traditionally considered to be Latin American
history, Noël is appropriating this history, emphasizing that it is
integral to Québécois heritage, identity, and culture and thereby to
Québécois fiction.

In another example of *rapprochement* between Latin American
and Québécois history and culture, Bertrand Russell, the early-
twentieth-century philosopher and mathematician, makes an appear-
ance in the Diable Vert's bar and attempts to explain to Myriam and
Agnes (Maryse's young daughter) the inherent ambiguity of the métis
identity. But before bringing up the quintessential Canadian example,
that of Louis Riel, Russell discusses the case of Garcilaso de la Vega,
also known as the Inca. The son of a Spanish conquistador and an
Inca princess in the late sixteenth and early seventeenth centuries,
he had to bear the weight of belonging to two camps: the conqueror
and the conquered. The duality of the métis is a difficult one to live
with, the Inca – who also happens to be in the surreal bar – explains,
because "des deux côtés de son ascendance, il est l'Autre. Le concept
de nation métisse, tel que rêvé et défendu par le Canadien Louis Riel,
me semble une aporie" (Noël 1999a, 289). His perspective contrasts
with that of Maryse's children and their circle of friends, who, for
the most part, all claim quite proudly their multiple cultural and
linguistic heritages even though this also raises questions regarding
their identity and sense of belonging to a single community. For this
métis character, the notion of happily reconciling multiple origins is

paradoxical, but his perspective is also grounded in a time when an ambiguous or impure identity was a reason for torture, if not a death sentence. It also predates the conceptualization of *criollo* culture that has been developed in Latin American societies, where, as Amaryll Chanady aptly points out, not only is the fact that they are hybrid recognized, but they are also "conceptualisées comme hybrides, soit comme multiculturelles (le Canada), soit comme métisses (l'Amérique latine), soit comme créole (les Antilles)" (1999, 13). This way of conceptualizing culture is common to most of the societies of the Americas, distinguishing them from European societies.

Finally, the treatment of time, crucial of course to our consideration of the historical discourse in this text, is of particular interest. The unity of time that was so important to classical theatre has long ago been rejected. But Noël's representation of time stands out for the historical span covered and the way it is narrated. Composed of five parts, the novel begins in 1992, and the first part covers events occurring during a span of five years in about sixty pages. In this part, the reader learns of the events that have occurred in Maryse's life since the end of the preceding part of the tetralogy – she has lived in Nicaragua and Mexico, has published many novels and plays, which make her famous in Quebec, and has had one child and adopted another. Then, over 300 pages are spent narrating events occurring during one week in 1999. During this week, the *Sommet de la Fraternité* is taking place at a university in Mexico City, with participants from all walks of life and from all over the world taking part. The aim of this conference is to reflect on the new millennium and on how to achieve peace and understanding throughout the world. But this material accounts for only the "present" of the narration. The tales being told and retold, and then written, take the characters and the readers back to the Middle Ages, "du temps où il n'y avait pas de pays" (Noël 1999a, 94) and, of course, to that fateful year of 1492. Thus periods that precede, include, and follow colonization are all represented in this novel. And we must also recall that *La Conjuration* is actually the third book in a tetralogy that begins with the coming of age of Maryse in the late 1960s and early 1970s, coinciding with the coming of age of Québécois literature, and ends with *J'ai l'angoisse légère*, published in 2008. Noël's novel is a saga, then, that could be the saga of Maryse, but perhaps we should also consider it a saga of Québécois literature. The saga has no conclusion, of course – in spite of Pierre Nepveu's famous words regarding the "end" of Québécois literature – but it does represent several of the "stages" in the evolution of modern Québécois literature and even a reconsideration of what this label means, which does connect with Nepveu's argument. He emphasizes that it is essential for a culture to define itself "par sa capacité d'auto-altération, de dépaysement, de migration" (1989, 19).

Let us come back to Nepveu's position in defence of a post-Québécois literature. By integrating historical references and narrative techniques that evoke Latin America into a novel written in French,[12] whose main character, Maryse, has often been identified as the archetypal modern female Québécois character, Noël imposes a reconsideration of what a "Québécois" novel is. Because this novel is clearly constructed as a hybrid text through its network of references, techniques, representations of time and space, and characters – who are themselves hybrids, or métis – as well as through themes that signal the importance of plurality and the myth of homogeneity, it is closer to the conceptualization of culture in Latin America than in France. Perhaps this tetralogy is thus truly postcolonial for recognizing Quebec's common heritage with Latin America rather than looking back to its connection with France.

This brings us to a brief consideration of the title. Noël appears to be offering, in her use of the word *bâtard*, an alternative to those that have already been mentioned in order to refer to an individual of mixed origins (hybrid, métis, creole); hence a *bâtard* is not simply one who is born of an illegitimate union – which of course is how the colonization of the Americas could be viewed – but is also an animal that is not of pure race.[13] In using this term, Noël rejects the pejorative sense of the word, suggesting that everyone is of mixed heritage; in fact, the concept of purity as a characteristic of cultural identity has no meaning. The term might also have some shock value in the context of a more traditional Quebec, where until the middle of the twentieth century, "bastard children" were given up for adoption and sometimes sent off to live in asylums. But by using this term in a completely different way, the author is suggesting that perhaps the expectations of what a Québécois novel is should also be re-examined and turned on their head.

Indeed, this text does venture beyond the traditional Québécois novel or even the postmodern one; could it be considered a postnational Québécois novel? Perhaps this is not the correct question to pose; it does however force us to reconsider what a Québécois novel is. One thing is certainly clear: the Québécois novel can no longer ignore its relations with other cultures with which it cohabits in the Americas. Other novels, such as *Volkswagen Blues* (1984) by Jacques Poulin and *Copies conformes* (1989) by Monique LaRue, to name only two, have amply demonstrated the "Americanness" of contemporary Québécois literature, although emphasizing to a certain extent the US element of America. Noël's novel, however, serves to remind us that the elephant that lies beyond Quebec's and Canada's southern border does not encompass all of the Americas. By looking beyond this elephant, it is in fact possible for Québécois literature to assert itself because it can develop significant connections with other American cultures, thus freeing itself from the conventional colonial paradigm of the centre and the periphery.

There are many aspects of Noël's work that I have not treated or that I have only touched upon, such as the treatment of time, space, intertextuality, and plurilingualism. However, the novel's themes, use of magical realism, and historiographic discourse clearly suggest that the conception of what makes a Québécois novel *Québécois* is problematic. I am not proposing that we should not consider it a Québécois novel at all, as labels do have some usefulness, and I do not believe that Noël aims to depreciate the aspirations of Quebec as a nation. In fact, by emphasizing Quebec's connection to Mexico and bypassing Canada altogether, she in a sense asserts the former's de facto independence – even if it has not yet been quite achieved politically. But she also implies that cultural identity does not end with the attainment of a sovereign nation; cultural identity is constantly mutating and must remain open to all the different unpredictable possibilities for mutation, even when – or rather, especially when – these possibilities originate beyond national boundaries.

NOTES

1 The novel was republished under the title *Nous avons tous découvert l'Amérique* in 1992 by Actes Sud.
2 The translation of Nepveu is from Patricia Godbout, quoted in Siemerling (2005, 28).
3 See, for example, Chassay (1995), which limits the notion of *américanité* to the United States. There are of course exceptions as well; see, for example, Killick (2005).

4 See Wyile's chapter in this volume.

5 It is amusing and interesting to note that Noël is not the first to link Quebec and Mexico. An alliance between Mexico and Quebec was envisaged by Abbé Henri-Raymond Casgrain in the late nineteenth century, as he hoped that the two Catholic nations would overcome the Anglo-Saxon protestant forces and defeat "les forces du matérialisme" (Nepveu 1998, 105).

6 It might be possible to interpret this betrayal through language as symbolic of Quebec's linguistic and political situation, especially as translation was often considered a step toward assimilation in the first few decades of the twentieth century, but it would be worthwhile to consider that French would also have been a "language of betrayal" contributing to the downfall of Native peoples in the sixteenth and seventeenth centuries.

7 Marie Vautier writes: "Although many studies of Québécois literature concentrate on *le merveilleux* and on *le fantastique* – especially with regard to their presence in the genre of *le conte*, magic realism as a postcolonial device – or even as a genre – has not received much critical attention in Quebec" (1998, 211).

8 Gabrielle first appears in the second instalment of the tetralogy, *Myriam Première*.

9 They met him as children when they hung out in his Montreal underground bar. They weren't allowed to drink alcoholic beverages of course!

10 Here, the reaction of the subway riders reflects the likely reaction of many of the work's ("real") readers.

11 In *La Conjuration*, Myriam is a young woman in her early twenties. But in the second volume of the tetralogy, *Myriam première*, she is a young girl.

12 I have not touched on the issue of language in this study, but of course it is an important direction to follow in future reflections on this novel.

13 These definitions are loosely borrowed from *Le Petit Larousse* 2003.

Contributors

ALBERT BRAZ is an associate professor of comparative literature and English at the University of Alberta, where he specializes in Canadian literature in both its national and inter-American contexts. He is particularly interested in literary representations of the encounters between Natives and newcomers in Canada and the rest of the Americas. Among other publications, he is the author of *The False Traitor: Louis Riel in Canadian Culture* (2003).

SARAH PHILLIPS CASTEEL is an associate professor of English at Carleton University, where she teaches postcolonial and diaspora literatures. She is the author of *Second Arrivals: Landscape and Belonging in Contemporary Writing of the Americas* (2007) and a co-editor, with Rachel Adams, of a special issue of *Comparative American Studies* on "Canada and the Americas" (2005). She is the recipient of a Horst Frenz Prize and a Polanyi Prize.

AMARYLL CHANADY is a professor of comparative literature at the Université de Montréal. Her areas of specialization are inter-American studies, space and collective identity, hybridity, and postcolonialism. Among her publications are *Entre inclusion et exclusion: La symbolisation de l'autre dans les Amériques* (1999) and *America's Worlds and the World's Americas* (2006, co-editor).

MONIKA GIACOPPE is an associate professor of comparative literature at Ramapo College of New Jersey. She is currently translating *Moi, Jeanne Castille de Louisiane* (I, Jeanne Castille of Louisiana), the autobiography of a Cajun/Cadien woman who advocated for the French language in Louisiana.

PATRICIA GODBOUT is an associate professor in the Lettres et Communications department at the Université de Sherbrooke. Her main fields of research are translation studies and the history of literary translation in Canada. Her French translation of Winfried Siemerling's *The New North American Studies* (2005) was published by Presses de l'Université Laval in 2009.

HUGH HAZELTON is a writer and translator who specializes in the comparison of Canadian and Quebec literatures with those of Latin America. His translation of *Vétiver*, by Joël Des Rosiers, won the Governor General's award for French-English translation in 2006. He teaches Spanish translation and Latin American civilization at Concordia University in Montreal.

CATHERINE KHORDOC is an associate professor of French at Carleton University. She is a co-editor, with Marie Carrière, of *Migrance comparée: Les littératures du Canada et du Québec/Comparing Migration: The Literatures of Canada and Québec*, and she has published articles in journals such *Voix et images*, the *International Journal of Canadian Studies*, and the *Irish Journal of French Studies* as well as in various essay collections.

DAVID LEAHY is currently the director of the graduate program in comparative Canadian literature at the Université de Sherbrooke. His chapter in this volume is part of a larger research project that critiques ways the neoliberal *embourgeoisement* of Quebec and Canada manifests itself culturally and its consequences for imaginative and political resistance.

MAUREEN MOYNAGH is an associate professor at St Francis Xavier University, where she teaches postcolonial literatures, modernism and gender, and theory. In addition to African Canadian postslavery literature, her research interests include hemispheric studies, travel and tourism, and the links between modernism, gender, and empire. Her recent books include *African-Canadian Theatre* (2005) and *Political Tourism and Its Texts* (2008).

WINFRIED SIEMERLING is a professor of English at the University of Waterloo and an associate of the W.E.B. Du Bois Institute for African and African American Research at Harvard. His books include

The New North American Studies (2005; French translation by Patricia Godbout, 2009), *Cultural Difference and the Literary Text* (1996–97, co-editor), *Writing Ethnicity* (1996, editor), and *Discoveries of the Other* (1994).

SHERRY SIMON is a professor in the Department of French at Concordia University. Her most recent book, *Translating Montreal: Episodes in the Life of a Divided City* (2006), appeared in French translation as *Traverser Montréal: Une histoire culturelle par la traduction* (2008). She is a co-editor, with Paul St-Pierre, of *Changing the Terms: Translating in the Postcolonial Era* (2000) and, with Pierre Anctil and Norm Ravvin, of *New Readings of Yiddish Montreal – Traduire le Montréal Yiddish* (2007). She is a member of the Royal Society of Canada and a Killam Research Fellow (2009–11).

CYNTHIA SUGARS is an associate professor in the Department of English at the University of Ottawa. She is the editor of *Unhomely States: Theorizing English-Canadian Postcolonialism* (2004), *Home-Work: Postcolonialism, Pedagogy, and Canadian Literature* (2004), and *Unsettled Remains: Canadian Literature and the Postcolonial Gothic* (2009), and she has co-edited an anthology of Canadian literature with Laura Moss, *Canadian Literature: Texts and Contexts* (2008).

HERB WYILE is a professor in the Department of English at Acadia University. His primary areas of interest are historical fiction, regionalism, Atlantic Canada, and globalization. His publications include *Speculative Fictions* (2002), a critical study of Canadian historical fiction, and *Speaking in the Past Tense* (2007), a book of interviews with Canadian historical novelists.

References

INTRODUCTION

Adams, Rachel, and Sarah Phillips Casteel. 2005. "Introduction." *Comparative American Studies* 3, no. 1 (special issue on "Canada and the Americas," ed. Rachel Adams and Sarah Phillips Casteel) (March): 5–13.

Appiah, Kwame Anthony. 2005. *The Ethics of Identity.* Princeton, NJ, and Oxford, UK: Princeton University Press.

Ashcroft, Bill, Gareth Griffiths, and Helen Tiffin. 1989. *The Empire Writes Back.* London, UK, and New York: Routledge.

Atwood, Margaret. 1972. *Surfacing.* Toronto: McClelland and Stewart.

– 1996. *Survival: A Thematic Guide to Canadian Literature.* 1972. Reprint, Toronto: McClelland and Stewart.

Balakian, Anna, and James J. Wilhelm, eds. 1985. *Proceedings of the Xth Congress of the International Comparative Literature Association.* New York: Garland.

Blodgett, Edward Dickinson. 2003. *Five-Part Invention: A History of Literary History in Canada.* Toronto: University of Toronto Press.

Braziel, Jana Evans. 2005. "C'est moi l'Amérique: Canada, Haiti and Dany Laferrière's Port-au-Prince/Montréal/Miami Textual Transmigrations of the Hemisphere." *Comparative American Studies* 3, no. 1 (special issue on "Canada and the Americas," ed. Rachel Adams and Sarah Phillips Casteel) (March): 29–46.

Brydon, Diana. 2004. "Postcolonialism Now: Autonomy, Cosmopolitanism, and Diaspora." *University of Toronto Quarterly* 73, no. 2: 691–706.

Buell, Lawrence. 1992. "American Literary Emergence as a Postcolonial Phenomenon." *American Literary History* 1: 411–42.

– 2000. "Postcolonial Anxiety in Classic United States Literature." In Amritjit Singh and Peter Schmidt, eds, *Postcolonial Theory and the United States: Race, Ethnicity, and Literature*, 196–219. Jackson: University Press of Mississippi.

Casteel, Sarah Phillips. 2007. *Second Arrivals: Landscape and Belonging in Contemporary Writing of the Americas*. Charlottesville: University of Virginia Press.

Cowan, Bainard, and Jefferson Humphries, eds. 1997. *Poetics of the Americas: Race, Founding, Textuality*. Baton Rouge: Lousiana State University Press.

Derrida, Jacques. 2001. *On Cosmopolitanism and Forgiveness*. Trans. Mark Dooley and Michael Hughes. London, UK, and New York: Routledge.

Elliott, Emory, ed. 1991. *The Columbia History of the American Novel*. New York: Columbia University Press.

Firmat, Gustavo Pérez. 1990. "Introduction: Cheek to Cheek." In Gustavo Pérez Firmat, ed., *Do the Americas Have a Common Literature?* 1–5. Durham, NC: Duke University Press.

Fitz, Earl E. 1991. *Rediscovering the New World: Inter-American Literature in a Comparative Context*. Iowa City: University of Iowa Press.

Flick, Jane. 1999. "Reading Notes for Thomas King's *Green Grass, Running Water*." *Canadian Literature*, nos 161–62: 140–72.

Frye, Northrop. 1965. "Conclusion." In Carl F. Klinck, ed., *Literary History of Canada: Canadian Literature in English*, 821–49. Toronto: University of Toronto Press. Reprinted as "Conclusion to a *Literary History of Canada*," in Northrop Frye, *The Bush Garden: Essays on the Canadian Imagination*, 213–51 (Toronto: Anansi, 1971).

– 1971. *The Bush Garden: Essays on the Canadian Imagination*. Toronto: Anansi.

– 1982. "'Conclusion' to *Literary History of Canada*, Second Edition (1976)." In *Divisions on a Ground: Essays on Canadian Culture*, 71–88. Toronto: Anansi.

Glickman, Susan. 1998. *The Picturesque and the Sublime: A Poetics of the Canadian Landscape*. Montreal and Kingston: McGill-Queen's University Press.

Glissant, Edouard. 1989. "L'autre Amérique." In *Caribbean Discourse*. Trans. J. Michael Dash. Charlottesville: University of Virginia Press.

Greenblatt, Stephen Jay. 1991. *Marvelous Possessions: The Wonder of the New World*. Chicago, IL: University of Chicago Press.

Gruesz, Kirsten Silva. 2002. *Ambassadors of Culture: The Transamerican Origins of Latino Writing*. Princeton, NJ: Princeton University Press.

Handley, George B. 2000. *Postslavery Literatures in the Americas: Family Portraits in Black and White*. Charlottesville: University of Virginia Press.

Hazelton, Hugh. 2002. "Latin America and Canadian Writing." In W.H. New, ed., *Encyclopedia of Writing in Canada*, 632–4. Toronto: University of Toronto Press.

– 2007. *Latinocanadá: An Anthology of Ten Latin American Writers of Canada*. Montreal and Kingston: McGill-Queen's University Press.

– and Gary Geddes, eds. 1990. *Compañeros: An Anthology of Writings about Latin America*. Dunvegan, ON: Cormorant Books.

Imbert, Patrick. 2004. *Trajectoires Culturelles Transaméricaines: Médias, Publicité, Littérature et Mondialisation*. Ottawa: University of Ottawa Press.

Jay, Gregory. 1991. "The End of 'American' Literature: Toward a Multicultural Practice." *College English* 53, no. 3: 264–81.

– 1997. *American Literature and the Culture Wars*. Ithaca, NY, and London, UK: Cornell University Press.

Kokotailo, Philip. 1992. "The Bishop and His Deacon: Smith vs Sutherland Reconsidered." *Journal of Canadian Studies* 27, no. 2: 63–81.

Lee, Dennis. 1985. "Cadence, Country, Silence: Writing in a Colonial Space." In Douglas M. Daymond and Leslie G. Monkman, eds, *Towards a Canadian Literature: Essays, Editorials and Manifestos*, vol. 2, 497–520. Ottawa: Tecumseh Press.

Martí, José. 2002. "Our America." In Paul Lauter, ed., *Heath Anthology of American Literature*, vol. 2, 4th ed., 879–86. Lexington, KY: D.C. Heath.

– 2003. "Nuestra América." In *Por Nuestra América*, 223–32. Havana, Cuba: Editorial José Martí.

Mignolo, Walter. 2000. "The Many Faces of Cosmo-polis: Border Thinking and Critical Cosmopolitanism." *Public Culture* 12, no. 3: 721–48.

Moya, Paula M.L., and Ramón Saldívar. 2003. "Fictions of the Trans-American Imaginary." *Modern Fiction Studies* 49, no. 1 (Spring): 1–18.

Moyes, Lianne. 2007. "Acts of Citizenship: Erin Mouré's *O Cidadán* and the Limits of Worldliness." In Smaro Kamboureli and Roy Miki, eds, *Trans.Can.Lit: Resituating the Study of Canadian Literature*, 111–28. Waterloo, ON: Wilfrid Laurier University Press.

Murphy, Gretchen. 2005. *Hemispheric Imaginings: The Monroe Doctrine and Narratives of United States Empire*. Durham, NC: Duke University Press.

Muthyala, John. 2001. "Reworlding America: The Globalization of American Studies." *Cultural Critique* 47 (Winter): 91–119.

Nepveu, Pierre. 1988. *L'Ecologie du réel: Mort et naissance de la littérature québécoise contemporaine*. Montreal: Boréal.

Ondaatje, Michael. 1978. "García Márquez and the Bus to Aracataca." In Diane Bessai and David Jackel, eds, *Figures in a Ground: Canadian Essays on Modern Literature*, 19–31. Collected in Honor of Sheila Watson. Saskatoon: Western Producer Prairie Books.

Patell, Cyrus R.K. 1999. "Comparative American Studies: Hybridity and Beyond." *American Literary History* 11, no. 1 (Spring): 166–86.

Pease, Donald E. 2001. "The Politics of Postnational American Studies." *European Journal of American Culture* 20, no. 2: 78–90.

– and Robyn Wiegman, eds. 2002. *The Futures of American Studies*. Durham, NC: Duke University Press.

Porter, Carolyn. 1994. "What We Know That We Don't Know: Remapping American Literary Studies." *American Literary History* 6, no. 3: 467–526.

Rodriguez, Richard. 2002. *Brown: The Last Discovery of America*. New York: Viking.

Rowe, John Carlos. 2003. "Nineteenth-Century United States Literary Culture and Transnationality." *PMLA* 118, no. 1 (January): 78–89.

Sadowski-Smith, Claudia, and Claire F. Fox. 2004. "Theorizing the Hemisphere: Inter-Americas Work at the Intersection of American, Canadian, and Latin American Studies." *Comparative American Studies* 2, no. 1: 5–38.

Saldívar, José David. 1997. *Border Matters: Remapping American Cultural Studies*. Berkeley: University of California Press.

Sale, Kirkpatrick. 1990. *The Conquest of Paradise: Christopher Columbus and the Columbian Legacy*. New York: Knopf.

Scott, Nina M. 1980. "Inter-American Literature: An Antidote to the Arrogance of Culture." *College English* 41, no. 6: 635–43.

Siemerling, Winfried. 2005. *The New North American Studies: Culture, Writing, and the Politics of Re/Cognition*. New York and London, UK: Routledge.

– 2007. "Trans-Scan: Globalization, Literary Hemispheric Studies, Citizenship as Project." In Smaro Kamboureli and Roy Miki, eds, *Trans.Can.Lit: Resituating the Study of Canadian Literature*, 129–40. Waterloo, ON: Wilfrid Laurier University Press.

Singh, Amritjit, and Peter Schmidt, eds. 2000. *Postcolonial Theory and the United States: Race, Ethnicity, and Literature*. Jackson: University Press of Mississippi.

Slemon, Stephen. 2007. "TransCanada, Literature: No Direction Home." In Smaro Kamboureli and Roy Miki, eds, *Trans.Can.Lit: Resituating the Study of Canadian Literature*, 71–83. Waterloo, ON: Wilfrid Laurier University Press.

Smith, A.J.M., ed. 1943. *The Book of Canadian Poetry: A Critical and Historical Anthology*. Chicago, IL: University of Chicago Press.

Spengemann, William. 1978. "What Is American Literature?" *Centennial Review* 22: 119–38.

Sugars, Cynthia. 2001. "Can the Canadian Speak? Lost in Postcolonial Space." *ARIEL: A Review of International English Literature* 32, no. 3: 115–52.

Sutherland, John. 1944. "Literary Colonialism." *First Statement* 2, no. 4: editorial. Reprinted in John Sutherland, *Essays, Controversies and Poems*, ed. Miriam Waddington, 31–2 (Toronto: McClelland and Stewart, 1972).

Turner, Margaret E. 1995. *Imagining Culture: New World Narrative and the Writing of Canada*. Montreal and Kingston: McGill-Queen's University Press.

Valdéz, Mario, and Djelal Kadir. 2004. *Literary Cultures of Latin America: A Comparative History*. New York: Oxford University Press.

Vautier, Marie. 1998. *New World Myth: Postmodernism and Postcolonialism in Canadian Fiction*. Montreal and Kingston: McGill-Queen's University Press.

Wald, Priscilla. 1998. "Minefields and Meeting Grounds: Transnational Analyses and American Studies." *American Literary History* 10, no. 1 (Spring): 199–218.

Walter, Roland. 2003. *Narrative Identities: (Inter)Cultural In-Betweenness in the Americas*. Bern, Switzerland: Peter Lang.

Winks, Robin W. 1997. *The Blacks in Canada: A History*. 1971. Reprint, Montreal and Kingston: McGill-Queen's University Press.

Zamora, Lois Parkinson. 1997. *The Usable Past: The Imagination of History in Recent Fiction of the Americas*. Cambridge, UK: Cambridge University Press.

CHAPTER ONE

Ahmad, Aijaz. 1994. *In Theory: Classes, Nations, Literatures*. Oxford, UK: Oxford University Press.

Atwood, Margaret. 1972. *Surfacing*. Toronto: McClelland and Stewart.

Bannerji, Himani. 2004. "Geography Lessons: On Being an Insider/ Outsider to the Canadian Nation." 1997. Reprinted in Cynthia Sugars, ed., *Unhomely States: Theorizing English-Canadian Postcolonialism*, 289–300. Peterborough, ON: Broadview.

Bhabha, Homi K. 1990. "Introduction: Narrating the Nation." In Homi K. Bhabha, ed., *Nation and Narration*, 1–7. London, UK: Routledge.

Birney, Earle. 1980. "Has Poetry a Future in Canada?" 1946. Reprinted in *Spreading Time: Remarks on Canadian Writing and Writers, Book I: 1904–1949*, 69–77. Montreal: Véhicule.

Brennan, Timothy. 1997. *At Home in the World: Cosmopolitanism Now*. Cambridge, MA: Harvard University Press.

– 2001. "Cosmo-Theory." *South Atlantic Quarterly* 100, no. 3: 659–91.

Brydon, Diana. 2003a. "Canada and Postcolonialism: Questions, Inventories, and Futures." In Laura Moss, ed., *Is Canada Postcolonial: Essays on Canadian Literature and Postcolonial Theory*, 49–77. Waterloo, ON: Wilfrid Laurier University Press.

– 2003b. "Writing Home." Munro Beattie Lecture, Carleton University, Ottawa, 7 March.

Buell, Frederick. 1998. "Nationalist Postnationalism: Globalist Discourse in Contemporary American Culture." *American Quarterly* 50, no. 3: 548–91.

Cheah, Pheng. 1999. "Spectral Nationality: The Living On [*sur-vie*] of the Postcolonial Nation in Neocolonial Globalization." *boundary* 2 26, no. 3: 225–52.

Frye, Northrop. 1971. "Conclusion to a *Literary History of Canada*." 1965. Reprinted in *The Bush Garden: Essays on the Canadian Imagination*, 213–51. Toronto: Anansi.

Gunew, Sneja. 2004. *Haunted Nations: The Colonial Dimension of Multiculturalisms*. London, UK: Routledge.

Hall, Stuart. 1997. "The Local and the Global: Globalization and Ethnicity." In Anne McClintock, Aamir Mufti, and Ella Shohat, eds, *Dangerous Liaisons: Gender, Nation, and Postcolonial Perspectives*, 173–87. Minneapolis: University of Minnesota Press.

Iyer, Pico. 2000. *The Global Soul: Jet Lag, Shopping Malls and the Search for Home*. London, UK: Bloomsbury.

– 2002. "The Last Refuge: On the Promise of the New Canadian Fiction." *Harper's Magazine*, June, 77–80.

Jameson, Fredric. 2000. "Globalization and Political Strategy." *New Left Review* 4: 49–68.

Johnston, Anna, and Alan Lawson. 2005. "Settler Colonies." In Henry Schwarz and Sangeeta Ray, eds, *A Companion to Postcolonial Studies*, 360–76. London, UK: Blackwell.

Kamboureli, Smaro. 2000. *Scandalous Bodies: Diasporic Literature in English Canada*. Toronto: Oxford University Press.

Lazarus, Neil. 1999. *Nationalism and Cultural Practice in the Postcolonial World*. Cambridge, UK: Cambridge University Press.

Lecker, Robert. 2000. "Where Is Here Now?" *Essays on Canadian Writing* 71: 6–13.

Mackey, Eva. 2002. *The House of Difference: Cultural Politics and National Identity in Canada*. Toronto: University of Toronto Press.

McClintock, Anne. 1995. *Imperial Leather: Race, Gender and Sexuality in the Colonial Contest*. New York: Routledge.

Miki, Roy. 1998. *Broken Entries: Race, Subjectivity, Writing*. Toronto: Mercury Press.

– 2005. "'Inside the Black Egg': Cultural Practice, Citizenship, and Belonging in a Globalizing Canadian Nation." *Mosaic* 38, no. 3: 1–19.

Mukherjee, Arun. 1998. *Postcolonialism: My Living*. Toronto: TSAR.

Pennee, Donna Palmateer. 2004. "Literary Citizenship: Culture (Un)Bounded, Culture (Re)Distributed." In Cynthia Sugars, ed., *Home-Work: Postcolonialism, Pedagogy, and Canadian Literature*, 75–85. Ottawa: University of Ottawa Press.

"Pico Iyer." 2005. *Wikipedia*. http://en.wikipedia.org/wiki/Pico_Iyer.

Robbins, Bruce. 1999. *Feeling Global: Internationalism in Distress*. New York: New York University Press.

Rowe, John Carlos. 2002. *The New American Studies*. Minneapolis: University of Minnesota Press.

Said, Edward. 2004. *Humanism and Democratic Criticism*. New York: Columbia University Press.

Saul, John Ralston. 2005. *The Collapse of Globalism and the Reinvention of the World*. Toronto: Viking.

Siemerling, Winfried. 2005. *The New North American Studies: Culture, Writing, and the Politics of Re/Cognition*. London, UK: Routledge.

Smith, Ray. 1989. *Cape Breton Is the Thought-Control Centre of Canada*. Erin, ON: Porcupine's Quill.

Spillers, Hortense. 2005. "The Arts of Gravity and Other Comforts." Keynote address. International American Studies Association Congress, University of Ottawa, 20 August.

Spivak, Gayatri Chakravorty. 1985. "The Rani of Sirmur." In Francis Barker et al., eds, *Europe and Its Others*, vol. 1, 128–51. Colchester, UK: University of Essex Press.

Sugars, Cynthia. 2001. "Can the Canadian Speak? Lost in Postcolonial Space." *ARIEL: A Review of International English Literature* 32, no. 3: 115–52.

– 2005. "'World Famous Across Canada': National Identity in the Global Village." In Janet Wilson and Clara Joseph, eds, *Global Fissures: Postcolonial Fusions*, 79–101. Amsterdam and New York: Rodopi.

Szeman, Imre. 2000. "Belated or Isochronic? Canadian Writing, Time, and Globalization." *Essays on Canadian Writing* 71: 186–94.
– 2003. *Zones of Instability: Literature, Postcolonialism, and the Nation.* Baltimore, MD: Johns Hopkins University Press.
Turner, Stephen. 1999. "Settlement as Forgetting." In Klaus Veumann et al., eds, *Quicksands: Foundational Histories in Australia and Aotearoa New Zealand*, 20–38. Sydney: University of New South Wales Press.
Wattenberg, Ben. 1990. *The First Universal Nation: Leading Indicators and Ideas about the Surge of America in the 1990s.* New York: Free Press.
Zamora, Lois Parkinson. 1997. *The Usable Past: The Imagination of History in Recent Fiction of the Americas.* Cambridge, UK: Cambridge University Press.

CHAPTER TWO

Bassnett, Susan. 1993. *Comparative Literature: A Critical Introduction.* Oxford, UK: Blackwell.
Bennett, Donna. 1994. "English Canada's Postcolonial Complexities." *Essays on Canadian Writing* 52: 164–210.
Brydon, Diana. 1995. "Introduction: Reading Postcoloniality, Reading Canada." *Essays on Canadian Writing* 56 (special issue on "Testing the Limits: Postcolonial Theories and Canadian Literatures"): 1–19.
– 2000. "It's Time for a New Set of Questions." *Essays on Canadian Writing* 71 (special issue on "Where Is Here Now?"): 14–25.
– 2007. "Metamorphoses of a Discipline: Rethinking Canadian Literature within Institutional Contexts." In Smaro Kamboureli and Roy Miki, eds, *Trans.Can.Lit: Resituating the Study of Canadian Literature*, 1–16. Waterloo, ON: Wilfrid Laurier University Press.
Buell, Frederick. 1994. *National Culture and the New Global System.* Baltimore, MD: Johns Hopkins University Press.
Clow, Michael. 2005. "Just More of the Same? Confederation and Globalization." In James Sacouman and Henry Veltmeyer, eds, *From the Net to the Net: Atlantic Canada and the Global Economy*, 25–50. Aurora, ON: Garamond.
Dirlik, Arif. 2000. *Postmodernity's Histories: The Past as Legacy and Project.* Boston, MA: Rowman and Littlefield.
Fitz, Earl E. 1991. *Rediscovering the New World: Inter-American Literature in a Comparative Context.* Iowa City: University of Iowa Press.
Freleng, Friz, dir. 1952. "14 Carrot Rabbit."

Jordan, David. 1994. *New World Regionalism*. Toronto: University of Toronto Press.

Kamboureli, Smaro, and Roy Miki, eds. 2007. *Trans.Can.Lit: Resituating the Study of Canadian Literature*. Waterloo, ON: Wilfrid Laurier University Press.

Moss, Laura, ed. 2003. *Is Canada Postcolonial? Unsettling Canadian Literature*. Waterloo, ON: Wilfrid Laurier University Press.

Moyes, Lianne. 1992. "'Canadian Literature Criticism': Between the Poles of the Universal-Particular Antinomy." *Open Letter*, 8th ser., no. 3 (special issue on "Canadian? Literature? Theory?" ed. Barbara Godard): 28–46.

Pennee, Donna Palmateer. 2004. "Literary Citizenship: Culture (Un)Bounded, Culture (Re)Distributed." In Cynthia Sugars, ed., *Home-Work: Postcolonialism, Pedagogy and Canadian Literature*, 75–85. Ottawa: University of Ottawa Press.

Siemerling, Winfried. 2005. *The New North American Studies: Culture, Writing and the Politics of Re/Cognition*. New York: Routledge.

Slemon, Stephen. 1990. "Unsettling the Empire: Resistance Theory for the Second World." *World Literature Written in English* 30, no. 2: 30–41.

– 2007. "TransCanada, Literature: No Direction Home." In Smaro Kamboureli and Roy Miki, eds, *Trans.Can.Lit: Resituating the Study of Canadian Literature*, 71–83. Waterloo, ON: Wilfrid Laurier University Press.

Smith, A.J.M. 1943. "Introduction." In A.J.M. Smith, ed., *The Book of Canadian Poetry*, 3–31. Chicago, IL: University of Chicago Press.

Sugars, Cynthia, ed. 2004. *Home-Work: Postcolonialism, Pedagogy and Canadian Literature*. Ottawa: University of Ottawa Press.

Vassanji, M.G. 1999. "Foreword." In Nurjehan Aziz, ed., *Floating the Borders: New Contexts of Canadian Criticism*, vii-viii. Toronto: TSAR.

Watson, William. 1998. *Globalization and the Meaning of Canadian Life*. Toronto: University of Toronto Press.

"Where Is Here Now?" 2000. *Essays on Canadian Writing* 71 (special issue).

CHAPTER THREE

Angenot, Marc. 1997. *Les idéologies du ressentiment*. Montreal: XYZ éditeur.

Ashcroft, Bill, Gareth Griffiths, and Helen Tiffin, eds. 2000. *Post-Colonial Studies: The Key Concepts*. London, UK, and New York: Routledge.

Atwood, Margaret. 1972. *Survival: A Thematic Guide to Canadian Literature*. Toronto: Anansi.

Bissoondath, Neil. 1994. *Selling Illusions: The Cult of Multiculturalism in Canada*. Toronto: Penguin.

Brand, Dionne. 1984. "Grenada, October 25th, 1983." *This Magazine*.

– 1990. *No Language Is Neutral*. Toronto: Coach House Press.

– 1997. "Dualities." *Brick: A Literary Journal*, no. 58: 4–8.

– 2001. *A Map to the Door of No Return*. Toronto: Doubleday.

– dir. 1996. *Listening for Something ... Adrienne Rich and Dionne Brand in Conversation*. Film. 55 mins. National Film Board of Canada.

Chamberland, Paul. 1964a. *L'afficheur hurle*. Montreal: Éditions Parti pris.

– 1964b. *Terre Québec*. Montreal: Librairie Déom.

– 1978. *Extrême survivance, extrême poésie*. Montreal: Éditions Parti pris.

– 1980. *Terre souveraine*. Montreal: L'Hexagone.

– 1990. "Independence Is for 1993." Trans. David Lenson. *The Massachusetts Review* 31, nos 1–2 (Spring-Summer): 61–74.

– 1991. *Le multiple événement terrestre: Géogrammes 1 (1979–1985)*. Montreal: L'Hexagone.

– 1994. *L'assaut contre les vivants: Géogrammes 2 (1986–1991)*. Montreal: L'Hexagone.

Cherry, Deborah. 2002. "Earth into World, Land into Landscape: The 'Worlding' of Algeria in Nineteenth-Century British Feminism." In Jill Beaulieu and Mary Roberts, eds, *Orientalism's Interlocutors: Painting, Architecture, Photography*, 103–30. Durham, NC, and London, UK: Duke University Press.

Douglas, Ann. 1995. *Terrible Honesty: Mongrel Manhattan in the 1920s*. New York: Noonday Press.

Englebrecht, Penelope J. 1990. "'Lifting Belly Is a Language': The Postmodern Lesbian Subject." *Feminist Studies* 16, no. 1 (Spring): 85–114.

Frye, Northrop. 1965. "Conclusion." In Carl F. Klinck, ed., *Literary History of Canada: Canadian Literature in English*, 821–49. Toronto: University of Toronto Press. Reprinted as "Conclusion to a *Literary History of Canada*," in Northrop Frye, *The Bush Garden: Essays on the Canadian Imagination*, 213–51 (Toronto: Anansi, 1971).

Grant, George. 1965. *Lament for a Nation: The Defeat of Canadian Nationalism*. Ottawa: Carleton University Press.

Lalonde, Michèle. 1979. "Speak White." In *Défense et illustration de la langue québécoise*, 37–40. Paris, France: Éditions Seghers/Laffont.

Mukherjee, Arun. 1994. *Oppositional Aesthetics: Readings from a Hyphenated Space.* Toronto and Cardiff: TSAR.

Parry, Benita. 2004. *Postcolonial Studies: A Materialist Critique.* London, UK, and New York: Routledge.

Siemerling, Winfried. 2005. *The New North American Studies: Culture, Writing and the Politics of Re/Cognition.* London, UK, and New York: Routledge.

Slemon, Stephen. 1990. "Unsettling the Empire: Resistance Theory for the Second World." *World Literature Written in English* 30, no. 2: 30–41.

Spivak, Gayatri Chakravorty. 1984–85. "Criticism, Feminism, and The Institution." Reprinted in *The Post-Colonial Critic: Interviews, Strategies, Dialogues,* 1–16. Ed. Sarah Harasym. London, UK, and New York: Routledge, 1990.

– 1985. "The Rani of Sirmur: An Essay in Reading the Archives." *History and Theory* 24, no. 3 (October): 247–72.

– 1986. "The Problem of Cultural Self-Representation." *Thesis Eleven* (Australia) 15, no. 1: 91–7.

– 1990. *The Post-Colonial Critic: Interviews, Strategies, Dialogues.* Ed. Sarah Harasym. London, UK, and New York: Routledge.

Zackodnik, Teresa. 1996. "'I Am Blackening in My Way': Identity and Place in Dionne Brand's *No Language Is Neutral.*" In Winfried Siemerling, ed., *Writing Ethnicity: Cross-Cultural Consciousness in Canadian and Québécois Literature,* 194–211. Toronto: ECW Press.

CHAPTER FOUR

Arguedas, José María. 1975. *Formación de una cultura nacional indoamericana.* Mexico City: Siglo Veintiuno.

Atwood, Margaret. 1972. "First People: Indians and Eskimos as Symbols." In *Survival: A Thematic Guide to Canadian Literature,* 87–106. Toronto: Anansi.

Basave Benítez, Agustín. 1992. *México mestizo: Análisis del nacionalismo mexicano en torno a la mestizofilia de Andrés Molina Enríquez.* Mexico City: Fondo de Cultura Económica.

Castro, Michael. 1983. *Interpreting the Indian: Twentieth-Century Poets and the Native American.* Albuquerque: University of New Mexico Press.

Chanady, Amaryll. 1999. *Entre inclusion et exclusion: La symbolisation de l'autre dans les Amériques.* Paris, France: Honoré Champion.

Clavijero, Francisco Xavier. 1958. *Historia antigua de México*. 4 vols.
Ed. R.P. Mariano Cuevas. 1780–81. Reprint, Mexico City: Editorial
Porrúa.

Connor, Walker. 1994. *Ethnonationalism: The Quest for Understanding*.
Princeton, NJ: Princeton University Press.

Fernández Retamar, Roberto. 1989. *Caliban and Other Essays*. 1971.
Reprint, Minneapolis: University of Minnesota Press.

Groening, Laura Smyth. 2004. *Listening to Old Woman Speak: Natives
and alterNatives in Canadian Literature*. Montreal and Kingston:
McGill-Queen's University Press.

Laurence, Margaret. 1986. "The Loons." 1966. Reprinted in Margaret
Atwood and Robert Weaver, eds, *The Oxford Book of Canadian Short
Stories*, 143–51. Toronto, Oxford, UK, and New York: Oxford University Press.

Martí, José. 1972. *Antología mínima*. Vol. 1. 1891. Reprint, Havana,
Cuba: Instituto cubano del libro.

Monkman, Leslie. 1981. *A Native Heritage: Images of the Indian in
English-Canadian Literature*. Toronto, Buffalo, and London, UK:
University of Toronto Press.

Seton-Watson, Hugh. 1982. *Nations and States*. London, UK: Methuen.

Thérien, Gilles. 1987. "L'Indien imaginaire: Une hypothèse." *Recherches
amérindiennes du Québec* 17, no. 3: 3–21.

Tompkins, Jane. 1986. "'Indians': Textualism, Morality, and the Problem
of History." *Critical Inquiry* 13, no. 1 (Fall): 101–19.

Traill, Catharine Parr. 1969. *The Canadian Settler's Guide*. 1855.
Reprint, Toronto: McClelland and Stewart.

– 1986. *The Backwoods of Canada*. 1836. Reprint, Toronto: McClelland
and Stewart.

Vasconcelos, José. 1961. *La raza cósmica*. 1925. Reprint, Mexico City:
Fondo de Cultura Económica.

Young, Robert J.C. 1995. *Colonial Desire: Hybridity in Theory, Culture
and Race*. London, UK: Routledge.

CHAPTER FIVE

Adams, Rachel, and Sarah Phillips Casteel. 2005. "Introduction: Canada
and the Americas." *Comparative American Studies* 3, no. 1 (special
issue on "Canada and the Americas") (March): 5–13.

Armstrong, Jeannette. 2000. *Whispering in Shadows*. Penticton, BC:
Theytus Books.

Bensen, Robert. 1994. "Catherine Weldon in *Omeros* and *The Ghost Dance*: Notes on Derek Walcott's Poetry and Drama." *Verse* 11, no. 2 (Summer): 119–25.

Berkhofer, Robert F., Jr. 1978. *The White Man's Indian: Images of the American Indian from Columbus to the Present*. New York: Knopf.

Brand, Dionne. 2005. *What We All Long For*. Toronto: Knopf.

Camayd-Freixas, Erik, and José Eduardo González, eds. 2000. *Primitivism and Identity in Latin America: Essays on Art, Literature, and Culture*. Tucson: University of Arizona Press.

Casteel, Sarah Phillips. 2007. *Second Arrivals: Landscape and Belonging in Contemporary Writing of the Americas*. Charlottesville: University of Virginia Press.

Chanady, Amaryll. 1994. "Introduction: Latin American Communities and the Postmodern Challenge." In Amaryll Chanady, ed., *Latin American Identity and the Construction of Difference*, ix-xlvi. Minneapolis: University of Minnesota Press.

Clifford, James. 1994. "Diasporas." *Cultural Anthropology* 9, no. 3 (August): 302–44.

Deloria, Philip J. 1998. *Playing Indian*. New Haven, CT: Yale University Press.

Goldie, Terry. 1989. *Fear and Temptation: Images of Indigenous Peoples in Australian, Canadian, and New Zealand Literature*. Montreal and Kingston: McGill-Queen's University Press.

Grinde, Donald A., Jr. 2002. "Iroquois Border Crossings: Place, Politics, and the Jay Treaty." In Claudia Sadowski-Smith, ed., *Globalization on the Line: Culture, Capital, and Citizenship at U.S. Borders*, 167–82. New York: Palgrave.

Fee, Margery. 1987. "Romantic Nationalism and the Image of Native People in Contemporary English-Canadian Literature." In Thomas King, Cheryl Calver, and Helen Hoy, eds, *The Native in Literature*, 15–33. Toronto: ECW Press.

Hamner, Robert. 1997. *Epic of the Dispossessed: Derek Walcott's Omeros*. Columbia: University of Missouri Press.

Highway, Tomson. 1999. *Kiss of the Fur Queen*. Toronto: Doubleday Canada.

Hundorf, Shari M. 2001. *Going Native: Indians in the American Cultural Imagination*. Ithaca, NY: Cornell University Press.

Julien, Isaac, dir. 2004. Installation. *True North*.

King, Thomas. 1993. "Borders." In *One Good Story, That One*, 133–47. Toronto: HarperPerennial Canada.

– 1999. *Truth and Bright Water*. Toronto: HarperCollins Canada.

Kogawa, Joy. 1992. *Itsuka*. Toronto: Penguin.

– 1994. *Obasan*. 1981. Reprint, New York: Anchor Books.

Luna-Firebaugh, Eileen M. 2002. "The Border Crossed Us: Border Crossing Issues of the Indigenous Peoples of the Americas." *Wicazo SA Review* (Spring): 159–81.

MacEwan, Grant. 1973. *Sitting Bull: The Years in Canada*. Edmonton: Hurtig.

Malamud, Bernard. 1989. *The People and Uncollected Stories*. New York: Farrar, Straus and Giroux.

Sadowski-Smith, Claudia, and Claire F. Fox. 2004. "Theorizing the Hemisphere: Inter-Americas Work at the Intersection of American, Canadian, and Latin American Studies." *Comparative American Studies* 2, no. 1: 5–38.

Torgovnick, Marianna. 1990. *Gone Primitive: Savage Intellects, Modern Lives*. Chicago, IL: University of Chicago Press.

Traister, Bryce. 2002. "Border Shopping: American Studies and the Anti-Nation." In Claudia Sadowski-Smith, ed., *Globalization on the Line: Culture, Capital, and Citizenship at U.S. Borders*, 31–52. New York: Palgrave.

Walcott, Derek. 1990. *Omeros*. New York: Noonday.

– 2002. *Walker* and *The Ghost Dance*. New York: Farrar, Straus and Giroux.

Wald, Patricia. 1998. "Minefields and Meeting Grounds: Transnational Analyses and American Studies." *American Literary History* 10, no. 1 (Spring): 199–218.

Wasserman, Renata R. Mautner. 1994. *Exotic Nations: Literature and Cultural Identity in the United States and Brazil, 1830–1930*. Ithaca, NY: Cornell University Press.

Yoon, Jin-me. 1998. *A Group of Sixty-Seven* (1996). Photograph. Reproduced in Jin-me Yoon, Monika Gagnon, Judy Radul, and Hyun Y. Kang, *Jin-me Yoon: Between Departure and Arrival*, 58–9. Vancouver: Western Front.

Zamora, Lois Parkinson. 1997. *The Usable Past: The Imagination of History in Recent Fiction of the Americas*. Cambridge, UK: Cambridge University Press.

CHAPTER SIX

Argüelles Arredondo, Carlos Gabriel. 2006. "Le Canada, les Amériques et la concurrence des blocs régionaux." In Amaryll Chanady, George

Handley, and Patrick Imbert, eds, *Americas' Worlds and the World's Americas/Les mondes des Amériques et les Amériques du monde*, 125–32. Ottawa: LEGAS.

Bahia, Márcio. 2006. "Americanidad: Towards the Mapping of a Concept." In Amaryll Chanady, George Handley, and Patrick Imbert, eds, *Americas' Worlds and the World's Americas/Les mondes des Amériques et les Amériques du monde*, 23–33. Ottawa: LEGAS.

Besner, Neil. 2005. "Postcolonial Theory, Difference, and National Traditions: The Case for a Brazilian-Canadian Dialogue." In Sandra Regina Goulart Almeida, ed., *Perspectivas transnacionais/Perspectives transnationales/Transnational Perspectives*, 23–9. Belo Horizonte, Brazil: Associação Brasileira de Estudos Canadenses (ABECAN) and Faculdade de Letras, Universidade Federal de Minas Gerais (UFMG).

Bolívar, Símon. 1960. "Contestacion de un americano meridional a un caballero de esta isla." In Charles V. Aubrun, ed., *Cuatro cartas y una memoria (1804–1815)*, 42–58. Paris, France: Centre de Recherches de l'Institut d'études hispaniques.

Braz, Albert. 2003. *The False Traitor: Louis Riel in Canadian Culture.* Toronto: University of Toronto Press.

– 2008. "Canada, America, and the Americas: The Quest for Continental Identity in the New World." *Canadian Review of Comparative Literature* 35, nos 1–2: 121–30.

Buchenau, Barbara, and Annette Paatz, eds. 2002. *Do the Americas Have a Common Literary History?* Frankfurt, Germany: Peter Lang.

Carvalho, Mathias. 1997. *Poemas americanos 1: Riel* (1886). In *Louis Riel, poèmes amériquains*, 15–57. Ed. and trans. Jean Morisset. Trois-Pistoles, QC: Éditions Trois-Pistoles.

Chanady, Amaryll, George Handley, and Patrick Imbert, eds. 2006. *Americas' Worlds and the World's Americas/Les mondes des Amériques et les Amériques du monde.* Ottawa: LEGAS.

Clarke, George Elliott. 2002a. "Canadian Biraciality and Its 'Zebra' Poetics." *Intertexts* 6, no. 2: 201–31.

– 2002b. *Odysseys Home: Mapping African-Canadian Literature.* Toronto: University of Toronto Press.

Colombo, John Robert, ed. 2000. *Famous Lasting Words: Great Canadian Quotations.* Vancouver: Douglas and McIntyre.

Cook-Lynn, Elizabeth. 1996. "American Indian Intellectualism and the New Indian Story." *American Indian Quarterly* 20, no. 1: 57–76.

Deacon, William Arthur. 1933. *My Vision of Canada.* Toronto: Ontario Publishing.

– 9 June 1935. Letter to Grey Owl. In W.A. Deacon Papers, box 10, folder 30, Thomas Fisher Rare Book Library, University of Toronto.

Diegues, Carlos, dir. and screenwriter. 1979. *Bye Bye Brasil*. Carnaval Films.

Fernández Retamar, Roberto. 1989. *Caliban and Other Essays*. Trans. Edward Baker. Minneapolis: University of Minnesota Press.

Frye, Northrop. 1965. "Conclusion." In Carl F. Klinck, ed., *Literary History of Canada: Canadian Literature in English*, 821–49. Toronto: University of Toronto Press.

García Márquez, Gabriel. February 1983. "Playboy Interview: Gabriel García Márquez," with Claudia Dreifus. *Playboy*, 65–77, 172–8.

Hodgins, Jack. 1987. Interview with Peter O'Brien. In Peter O'Brien, ed., *So to Speak: Interviews with Contemporary Canadian Writers*, 195–228. Montreal: Véhicule.

Johnson, E. Pauline (Tekahionwake). 2002. *Collected Poems and Selected Prose*. Ed. Carole Gerson and Veronica Strong-Boag. Toronto: University of Toronto Press.

Manguel, Alberto. 17 October 1998. "Borges: Still Failed by English Translators." Review of Jorge Luis Borges's *Collected Fictions* (trans. Andrew Hurley). *Globe and Mail*, D9.

Martí, José. 2000. *Selected Writings*. Trans. Esther Allen. Ed. Roberto González Echevarría. New York: Penguin.

Mayr, Suzette. 1998. *The Widows*. Edmonton: NeWest.

– 2004. "Exploring the Middle Spaces: An Interview with Suzette Mayr on Genre, Gender, and Race," with Albert Braz. In Laura P. Alonso Gallo, ed., *Voces de América: Entrevistas a escritores americanos/ American Voices: Interviews with American Writers*, 433–52. Cádiz, Spain: Aduana Vieja.

Morrison, Katherine L. 2003. *Canadians Are Not Americans: Myths and Literary Traditions*. Toronto: Second Story.

Page, P.K. 1987. *Brazilian Journal*. Toronto: Lester and Orpen Dennys.

– 2006. *Hand Luggage: A Memoir in Verse*. Erin, ON: Porcupine's Quill.

Parameswaran, Uma. 2000. "Driving into the New Millennium on a Trans-Canada Highway That Has Only Entry Ramps." In Marc Maufort and Franca Bellarski, eds, *Reconfigurations: Canadian Literatures and Postcolonial Identities/Littératures canadiennes et identités postcoloniales*, 91–108. Brussels, Belgium: Peter Lang.

Riel, Louis. 1985. *The Collected Writings of Louis Riel/Les écrits complets de Louis Riel*. 5 vols. General editor George F.G. Stanley. Edmonton: University of Alberta Press.

Rishchynski, Guillermo. 9 November 2005. "Discurso do Senhor Embaixa-dor Guillermo Rishchynski." Speech to the 8th International Congress of the Brazilian Association of Canadian Studies, Gramado, RS, Brazil.

Rodriguez, Richard. 2002. *Brown: The Last Discovery of America.* New York: Penguin.

Schwarz, Roberto. 1992. *Misplaced Ideas: Essays on Brazilian Culture.* Ed. John Gledson. London, UK: Verso.

Stavans, Ilan, ed. 1999. *Mutual Impressions: Writers from the Americas Reading One Another.* Durham, NC: Duke University Press.

Strong-Boag, Veronica, and Carole Gerson. 2000. *Paddling Her Own Canoe: The Times and Texts of E. Pauline Johnson (Tekahionwake).* Toronto: University of Toronto Press.

Toomer, Jean. 1993. "The New Race." In Frederik L. Rusch, ed., *A Jean Toomer Reader: Selected Unpublished Writings,* 105–14. New York: Oxford University Press.

Vasconcelos, José. 1997. *The Cosmic Race/La raza cósmica.* Trans. Didier T. Jaén. Baltimore, MD: Johns Hopkins University Press.

CHAPTER SEVEN

Benjamin, Walter. 1969. "Theses on the Philosophy of History" (1940). In *Illuminations,* 253–64. Ed. H. Arendt. New York: Schocken.

Berger, Carl. 1966. "The True North Strong and Free." In P. Russell, ed., *Nationalism in Canada,* 3–26. Toronto: McGraw Hill.

– 1970. *The Sense of Power: Studies in the Ideas of Canadian Imperialism.* Toronto: University of Toronto Press.

Berlant, Lauren. 1997. *The Queen of America Goes to Washington City.* Durham, NC: Duke University Press.

Brand, Dionne. 1996. *In Another Place, Not Here.* Toronto: Knopf Canada.

– 1999. *At the Full and Change of the Moon.* Toronto: Knopf Canada.

– 2001. *A Map to the Door of No Return: Notes to Belonging.* Toronto: Doubleday Canada.

Carby, Hazel. 1987. *Reconstructing Womanhood: The Emergence of the Afro-American Woman Novelist.* New York: Oxford University Press.

Castronovo, Russ. 1995. *Fathering the Nation: American Genealogies of Slavery and Freedom.* Berkeley: University of California Press.

Clarke, George Elliott. 1998. "Contesting a Model Blackness: A Medita-tion on African-Canadian African Americanism, or the Structures of African Canadianité." *Essays on Canadian Writing* 63: 1–55.

– 1999. *Beatrice Chancy.* Vancouver: Polestar.

– ed. 1991. *Fire on the Water: An Anthology of Black Nova Scotian Writing.* Vol. 1. Lawrencetown Beach, NS: Pottersfield Press.

Coleman, Daniel. 2001. "The National Allegory of Fraternity: Loyalist Literature and the Making of Canada's White British Origins." *Journal of Canadian Studies* 36 (Fall): 131–56.

Cuder-Domínguez, Pilar. 2003. "African-Canadian Writing and the Narration(s) of Slavery." *Essays on Canadian Writing* 79: 55–75.

Dash, J. Michael. 1998. *The Other America: Caribbean Literature in a New World Context.* Charlottesville and London, UK: University Press of Virginia.

Davis, Angela. 1981. *Woman, Class, and Race.* New York: Random House.

Fee, Margery. 1992. "Canadian Literature and English Studies in the Canadian University." *Essays on Canadian Writing* 48: 20–40.

Foucault, Michel. 1980. *Power/Knowledge: Selected Interviews and Other Writings, 1972–1977.* New York: Pantheon.

– 1984. "Nietzsche, Genealogy, History." In *The Foucault Reader,* 76–100. Ed. P. Rabinow. New York: Pantheon.

Gilroy, Paul. 1993. *The Black Atlantic: Modernity and Double Consciousness.* Cambridge, MA: Harvard University Press.

Godard, Barbara. 2000. "Notes from the Cultural Field: Canadian Literature from Identity to Hybridity." *Essays on Canadian Writing* 72 (Winter): 209–47.

Hall, Stuart. 1994. "Cultural Identity and Diaspora." In P. Williams and L. Chrisman, eds, *Colonial Discourse and Post-Colonial Theory,* 392–403. New York: Columbia University Press.

Handley, George B. 2000. *Postslavery Literatures in the Americas: Family Portraits in Black and White.* Charlottesville and London, UK: University Press of Virginia.

Harper, Frances. 1892. *Iola Leroy, or Shadows Uplifted.* Philadelphia, PA: Garrigues Bros.

Hill, Lawrence. 1997. *Any Known Blood.* Toronto: HarperCollins.

– 2001. *Black Berry, Sweet Juice: On Being Black and White in Canada.* Toronto: HarperFlamingo.

Huggan, Graham, and Winfried Siemerling. 2000. "US/Canadian Writers' Perspectives on the Multiculturalism Debate." *Canadian Literature* 164 (Spring): 82–111.

Hulme, Peter. 1994. "The Locked Heart: The Creole Family Romance of *Wide Sargasso Sea.*" In F. Barker, P. Hulme, and M. Iversen, eds,

Colonial Discourse/Postcolonial Theory, 72–88. Manchester, UK: Manchester University Press.

Kertzer, Jonathan. 1998. *Worrying the Nation: Imagining a National Literature in English Canada*. Toronto: University of Toronto Press.

Kirby, William. 1973. *The U.E.: A Tale of Upper Canada* (1859). Toronto Reprint Library of Canadian Prose and Poetry. Toronto: University of Toronto Press.

Law, Howard. 1988. "'Self-Reliance Is the True Road to Independence': Ideology and the Ex-Slaves in Buxton and Chatham." In F. Iacovetta, ed., *A Nation of Immigrants: Women, Workers, and Communities in Canadian History*, 82–97. Toronto: University of Toronto Press.

Mannette, Joy. 1984. "'Stark Remnants of Blackpast': Thinking on Gender, Ethnicity and Class in 1780s Nova Scotia." *Canadian Review of Sociology and Anthropology* 31, no. 4: 365–91.

McCallum, Pamela, and Christian Olbey. 1999. "Written in the Scars: History, Genre, and Materiality in Dionne Brand's *In Another Place, Not Here*." *Essays on Canadian Writing* 68: 159–82.

Moya, Paula M., and Ramón Saldívar. 2003. "Fictions of the Transamerican Imaginary." *Modern Fiction Studies* 49, no. 1 (special issue): 1–18.

Moynagh, Maureen. 1996. "Mapping Africadia's Imaginary Geography: An Interview with George Elliott Clarke." *ARIEL: A Review of International English Literature* 27, no. 4: 71–94.

– 2002. "'This History's Only Good for Anger': Gender and Cultural Memory in *Beatrice Chancy*." *Signs: Journal of Women in Culture and Society* 28, no. 1: 97–124.

Nelson, Cary. 2002. "The International Context for American Poetry about the Spanish Civil War." In Cary Nelson, ed., *The Wound and the Dream: Sixty Years of American Poems about the Spanish Civil War*, 1–61. Chicago: University of Illinois Press.

Nichols, Charles H. 1985. "The Slave Narrators and the Picaresque Mode: Archetypes for Modern Black Personae." In C.T. Davis and H.L. Gates Jr, eds, *The Slave's Narrative*, 283–97. Oxford, UK, and New York: Oxford University Press.

Spillers, Hortense. 1987. "Notes on an Alternative Model: Neither/Nor." In M. Sprinker, M. Davis, and M. Marable, eds, *Year Left 2*, 176–94. New York: Verso.

Walcott, Derek. 1981. "Ruins of a Great House." In *Selected Poetry*, 4–5. Oxford, UK: Heinemann.

Walcott, Rinaldo. 1999. "The Desire to Belong: The Politics of Texts and Their Politics of Nation." In N. Aziz, ed., *Floating the Borders: New Contexts in Canadian Criticism*, 61–79. Toronto: TSAR.

Walker, James W. St. G. 1992. *The Black Loyalists: The Search for the Promised Land in Nova Scotia and Sierra Leone*. Toronto: University of Toronto Press.

Ward, Samuel Ringgold. 1968. *Autobiography of a Fugitive Negro*. 1855. Reprint, New York: Arno.

Winks, Robin. 1970. *The Blacks in Canada*. New Haven, CT: Yale University Press.

Zamora, Lois Parkinson. 1997. *The Usable Past: The Imagination of History in Recent Fiction of the Americas*. Cambridge, UK: Cambridge University Press.

CHAPTER EIGHT

Alexis, André. 1995. "Borrowed Blackness." *This Magazine* 28, no. 8: 14–20, available online through ProQuest at http://www.proquest.com.

Anderson, Osborne Perry. 2000. *A Voice from Harpers Ferry*. 1861. Reprint, New York: World View Forum.

Appiah, K. Anthony. 1986. "The Uncompleted Argument: Du Bois and the Illusions of Race." In Henry Louis Gates Jr, ed., *'Race,' Writing, and Difference*, 21–37. Chicago, IL, and London, UK: University of Chicago Press.

– and Amy Gutmann. 1996. *Color Conscious: The Political Morality of Race*. Princeton, NJ: Princeton University Press.

Banks, Russell. 1998. *Cloudsplitter*. Toronto: Vintage.

Brand, Dionne. 1999. *At the Full and Change of the Moon*. Toronto: Vintage.

Butler, Judith. 1993. *Bodies That Matter: On the Discursive Limits of "Sex."* New York and London, UK: Routledge.

Clarke, Austin. 2002. *The Polished Hoe*. Toronto: Thomas Allen.

Clarke, George Elliott. 1998. "Contesting a Model Blackness: A Meditation on African-Canadian African Americanism, or the Structures of African-Canadianité." *Essays on Canadian Writing* 63: 1–55. Reprinted in George Elliott Clarke, *Odysseys Home: Mapping African-Canadian Literature*, 27–70 (Toronto: University of Toronto Press, 2002).

– 1999. *Beatrice Chancy*. Victoria: Polestar.

– 2002. *Odysseys Home: Mapping African-Canadian Literature*. Toronto: University of Toronto Press.

Cooper, Richard S., Jay S. Kaufman, and Ryk Ward. 2003. "Race and Genomics." *New England Journal of Medicine* 348, no. 12: 1166–70.

Cuder-Domínguez, Pilar. 2003. "African Canadian Writing and the Narration(s) of Slavery." *Essays on Canadian Writing* 79: 55–75.

Douglass, Frederick. 1997. *Narrative of the Life of Frederick Douglass, an American Slave, Written by Himself* (1845). In Henry Louis Gates Jr and Nellie Y. McKay, eds, *The Norton Anthology of African American Literature*, 299–401. New York and London, UK: Norton.

– 1999. *Life and Times of Frederick Douglass.* 1881. Reproduced in Encarta Africana 2000. CD-ROM. Microsoft Corporation.

Drew, Benjamin. 2000. *The Refugee, or The Narratives of Fugitive Slaves in Canada, Related by Themselves, with an Account of the History and Condition of the Colored Population of Upper Canada.* 1856. Reprint, Toronto: Prospero.

Du Bois, W.E.B. 2001. *John Brown.* 1909. Reprint, edited and introduced by David Roediger, New York: Modern Library.

Fanon, Frantz. 1963. *The Wretched of the Earth.* Trans. Constance Farrington. New York: Grove.

Fuss, Diana. 1995. *Identification Papers.* New York and London, UK: Routledge.

Gates, Henry Louis, Jr. 1987. *Figures in Black: Words, Signs, and the "Racial" Self.* New York and Oxford, UK: Oxford University Press.

– 1988. *The Signifying Monkey: A Theory of Afro-American Literary Criticism.* New York: Oxford University Press.

– 1997. "The Passing of Anatole Broyard." In *Thirteen Ways of Looking at a Black Man,* 180–214. New York: Random House.

Hacking, Ian. 1986. "Making up People." In Thomas C. Heller, Morton Sosna, and David E. Wellbery, eds, *Reconstructing Individualism: Autonomy, Individuality and the Self in Western Thought,* 222–36. Stanford, CA: Stanford University Press.

Hill, Lawrence. 1992. *Some Great Thing.* Winnipeg: Turnstone.

– 1993. *Trials and Triumphs: The Story of African-Canadians.* Toronto: Umbrella.

– 1994. "Zebra: Growing up Black and White in Canada." In Carl James and Adrienne Shadd, eds, *Talking about Difference: Encounters in Culture, Language and Identity,* 41–7. Toronto: Between the Lines.

– 1996. *Women of Vision: The Story of the Canadian Negro Women's Association, 1951–1976.* Toronto: Umbrella.

– 1997a. *Any Known Blood.* Toronto: HarperCollins.

– 25 October 1997b. "Black Like Us, Eh?" *Toronto Star,* J20.

– 1998. "Gory, Gory, Hallelujah." Review of *Cloudsplitter*, by Russell Banks. *Maclean's* 111, no. 15: 64.

– 9 February 2000. "Black Like Us." *Globe and Mail*, A13.

– 2001a. *Black Berry, Sweet Juice: On Being Black and White in Canada*. Toronto: HarperFlamingo.

– 2001b. "Black + White ... Equals Black." *Maclean's* 114, no. 35, http://www.lawrencehill.com/black_plus_white_equals_black.pdf (viewed 22 June 2009).

Jacobs, Diane. 1996. "On Becoming a Black Canadian." *Kola* 8, no. 2: 71–2.

Jacquard, Albert. 1996. "An Unscientific Notion." UNESCO *Courier* 49, no. 3: 22–5.

Kristeva, Julia. 1982. *Powers of Horror: An Essay on Abjection*. Trans. Leon S. Roudiez. New York: Columbia University Press.

Lindberg, Kathryne. 1997. "Raising Cane on the Theoretical Plane: Jean Toomer's Racial Personae." In Winfried Siemerling and Katrin Schwenk, eds, *Cultural Difference and the Literary Text: Pluralism and the Limits of Authenticity in North American Literatures*, 49–74. Iowa City: University of Iowa Press.

MacLeod, Alistair. 1999. *No Great Mischief*. Toronto: McClelland and Stewart.

Rotman, David. 2003. "Genes, Medicine, and the New Race Debate." *Technology Review* 106, no. 5: 41–7.

Sollors, Werner. 1997. *Neither Black nor White yet Both: Thematic Explorations of Interracial Literature*. New York: Oxford University Press.

Spillers, Hortense J. 2003. *Black, White, and in Color: Essays on American Literature and Culture*. Chicago, IL, and London, UK: University of Chicago Press.

Toomer, Jean. 1988. "['Autobiographical Selection']." In *Cane: An Authoritative Text, Backgrounds, Criticism*, 140–5. Ed. Darwin T. Turner. New York and London, UK: Norton.

Walcott, Rinaldo. 2003. *Black Like Who? Writing Black Canada*. Toronto: Insomniac Press.

Winks, Robin W. 1997. *The Blacks in Canada: A History*. 1971. Reprint, Montreal and Kingston: McGill-Queen's University Press.

– 2002. "Slavery." In *The 2003 Canadian Encyclopedia/L'Encyclopédie Canadienne 2003*, n.p. Historica Foundation of Canada.

CHAPTER NINE

Apter, Emily. 2001. "On Translation in a Global Market." *Public Culture* 13, no. 1 (special issue on translation): 1–12.

– 2005. *The Translation Zone*. Princeton, NJ: Princeton University Press.

Blum, Alan. 2003. *The Imaginative Structure of the City*. Montreal and Kingston: McGill-Queen's University Press.

Brand, Dionne. 2005. *What We All Long For*. Toronto: Knopf Canada.

Canclini, Nestor Garcia. 1995. *American Ethnologist* 22, no. 4 (November): 743–55.

Cronin, Michael. 2003. *Translation and Globalization*. London, UK: Routledge.

– 2006. *Translation and Identity*. London, UK: Routledge.

Egoyan, Atom. 1991. *En Passant*. In Denise Robert, producer, *Montréal vu par ...* 6 short films on Montreal.

Frey, William H. 2002. "Multilingual America." *American Demographics* 24, no. 7 (July-August): 20–3.

Gaonkar, Dilip Parameshwar, and Elizabeth A. Povinelli. 2003. "Technologies of Public Forms: Circulation, Transfiguration, Recognition." *Public Culture* 15, no. 3: 385–97.

Germain, Annick, and Damaris Rose. 2000. *Montréal: The Quest for a Metropolis*. Chichester, UK: John Wiley and Sons.

Holston, James, and Arjun Appadurai. 1996. "Cities and Citizenship." *Public Culture* 8, no. 2: 187–204.

King, Anthony D. 1990. *Urbanism, Colonialism and the World Economy: Cultural and Spatial Foundations of the World Urban System*. London, UK, and New York: Routledge.

Kingwell, Mark. 2000. "Building, Dwelling, Acting." *Queen's Quarterly* 107, no. 2 (Summer): 177–201.

Médam, Alain. 1978. *Montréal interdite*. Paris, France: Presses Universitaires de France.

– 2002. *Labyrinthes des rencontres*. Collection Métissages. Montreal: Fides.

Pratt, Mary Louise. 2002. "The Traffic in Meaning: Translation, Contagion, Infiltration." *Profession 2002*, MLA: 25–36.

– 2003. "Building a New Public Idea about Language." *Profession 2003*, MLA: 110–19.

Rama, Angel. 1996. *The Lettered City*. Trans. John Charles Chasteen. Durham, NC, and London, UK: Duke University Press.

Ross, Robert J., and Gerard J. Telkamp, eds. 1985. *Colonial Cities: Essays on Urbanism in a Colonial Context*. Dordrecht, Netherlands, and Boston, MA: Martinus Nijhoff.

Shell, Marc. 2001. "Language Wars." CR: *The New Centennial Review* 1, no. 2: 1–17.

Siemerling, Winfried. 2005. *The New North American Studies: Culture, Writing and the Politics of Re/Cognition.* London, UK: Routledge.

Simon, Sherry. 1999. *Hybridité culturelle.* Montreal: L'île de la tortue.

Sommer, Doris. 1998. "Choose and Lose." In Werner Sollors, ed., *Multilingual America: Transnationalism, Ethnicity, and the Languages of American Literature,* 297–309. New York: New York University Press.

– 2004. *Bilingual Aesthetics: A Sentimental Education.* Durham, NC, and London, UK: Duke University Press.

– ed. 2003. *Bilingual Games: Some Literary Investigations.* New York: Palgrave, Macmillan.

Spector, Scott. 2000. *Prague Territories: National Conflict and Cultural Innovation in Franz Kafka's Fin de Siècle.* Berkeley: University of California Press.

CHAPTER TEN

Anaya, Rudolfo. 1989. *Bless Me, Ultima.* 1972. Reprint, Berkeley: Tontiuh-Quinto Sol International.

Anzaldúa, Gloria. 1987. *Borderlands/La Frontera: The New Mestiza.* San Francisco, CA: Aunt Lute Press.

– 1989. "Interview with Susanne de Lotbinière-Harwood." *Trivia* 14: 37–45.

Aranda, José F., Jr. 2005. *When We Arrive: A New Literary History of Mexican America.* Tucson: University of Arizona Press.

Bouchard, Chantal. 1998. *La langue et le nombril: Histoire d'une obsession québécoise.* Nouvelles études québécoises. Montreal: Fides.

Boucher, Denise. 1979. *Les Fées ont soif.* 1978. Reprint, Montreal: Éditions Intermède.

Cisneros, Sandra. 1989. *The House on Mango Street.* 1984. Reprint, Houston: Arte Público Press.

Cooper Alarcón, Daniel. 1997. *The Aztec Palimpsest: Mexico in the Modern Imagination.* Tucson: University of Arizona Press.

de Lotbinière-Harwood, Susanne. 1991. *Re-belle et infidèle: La traduction comme pratique de ré-écriture au féminin/The Body Bilingual: Translation as a Re-writing in the Feminine.* Toronto: Women's Press; Montreal: Editions du Remue-ménage.

Fitz, Earl E. 1991. *Rediscovering the New World: Inter-American Literature in a Comparative Context.* Iowa City: University of Iowa Press.

Gauvin, Lise. 1983. "From Octave Crémazie to Victor-Lévy Beaulieu: Language, Literature and Ideology." Trans. Emma Henderson. *Yale*

French Studies 65 (special issue on "The Language of Difference: Writing in QUEBEC[ois]"): 30–49.

Hébert, Anne. 1975. *Les Enfants du sabbat*. Paris, France: Éditions du Seuil.

Hémon, Louis. 1990. *Maria Chapdelaine*. 1917. Reprint, Montreal: Bibliothèque québécoise.

Homel, David. 1988. "The Way They Talk in *Broke City*." In David Homel and Sherry Simon, eds, *Mapping Literature: The Art and Politics of Translation*, 56–60. Montreal: Véhicule Press.

Innis, Hugh R. 1973. *Bilingualism and Biculturalism: An Abridged Version of the Royal Commission Report*. Toronto: McClelland and Stewart, in cooperation with the Secretary of State Department and Information Canada.

Kaup, Monika. 2002. "Constituting Hybridity as Hybrid: Métis Canadian and Mexican American Formations." In Monika Kaup and Debra J. Rosenthal, eds, *Mixing Race, Mixing Culture: Inter-American Literary Dialogues*, 185–210. Austin: University of Texas Press.

Lalonde, Michèle. 1992. "Speak white" (1970). In Michel Erman, ed., *Anthologie critique: Littérature canadienne-française et québécoise*, 148–51. Laval, QC: Éditions Beauchemin.

Moraga, Cherríe. 1983. *Loving in the War Years: Lo que nunca pasó por sus labios*. Boston, MA: South End Press.

New, W.H. 1991. *A History of Canadian Literature*. Macmillan History of Literature. 1989. Reprint, London, UK: Macmillan.

Paz, Octavio. 1983. *El Laberinto de la soledad*. 1950. Reprint, Mexico, DF: Fondo de Cultura Económica.

Rioux, Marcel. 1980. *Les Québécois*. New edition. Le Temps qui Court Series. Paris, France: Éditions du Seuil.

Robin, Régine. 1983. *La Québécoite*. Montreal: Éditions Québec-Amérique.

– 1993. "Un Québec pluriel." In Claude Duchet and Stéphane Vachon, eds, *La Recherche littéraire: Objets et méthodes*, 301–9. Montreal: XYZ éditeur.

Saldívar, Ramón. 1991. "Narrative, Ideology, and the Reconstruction of American Literary History." In Héctor Calderón and José David Saldívar, eds, *Criticism in the Borderlands: Studies in Chicano Literature, Culture, and Ideology*, 11–20. Durham, NC, and London, UK: Duke University Press.

Santos, John Phillip. 1999. *Places Left Unfinished at the Time of Creation*. New York: Viking.

Sarkonak, Ralph. 1983a. "Accentuating the Differences." *Yale French Studies* 65 (special issue on "The Language of Difference: Writing in QUEBEC[ois]"): 3–20.

– 1983b. "A Brief Chronology of French Canada, 1534–1982." *Yale French Studies* 65 (special issue on "The Language of Difference: Writing in QUEBEC[ois]"): 275–82.

Savard, Félix-Antoine. 1992. *Menaud, maître-draveur*. 1937. Reprint, Montreal: Bibliothèque québécoise.

See, Katharine O'Sullivan. 1986. *First World Nationalisms: Class and Ethnic Politics in Northern Ireland and Quebec*. Chicago, IL, and London, UK: University of Chicago Press.

Simon, Sherry. 1999. "Translating and Interlingual Creation in the Contact Zone: Border Writing in Quebec." In Susan Bassnett and Harish Trivedi, eds, *Post-Colonial Translation: Theory and Practice*, 58–74. London, UK, and New York: Routledge.

Stavans, Ilan. 2001. *The Hispanic Condition: The Power of a People*. 1995. Reprint, New York: Rayo-HarperCollins.

Torres, Lourdes. 1991. "The Construction of the Self in U.S. Latina Autobiographies." In Chandra Talpade Mohanty, Ann Russo, and Lourdes Torres, eds, *Third World Women and the Politics of Feminism*, 271–87. Bloomington and Indianapolis: Indiana University Press.

Tuveson, Ernest Lee. 1968. *Redeemer Nation: The Idea of America's Millennial Role*. Chicago, IL: University of Chicago Press.

Vallières, Pierre. 1971. *White Niggers of America: The Precocious Autobiography of a Quebec "Terrorist."* Trans. Joan Pinkham. New York: Monthly Review Press.

CHAPTER ELEVEN

Choquette, Robert. 1931. *Metropolitan Museum*. Montreal: Herald Press.

Clarke, George Elliott. 2002. *Odysseys Home: Mapping African-Canadian Literature*. Toronto: University of Toronto Press.

Correspondence between Louis Dantin and Rosaire Dion-Lévesque, 1928–1944 (extracts). 1982. *Écrits du Canada français*, nos 44–5 (special issue on Louis Dantin): 282–321.

Dantin, Louis. 1928. *Poètes de l'Amérique française*. Vol. 1. Montreal: Éditions du Mercure.

– 1930. *La Vie en rêve*. Montreal: Librairie d'Action canadienne-française.

– 1931. *Gloses critiques*. Vol. 1. Montreal: Éditions Albert Lévesque.

- 1934. *Poètes de l'Amérique française*. Vol. 2. Montreal: Éditions Albert Lévesque.
- 1936. *Contes de Noël*. Montreal: Éditions Albert Lévesque.
- 27 May 1939. "Chômage et paresse." *Le Jour*, 8.
- 6 December 1941. "Deux traductions de romans étrangers." *Le Jour*, 7.
- 1951. *Les enfances de Fanny*. Montreal: Chanteclerc. Trans. Raymond Y. Chamberlain as *Fanny*, French Writers of Canada series (Montreal: Harvest House, 1973).
- 1962. *Poèmes d'outre-tombe*. Cahiers Louis Dantin 1. Trois-Rivières, QC: Éditions du bien public.
- 1963. *Les sentiments d'un père affectueux: Lettres de Louis Dantin à son fils*. Preface by Gabriel Nadeau. Cahiers Louis Dantin 2. Trois-Rivières, QC: Éditions du bien public.
- 1997. *Émile Nelligan et son œuvre*. Critical edition prepared by Réjean Robidoux. Bibliothèque du Nouveau Monde series. Montreal: Presses de l'Université de Montréal.
- 2002. *Essais critiques I* and *II*. Critical edition prepared by Yvette Francoli. Bibliothèque du Nouveau Monde series. Montreal: Presses de l'Université de Montréal.
- Dion-Lévesque, Rosaire. 1933. *Walt Whitman: Ses meilleures pages traduites de l'anglais par Rosaire Dion-Lévesque*. Montreal: Les Elzévirs.
- Fonds Alfred-DesRochers (FAD). Bibliothèque et Archives nationales du Québec, Sherbrooke, QC.
- Francoli, Yvette. 2002. "Introduction." In Louis Dantin, *Essais critiques I*, 7–74. Critical edition prepared by Yvette Francoli. Bibliothèque du Nouveau Monde series. Montreal: Presses de l'Université de Montréal.
- Giguère, Richard. 1996. "Les années de la Crise dans la correspondance Louis Dantin-Alfred DesRochers (1929–1935)." In Michel Biron and Benoît Melançon, eds, *Lettres des années trente*, 85–107. Ottawa: Le Nordir.
- Godbout, Patricia. 1996. "Poésie, source de vie: Alfred DesRochers et Ralph Gustafson." *Revue d'études des Cantons de l'Est* 9: 11–20.
- Hall, Max. 1986. *Harvard University Press: A History*. Cambridge, MA, and London, UK: Harvard University Press.
- Hébert, Pierre. 2004. "L'homme derrière une vitre: Pseudonymie et transgression chez Eugène Seers/Louis Dantin." *Voix et images* 30, no. 1: 81–92.
- Kesteman, Jean-Pierre, Peter Southam, and Diane Saint-Pierre. 1998. *Histoire des Cantons de l'Est*. Quebec City: Institut québécois de recherche sur la culture.

Lüsebrink, Hans-Jürgen. 2004. "Introduction." *Globe* 7, no. 2 (special issue on "Américanités francophones: Ancrages médiatiques, mises en perspective historiques et comparatistes"): 11–20.

Melançon, Robert. 2004. *Qu'est-ce qu'un classique québécois?* Les grandes conférences series. Montreal: Fides and Presses de l'Université de Montréal.

Morency, Jean. 2004. "L'américanité et l'américanisation du roman québécois: Réflexions conceptuelles et perspectives littéraires." *Globe* 7, no. 2 (special issue on "Américanités francophones: Ancrages médiatiques, mises en perspective historiques et comparatistes"): 31–58.

– 2005. "La (re)découverte de l'Amérique: Le rôle de quelques médiateurs culturels dans le Québec de l'entre-deux-guerres." In Jean Morency et al., eds, *Des cultures en contact: Visions de l'Amérique du Nord francophone*, 299–311. Quebec City: Nota bene.

Nadeau, Gabriel. 1948. *Louis Dantin: Sa vie et son œuvre*. Manchester, NH: Éditions Lafayette. Previously published in serial form in the Franco-American newspaper *Le Travailleur* in Worcester, MA, in 1945, 1946, and 1947.

– 1968. *Dantin parmi les nègres: Dantin et l'Universal Bureau*. Cahiers Louis Dantin: Cahier Hors Série. Trois-Rivières, QC: Éditions du bien public.

Narrache, Jean. 1993. *Quand j'parl' pour parler: Poèmes et proses*. Anthology presented by Richard Foisy. Anthologie series. Montreal: L'Hexagone.

Nepveu, Pierre. 1998. *Intérieurs du Nouveau Monde*. Papiers collés series. Montreal: Boréal.

Pelletier-Baillargeon, Hélène. 1996. *Olivar Asselin et son temps*. Vol. 1, *Le militant*. Montreal: Fides.

– 2001. *Olivar Asselin et son temps*. Vol. 2, *Le volontaire*. Montreal: Fides.

Pepall, Rosalind. 2002. "Un art de vigueur et de mesure." Trans. Christine Gendreau. In Rosalind Pepall and Brian Foss, eds, *Edwin Holgate*, 12–27. Montreal: Musée des beaux-arts de Montréal.

Siemerling, Winfried. 2005. *The New North American Studies: Culture, Writing and the Politics of Re/Cognition*. London, UK: Routledge.

Smith, A.J.M, trans. 1970. *The Poetry of French Canada in Translation*. Ed. John Glassco. Toronto: Oxford University Press.

Wintz, Cary D., and Paul Finkelman, eds. 2004. *Encyclopedia of the Harlem Renaissance*. Vol. 2. New York: Routledge.

CHAPTER TWELVE

Bellemare, Gaston. 28 November 2004. Personal conversation.

Bernd, Zilá, and Joseph Melançon, eds. 1991. *Vozes do Quebec: Antologia*. Porto Alegre, Brazil: Universidade Federal do Rio Grande do Sul.

Betanzos Santos, Manuel. 1974. "Poesía canadiense actual." *Revista de la Universidad Complutense* 93: 9–27.

– 1989. "Un poète espagnol au Québec." *Écrits du Canada français* 66: 145–56.

Etcheverry, Jorge. 2005. "Una literatura en castellano en medio anglófono." http://poesias.cl/latinocanadienseo1.htm (viewed 20 June 2009).

Gunn, Drewey Wayne. 1992. *Escritores norteamericanos y británicos en México*. Trans. Ernestina de Champourcin. 1977. Reprint, Mexico City: Fondo de Cultura Econónica.

Hazelton, Hugh. 2007. *Latinocanadá: An Anthology of Ten Latin American Writers of Canada*. Montreal and Kingston: McGill-Queen's University Press.

Jolicoeur, Louis, ed. and trans. 1993. *Nouvelles mexicaines d'aujourd'hui*. Quebec City: L'instant même.

Lara Zavala, Hernán. 2002. "Las poéticas de *Bajo el volcán*." *E-Journal*. http://www.ejournal.unam.mx/losuniversitarios/02 (viewed 10 August 2006).

López Morales, Laura, ed. and trans. 1996. *Literatura francófona II: América*. Mexico City: Fondo de Cultura Económica.

Lucotti, Claudia, ed. 2002. *¿Dónde es aquí? 25 cuentos canadienses*. Mexico City: Fondo de Cultura Económica.

Malinowski, Bronislaw. 1963. "Introducción." In Fernando Ortiz, *Contrapunteo cubano del tabaco y el azúcar*, xi–xix. Havana, Cuba: Universidad Central de las Villas.

Moussong, Lazlo. 1994. "Malcolm Lowry: El volcán no es como lo pintan." *Ruptures* 6: 203–8.

Noël, Francine. 1999. *La Conjuration des bâtards*. Montreal: Leméac.

Nómez, Naín. 1986. *Identidad y exilio: Poetas chilenos en Canadá*. Santiago, Chile: CENECA.

Ortiz, Fernando. 1963. *Contrapunteo cubano del tabaco y el azúcar*. 1940. Reprint, Havana, Cuba: Universidad Central de las Villas.

Page, P.K. 1989. *Brazilian Journal*. Toronto: Lester and Orpen Dennys.

Peterson, Michel, and Zilá Bernd. 1992. *Confluences littéraires Brésil-Québec: Les bases d'une comparaison*. Montreal: Balzac.

Sagaris, Lake. 1993. *Medusa's Children: A Journey from Newfoundland to Chiloe*. Regina: Coteau.

– ed. and trans. 1986. *Un pájaro es un poema: 12 poetas canadienses*. Santiago, Chile: Pehuén.

Saravia, Alejandro. 2003. *Rojo, amarillo y verde*. Toronto: Artifact; Montreal: Enana Blanca.

– 15 August 2005. Personal conversation.

Stratford, Madeleine. 2007. "La identidad quebequense traducida al español: Difusión de la poesía quebequense en el mundo hispánico." In Ana María Granero de Goenaga et al., eds, *La traducción: Hacia un encuentro de lenguas y culturas: Actas de las Primeras Jornadas Internacionales de Traductología*, 147–59. Córdoba, Argentina: Comunicarte and Centro de Investigación en Traducción.

CHAPTER THIRTEEN

Works by Francine Noël

1985. *Chandeleur, cantate parlée pour cinq voix et un mort*. Montreal: VLB Éditeur.

1990. *Babel, prise deux ou Nous avons tous découvert l'Amérique*. Montreal: VLB Éditeur.

1994. *Maryse*. 1983. Reprint, Montreal: Bibliothèque Québécoise.

1998. *Myriam première*. 1987. Reprint, Montreal: Bibliothèque Québécoise.

1999a. *La Conjuration des bâtards*. Montreal: Leméac.

1999b. *Nous avons tous découvert l'Amérique*. 1992. Reprint, Montreal: Babel.

2008. *J'ai l'angoisse légère*. Montreal: Leméac.

Secondary Sources

Chanady, Amaryll. 1999. *Entre inclusion et exclusion: La symbolisation de l'autre dans les Amériques*. Paris, France: Honoré Champion.

Chassay, Jean-François. 1995. "Littérature et américanité: La piste scientifique." In Yvan Lamonde et Gérard Bouchard, eds, *Québécois et Américains: La culture québécoise aux XIXᵉ et XXᵉ siècles*, 175–93. Montreal: Fides.

Faris, Wendy B. 1995. "Scheherazade's Children: Magical Realism and Postmodern Fiction." In Lois Parkinson Zamora and Wendy B. Faris, eds, *Magical Realism: Theory, History, Community*, 163–90. Durham, NC, and London, UK: Duke University Press.

García Márquez, Gabriel. *One Hundred Years of Solitude*. Trans. Gregory Rabassa. New York: Harper and Row, 1970.

Gauvin, Lise. 2000. *Langagement: L'écrivain et la langue au Québec*. Montreal: Boréal.

Joubert, Lucie. 1993. "La lecture de *Maryse*: Du portrait social à la prise de parole." *Voix et images* 53 (Winter): 273–86.

Killick, Rachel. 2005. "Going West, Going South and the Québec Space of Writing in Noël Audet's *Frontières ou tableaux d'Amérique*." In Rachel Killick, ed., *Uncertain Relations: Some Configurations of the 'Third Space' in Francophone Writings of the Americas and Europe*, 63–79. Bern, Switzerland: Peter Lang.

Lamonde, Yvan, and Gérard Bouchard. 1995. "Introduction." In Yvan Lamonde et Gérard Bouchard, eds, *Québécois et Américains: La culture québécoise aux XIXᵉ et XXᵉ siècles*, 7–11. Montreal: Fides.

Lamontagne, André. 2004. *Le Roman québécois contemporain: Les voix sous les mots*. Nouvelles études québécoises. Montreal: Fides.

Mikics, David. 1995. "Derek Walcott and Alejo Carpentier: Nature, History and the Caribbean Writer." In Lois Parkinson Zamora and Wendy B. Faris, eds, *Magical Realism: Theory, History, Community*, 371–404. Durham, NC, and London, UK: Duke University Press.

Nepveu, Pierre. 1989. "Qu'est-ce que la transculture?" *Paragraphes* 2: 15–31.

– 1998. *Intérieurs du Nouveau Monde: Essais sur les littératures du Québec et des Amériques*. Papiers collés. Montreal: Boréal.

– 1999. *L'écologie du réel: Mort et naissance de la littérature québécoise contemporaine*. 1988. Reprint, Montreal: Boréal.

Semujanga, Josias. 2004. "Liminaire." *Tangence*, no. 75 (Summer): 5–13.

Siemerling, Winfried. 2005. *The New North American Studies: Culture, Writing and the Politics of Re/Cognition*. London, UK, and New York: Routledge.

Todorov, Tzvetan. 1982. *La Conquête de l'Amérique: La Question de l'autre*. Paris, France: Seuil.

Vautier, Marie. 1998. *New World Myth: Postmodernism and Postcolonialism in Canadian Fiction*. Montreal and Kingston: McGill-Queen's University Press.

Index